THE MACMILLAN COMPANY
NEW YORK · CHICAGO
DALLAS · ATLANTA · SAN FRANCISCO

THE MACMILLAN COMPANY
OF CANADA, LIMITED
TORONTO

George N. Shuster

RELIGION BEHIND
THE IRON CURTAIN

New York   *The Macmillan Company*   *1954*

CONTENTS

FOREWORD

THIS IS NOT a pleasant book. It is not a book anybody would
write with a feeling that his next chapter was sure to keep
people on the edge of their chairs. There are murders in it, to be
sure, but no District Attorney demonstrates that crime does not
pay. The difficulty it confronts is not that it is about persecution, loss of liberty, propaganda no one can talk back to, torture
and death. Men and women are never nobler or more significant than when they suffer for justice's sake, or when like the
Netherlanders Motley so well portrays they pay the heaviest
price human beings can pay for freedom. No. The trouble with
this book is that it deals with a social machine which grinds
souls and bodies into a kind of depersonalized, stinking flour
one cannot think about without nausea. Nathan Hale, regretting
that he had only one life to lose for his country, emerges clear
against the setting of history. You can see him, hear him, share
his decision and the bloody glory of what he paid for it. But ten
million, thirty million, in a sense a hundred million mortals
silent in a chain gang from which no one can possibly rescue
them, a chain gang in which one figure is just like the rest and
all are countless, voiceless, hopeless, to borrow a phrase from

vii

Chesterton—what shall we do with them, how on earth can anyone write about them?

It so happens that I have known most of the countries now governed by those who say they are building the "People's Democracies." They were not paradises. There was poverty of the worst kind in many of them. There was injustice. There was hatred. But there was also humanity. One day, driving through Poland, we had a flat tire on the main street of what in our own Middle West would be a rather small county-seat town. We were always having flats because square iron nails lay along the highways, traveled for the most part by teamsters and their horses, thicker than locusts in the Middle East. Our spares were flat, too. I had stupidly forgotten to bring a hand pump, and we could not move unless we somehow got hold of one. There was no pump in the town for the simple reason that there was no automobile in the town. One of the two-thousand-odd citizens who gathered round the stricken car volunteered (for these people were innately kind) to ride on his bicycle to the manor of an estate owner some five miles away and see whether he could borrow the precious device. He returned in due time, escorting one of the most muscular human beings I have ever seen. Under his arm he carried the inflationary instrument. He rolled up his sleeves, bowed majestically to me and to the crowd, and went to work with a vengeance. The faster he pumped, the more vigorous were the salvos of applause. Finally we were on our way, with urchins scampering behind for a couple of hundred yards, leaving in the wake of us a town agog at having seen an American millionaire seated in his limousine. What did it matter that the car was really a well used Pontiac, and the driver poorer than he would like to admit!

Yet for all the elemental peasant squalor and need, and despite the vital unsolved social problems presented by the difference between affluent squire and penniless peasant, there was a great human stir in Poland. It felt good, being there and talking to people, even if I had only forty words of Polish, carefully memorized from a piece of paper, and supplemented with German when there was somebody present who could understand that language, as there usually was. Everybody had a share in at least three great ideas. There was the dream of economic improvement, no longer wholly a dream. Then there was the ideal of nationhood, unfortunately too irrationally cherished, as was very natural in view of the people's past. And finally there was the mystical solidarity of the Christian (or the Jewish) community, real and vital though encrusted no doubt with what some would call poetry and others superstition. One could see a good deal of the ugly passions of the illiterate and the prejudiced. But there were also the great loves which Ladislas Reymont has described: love of the tiller for the soil, of the boys for the girls, of a people for the Virgin Mary, full of grace and goodness.

And now? I repeat. It is not tragedy that has thrown a black blanket over all this. It is just that the iron heel has come down behind the iron curtain. Here are the unadorned population statistics of the "People's Democracies" as they were available prior to World War II:

Bulgaria	6,106,000	Poland	31,000,000
Czechoslovakia	14,726,000	Rumania	18,025,277
Hungary	8,683,000	East Germany	17,313,734
		(census of 1946)	

In addition, here are the statistics for the Baltic States absorbed by Russia:

Estonia	1,114,900
Latvia	1,900,045
Lithuania	2,361,142

These figures are subject to correction, but are adequate for the present purpose. They indicate that the population of Stamford, Connecticut, could be multiplied into this total subjected European population about fourteen hundred times. That is, every man, woman, and child in such a community has fourteen hundred counterparts over there. Fourteen hundred Stamfords with its schools and churches, its jails and railroad station, its doctors and lawyers, its butchers and bakers, its little children and its grandfathers—all of them, every day and every night, first under the heel of Hitler and then under the heel of Stalin. And every living soul has been steeped in a bath of propaganda for twelve years, one version being that there exists a master race, and another that "Anglo-American imperialism" does an endless series of misdeeds, such as sending potato bugs to Eastern Germany and disease-spreading insects to Korea. He may not believe all this, but he must not say so even to himself.

For the nerve center of this propaganda is terror. The Communist always begins with the devices of infiltration. These he is taught to handle adroitly. He can take over a labor union almost before its members suspect that he has any desire to do so. In the presence of liberals he can be a boon companion, and discreetly assent to his neighbor's views about Whitehead or St. Thomas Aquinas. But when the Russian Army is on hand to support him he is camouflaged only moderately. Everyone knows that his bosses have arrived from Moscow after a period of intensive training. But so long as "imperialist powers" are in relative control he appreciates each and every opportunity to pretend that he is some one else.

He uses the radio and the newspaper, the friendly gathering of citizens, and the picture magazine. But the instrumentalities upon which he really relies are the secret police and the concentration camp. The police are not primarily there to ferret out plots. It is their business to cajole a vast army of informers into thinking that if they report the conversations and the past histories of others they themselves will be able to keep their skins relatively intact. The concentration camp is, however, the Communists' trump card. Anyone who causes trouble can be sent to one, and the supply is unlimited. The existence of such camps is, to be sure, so well known to the average person outside the Russian orbit that mention of them arouses relatively little interest. How many remember any longer the names of Dachau and Auschwitz?

Nevertheless the concentration camps operated by the Russians are very serious matters even to Americans, and may the Lord forbid that we ever get into them. But if we suppose that Thomas Murphy of Dubuque, Iowa, proprietor of a stationery store, were suddenly put into one before his wife could get much more than his toothbrush into his briefcase, we shall have a fairly good idea of what has been happening to hundreds of thousands of poor people in Eastern Europe for a long time and to all Central Europeans since 1945.

We know rather less about Russia's slave-labor camps than, perhaps, we should; but even so the information is considerable. Some of what is known comes from sources which cannot be divulged. A good deal has also been supplied by persons who once resided in such camps. The system as such is thirty years old, though it has probably never been so extensive and well organized as it now is. Two purposes are served by it, which we may assume are those which the Nazis also posited as goals, even if their social objectives and methods were in some respects different from those of the Communists. Human beings can be used as beasts of burden in carrying out enterprises sponsored by the government. Secondly, if anyone is suspected of disloyalty, "sabotage," or difference of opinion, he can be removed from normal social life. Soviet society is a Gargantuan feat of human engineering. In the present state of technological advancement it is possible for its masters to compute the development of industry and transportation in terms of the work hours men and women can perform. Similarly the "planners" can estimate quite precisely what each such hour is worth. Farms are collectivized not merely because the individual landowner is likely to retain ideas of freedom, but because it is possible to acquire a surplus rural population which can then be put to work on projects which will bring about a more rapid industrialization. And what Communism terms the "bourgeoisie"—that is, the urban group which makes a living by buying and selling—can be transformed into a "vagrant" and therefore usable population by nationalizing trade and confining it to the smallest possible number of stores and commercial agencies.

I have tried to form an over-all impression of this system by imagining that the United States set out to create the largest conceivable WPA. To this would be assigned all older people, all gentlemen of leisure, and all unemployed housewives. It would be announced that every person so employed would be paid just what his collective work produced in terms of immediate economic value, and no more. If no such value could be perceived, the government would furnish a food ration calculated to keep the worker alive, and barely alive. Let us assume that one project was to nationalize a group of abandoned farms in upstate New York and combine them into a single collectively operated estate. Workers could then be paid in produce. Granted that Americans as a nation could even conceive of doing something of the sort, we should still have a long way to go before establishing anything like the Soviet system. For example, in our passion to get hold of every possible man hour we should cut down the amount of time during which pregnant women could remain away from work. This the Communists have done no doubt everywhere, but demonstrably in Eastern

Germany, where the time was cut recently by nearly five months. We should also have to develop a fanatical pleasure in devising ways and means for putting everybody who disapproved of our WPA projects to work on them.

Yet it must be conceded that such a system has one very great advantage. Instead of mortgaging the future by piling up a huge collective debt in order to maintain a vast and costly military organization (as we in the United States are doing), it takes from the poor humankind which falls into its clutches literally everything. And so no doubt there is in this dour and cruel Soviet experiment a lesson which every American ought to take to heart—the lesson that we shall be able to compete in the long run only by voluntarily making sacrifices, of labor and of money, of pleasures and rewards.

At any rate, the concentration camps in Russia are roughly of three kinds: the stockades in industrial areas where there are housed men and women who are the unskilled slave labor of local industry or of the *kolkhozes* (collective farms); the penal districts properly so called, in the far North and East of the Soviet Union; and the colonization projects—for example, that in Takistan—which involve the compulsory resettlement of whole folk groups such as the Tartars of the Crimea. While the system operates in accordance with a scale of prison strictness, not one place of confinement has been reported in which the minimum standards of penal practice observed anywhere in the United States are in force. Indeed, sources which appear to be reliable indicate that Buchenwald and Dachau have been duplicated many times. The same methods of camp rule through the enlistment of criminals and rowdies as trusties, the same lack of food and clothing, the same abominably bad medical attention, have been described over and over again by survivors. The average inmate of such a camp lives five years. He is hounded and starved, vilified and dehumanized.

But what most astonishes everyone who studies the evidence about the situation is the total dimension of the slave-labor population. German ex-prisoners have reported that in some areas one in every seven Russians is systematically sent to a concentration camp. The camps seem to be taken for granted, just as are disease and death. Even if one discounts heavily the available estimates, it seems highly probable that at least 20,000,000 Russians have been among the victims. Thus forced labor has become one of the most virulent plagues in history. For, if one adds together those who were enslaved by the Nazis and those corralled by the Communists, the total figures far outdistance the number of those who died as a result of World Wars I and II.

Here is a description of slave-camp life, based on a great variety of accounts by eyewitnesses:

Existence is subhuman. This word tells everything. Hunger, toil, illness, theft, murder, corruption, bribery, and mental suffering are dominant. The prisoners are corralled by the thousands in isolated zones of the camp. The barracks have beds of wooden slabs arranged in tiers of two, with occasional tables and stools. Very few have either straw sacks or covers. There is not a book or a newspaper in the camp. Possession of a lead pencil is a punishable offense. During winter the barracks are warmed a little by the presence of so many human beings. Heating is sporadic, because the coal supply is never adequate. There is no opportunity to wash. The prisoners are in tatters and covered with lice. All good articles of clothing are taken away and sold. The camp is ruled with an iron fist. The criminals in control make the camp, in accordance with a kind of unwritten law, into a place where they have a chance to give vent to their urges and exercise bloody dominion with knives and clubs. Persons who are not liked or are deemed undesirable competitors for power are placed on a death list. The killers are

FOREWORD xv

chosen by lot. Then at the appointed hour in the night they pounce on their victim and hack him to pieces in a bestial fashion.

Such is the situation in Russia. There are also concentration camps in the satellite countries, called in Communist language "People's Democracies." It has been estimated that more than 1,000,000 persons have been sent to such camps, and the number may be far greater. Not included in this figure, for example, are Eastern Germany and the former Baltic States. The existence of concentration camps has been widely advertised, and decrees establishing them are on the statute books of all the People's Democracies. The decrees merely apply to the country in question the provisions of Article 59 of the Criminal Code of U.S.S.R. The first Article of the Criminal Code of Rumania, for example, as reported by Albert K. Herling, reads as follows:

Criminal law has for its purpose defending the Rumanian People's Republic and its legal order against actions dangerous to society by enforcing legal measures of social defense against persons who commit such actions. In the meaning of the preceding paragraph any action and omission that brings harm to the economic, social and political structure, or to the security of the Rumanian People's Republic, or which disturbs the legal order established by the people under the leadership of the working class is to be considered dangerous to society. The actions which are considered dangerous for society can be punished even when they are not expressly prohibited by law. In such cases the extent and limit of criminal responsibility is to be determined in accordance with the legal provisions in force for similar crimes.*

The number of camps in the area reported by persons who assert that they were present in them is so vast that the names by

* Statement issued on June 18, 1952, in behalf of the International League for the Rights of Man.

which they go and the places where they are situated would fill a small directory. Thus 179 have been reported from Czechoslovakia alone. If the information gathered is correct, there are at least six hundred slave-labor institutions in the People's Democracies. The use to which this labor is put, according to reports, is significant. In Rumania slave laborers, for example, work on farms, at power plants, on the construction of railroads and bridges, on the digging of canals, and in factories. Of interest also is the manner in which the system has been developed. Both Poland and Czechoslovakia witnessed the deportation to Russia, during the early stages of the occupation, of hundreds of thousands of people deemed hostile to Communism. Popular resentment of this brought about a temporary lull. What happened next, if one can judge by the experience of the Czechs and Slovaks, is that the government was authorized to compel workers to remain on jobs deemed to be in the national interest. This action was described as an emergency measure. The net result, however, was that young workers suspected of being hostile to the Communist regime were disciplined.

After the seizure of power by the Communists in 1948, several decrees were issued authorizing the government of Czechoslovakia to establish commissions of three to determine whether citizens should be sentenced to forced labor. Liability was very broadly defined. Thus one decree stipulated that "persons who are not less than eighteen and not more than sixty years of age, and are physically and mentally capable of working but evade work or threaten the establishment of the people's democratic order," might be sent to work camps for periods not less than three months and not longer than two years. In addition very stringent regulations were laid down concerning the supply of labor. No one was any longer to change his place of employment unless the responsible authorities had received the request and acceded to it. Perhaps the most stringent regulation was that which held the trade unions responsible for the production outlined in the Five-Year Plan but deprived them of every right to defend workers against the state. Boiled down to its essentials, the system compels every laboring man to expend the last ounce of his energy regardless of whether he is employed normally or under duress. In the circumstances, it is rather strange that while the forced laborer's dinner normally consists of coffee and three potatoes, it is followed by a lecture on the blessings of Marxism.

A social system of this character cannot tolerate sabotage, even if that is mere opposition to the aims and purposes of the rulers; for any thought, word, or deed which deprives the masters of even so much as an hour of a worker's time, or which places upon them the burden of defending any action they have taken, represents a loss of precious human energy. Sins are committed against the highest authority on earth (and of course there is no power beyond the world of appearance and matter), Stalin or his successors, by those who feel that the traditional forms of European living offer the greatest hope of human happiness. Therefore the Church was from the outset doomed, not only because it professed a spiritual view of life at odds with dialectical materialism but also because it was an obstacle to the full and unrestricted use of human beings. An American may find it hard to understand fanaticism of this sort, but every thoughtful churchman doomed to live under Communist domination knows the truth full well.

But how can a compact religious body be infiltrated? The answer is of course that, if the churches were not human but representative of every ideal which they purport to profess, the high tide of Communism would break at their doorsteps. So profoundly spiritual, however, they are not. Some of the clergy will succumb to blandishments, to fear, and to the no doubt inevitable despair resulting from a feeling that things will never change anyway. At first, in nearly all the People's Democracies, peasant congregations attempted to defend their pastors, and there are numberless stories of clashes with Communist police in which the congregations emerged temporarily victorious. Gradually, however, even these forms of hastily improvised self-defense became impossible. Today life goes wearily on. The heroes remain, as did the brave Protestant Confessional Church in Hitler's Germany, but the others compromise. We may as well admit that there is a good supply of these others. Religious faith loses for many its strength and savor when the mind is assailed by that semantic confusion which is the primary objective sought by Communist propaganda.

I cannot speak with any measure of authority on what appears to be Soviet use of Pavlov's theory of the conditioned reflex. Yet there would seem to be little doubt that commitment by propagandists to such a conception of human psychology brings about a reliance on a repetitive, symbolistic impact on the subconscious (if one concedes that for materialists there exists anything akin to what we familiarly term "consciousness") which people outside the Russian orbit find bizarre but which one long exposed to it may well find a pattern of suggestion difficult if not impossible to escape. Thus the British Broadcasting Corporation reports that a young Russian escapee answered an inquiry about its broadcasts by saying that he was disappointed to hear so many references to democracy. This, he thought, was what existed in Russia, and was therefore precisely what he was anxious to get away from. From a religious point of view, constant reiteration of the statement that miracles do not occur, and that reports concerning them are based on delusions, conflict with the traditional Christian view that God will answer prayer. And when no direct and tangible Divine response is received, men and women whose faith is not firmly anchored in contemplation may well begin to doubt. It is upon this doubt, however embryonic, that Communism pounces. The victim whose psyche is thus devoured may not even be aware of what is happening. But he will become spiritually listless and anemic. He will no longer see essential things clearly.

It follows that those who are most nearly immune are either the very intelligent who have acquired mastery of the inner life, or the simple and clean of heart who cling to deeply embedded ideas of right and wrong. The former are successful because they have a highly conscious awareness of what alone is permanent and so deserving of the full commitment of personality. The latter remain uncontaminated because the verbal impact of propaganda merely rolls off the granite walls of the decisions by which their consciences abide. Therefore, it has often been said by churchmen that from a Christian point of view nothing could be more important than continuous prayer by the free world for the Russian and the satellite peoples. For (it is alleged) if we disregard entirely our, alas, necessarily inconclusive and anthropomorphic views of what this prayer may be able to obtain from the Maker of us all, it will still be profoundly true that only in this wise can we ourselves acquire the spiritual habits certain to render us immune to Communist enticements, and the gift of insight into the day-by-day situation in which the conquered peoples find themselves. And in all truth we must, despite a legitimate aversion from the Communist view of life, never forget that we are the brothers even of those who have, it may well be, winced or flinched under the scourging. We and they alike must hope for compassion.

The Russian people, if one can form an impression of them on the basis of innumerable accounts, were at least as guilty of collusion with the powers of evil as any other nation. By and large they rejoiced in the opportunity to disposses fellow citizens who had somewhat more of this world's goods than they. It has now become quite as impossible to chant a hymn of praise in their honor as it is to laud unreservedly their fellow human beings. But that many have remained loyal to faith, hope, and love in the sense in which St. Paul described them is supported by so much evidence that we can both credit and reverence it. The passion for holiness—oldest, deepest, and most beautiful of human desires—may, indeed, be stronger among them than it is in our midst. But there is no medium through which it can find expression; and perhaps, were one provided, there would not be a man who would know how to use it and could speak other than tritely, in words lacking the halo of joy. It is not easy to sing after heartbreak. Nevertheless we know that the faithful ones are there. We must make every effort to reach out to them, as unfortunately we failed to do to the Germans who stood against Hitler. Nor may we judge too hastily people who no longer struggle or who even mouth phrases of betrayal. It is, for example, very true that, although only the Sovereign Pontiff himself can lift the ban of excommunication from Catholic traitors, he must do so if they ask it some time.

And so I pray that the pages I have written about our brethren under Communist bondage may always reflect an underlying humility and that there may be no pride based on the assumption that we are better or quite different men. There is a legitimate debt of gratitude to be paid always for our birthright in the West, and we must be strong and brave enough to keep this intact. Our goal, however, is always the liberation of the others not through war, which would doom countless millions and perhaps even obliterate the present and the past of man, but through some profound change of the spirit and a great uprising for freedom. Nothing has been more impressive to me, speaking with men and women who have escaped to us, than their obvious quest for such a change. How it is to be brought about, no one knows at present. The time is very dark. But one must believe and hope that so much agony of body and spirit will constitute the great tribulation from out of whose womb humanity will be reborn through the mercy of God.

I should like to add just a few words of gratitude to all who have helped me gather the information on which this book is based. The several chapters have profited from memoranda prepared by a number of refugee scholars, who will be mentioned wherever possible in subsequent bibliographical notes. Here I should like to thank particularly John B. Woodall and Levering Tyson of the Mid-European Studies Center, who have done everything they possibly could to help; Professor Adolf Berger, who has patiently read through *Osservatore Romano* for me; the librarian of the Council on Foreign Relations; and Paul Fabry, Director of the Hungarian Section of the Mid-European Studies Center. Those refugees or persons having to do with refugees with whom I talked while I was in Germany must be nameless here. But I hope they will somehow know how deeply indebted to them I am.

1 HISTORICAL PERSPECTIVE

For a year and a half I had some concern with the Iron Curtain as United States Land Commissioner for Bavaria. It took seven days of hard driving to inspect all of it that was of interest to our side. Across one part of it, that contiguous to East Germany, you could move rather freely if you were not an American. The other part, bordering on Czechoslovakia, was quite different. For here the Curtain on the Czech side was a strip of evacuated terrain, normally about four miles wide, inside which houses were falling into ruin and grass was growing up through the pavement. This was patrolled by young men in nondescript uniforms carrying tommy guns. Sometimes strange things happened, as when a group of Czechs commandeered a train and simply steamed across the border into the land of at least relative freedom. Or there was the afternoon when a coachful of aged and sick nuns was suddenly dumped on the platform of the German frontier station. Some of them died right there, and others were driven off by the Bavarians to friendly convents where they could pass their last days. One never knew what was coming—bullet or straggler or escapee seeking asylum. There was a campful of escapees, mostly Czechs and Slovaks, at Valka near Nuremberg.

We Americans used before the war to roam freely in the countries on the other side. Many of us either came from there or are descended from people who did. It is strange not to be able to cross the border now, and of course the fact makes it only too easy to consign the whole region to a sort of monochrome limbo. We need to remind ourselves constantly that here are some of the oldest, most cultivated, most individualistic, and most heroic of the nations of the West. Were one merely to list all the deeds of great valor which have been wrought here in more than two thousand years, or all the notable works of art, music, and literature which were created by men at home in these regions, the summary would be a brilliant one, indeed. Yet it is no doubt primarily dedication to religion that gave these cultures their individuality and vitality.

For convenience's sake we may follow Julius Caesar's example and divide the whole area into three parts. The first embraces the lands which were once portions of the Austro-Hungarian Empire, which collapsed in 1918 but, despite its faults, must in retrospect be termed one of the most coherent and civilized states known to modern history. Once I compared notes with Arnold Toynbee about the singular fact that wherever one crossed those vanished boundaries, whether to the north of Cracow or to the east of Budapest, the sense of coming into the familiar world of the West was immediate and unmistakable. There was a manifest ease and gracefulness of the art of living, reflected in all the many buildings, humble or ornate, in which that art found expression. Vienna, Prague, Budapest, Cracow, Zagreb, Bratislava—these cities were built by the collective genius which Austria somehow managed to evoke and nurture, even though the people who lived in them might more often than not talk of tyranny.

The second part used to be called the Balkans, because these lands, north of the Greek seas, were identified with the mountains which traversed them. Ancient Rome had established its power on their slopes, and later the peoples who settled there after the Slovenian invasions of the Dark Ages accepted the faith of the Eastern Church. To this they clung with fidelity during centuries of subjection to the Turks; and as soon as their freedom had been regained this faith was everywhere restored in cities and rural communes alike. It is unfortunate that so little about this aspect of Rumanian and Bulgarian history has been known to us generally. Recalled recently with philosophic nostalgia in such books as Gheorghiu's *Twenty-fifth Hour*, some awareness of it is an indispensable prerequisite for judging what has happened during the last terrible years.

The third part consists of Poland outside the old Austrian border, the small Baltic States to the north (Latvia, Estonia, and Lithuania) given back to bondage by Hitler in an hour of mad bargaining for power, and those territories taken from Germany in the aftermath of the Yalta and Potsdam conferences. The tragedy which has befallen these peoples is heart-rending. It is believed, for example, that one-fourth of the population of Estonia has been deported to Siberia by the Russians. Whatever the blunders of all governments concerned may have been, it is difficult to read the chronicles of horror inflicted on their erstwhile subjects without shuddering. There is little even in the history of Nazi savagery which can outdo, for example, the conquest of German Silesia. Consider, by way of illustration, the fate of Neisse, center of Silesian Catholic activity, which was entered by the Russian army on Palm Sunday, 1945. After scenes of rape, murder, and violence almost unparalleled even in the long history of war, the little city with its priceless churches was put to the torch, so that the thousand inmates of the great home for the aged burned to death in their beds. All these lands will never again become what they once were—regions of constant struggle and short-lived serenity, of poverty and its exploitation, of poetry, fervor, and sadness. Those of us who have, for example, seen peasant women trudging for many miles through the omnipresent dust to kneel for an hour at the shrines of Silesia will never forget either the fact or its meaning.

There is not a foot of the old soil of Central Europe which has not been consecrated by endurance for the sake of the things of the spirit and the mind. Indeed, I have sometimes wondered, reading the Polish and Silesian poets and novelists, why the longing to hold out should have persisted during many difficult centuries—why, for instance, Polish forests in thrall to the Czars should have hidden priest and ritual with such fidelity. Perhaps the explanation, in so far as it is of this world, can be found in the deep human urge for the preservation of identity. Custom and language were vital symbols of the self, and without them men felt they could not live. But stronger than all else was the deep, primitive, mystical desire for identification with Eternal Righteousness, manifest to the believer in the life of the Redeemer. To give up the faith was to surrender not merely one's self but the world as well.

To be sure these men and women were very human, often poverty-stricken and untutored, sometimes intolerant and oppressive. The effort to conserve themselves and their identity spilled over into moments of vengeful outrage inflicted upon others because they were different. Thus anti-Semitism has a long history in Eastern Europe studded with bloody pogroms. Although curbed in Austro-Hungarian regions it was latent there, too, as the shameful events of 1938 proved, but manifest elsewhere continuously with varying intensity. Or who can forget the repression of the Ukrainians in Poland under the Pilsudski government, the conflict between Czechs and Slovaks, or the expulsion of the Sudeten Germans from their homes during 1945, an action flagrantly in violation of the principles for which the war against Nazism had been fought?

Against this background one must set the figures of those who, whether of the clergy or of the laity, lived and preached the law of charity. Nowhere more than amongst such men—Princes of the Church, professors, men of affairs, labor leaders, simple religious, and common people—was this law manifest. It is imperative that their memory be not obscured, now that so mighty an army of the mean and servile has arisen. Let us note what we shall have mournful occasion to repeat again and again. Marxism, which had its rise in the concern of intellectuals for the worker, and which formulated that concern in terms of a materialist version of the Hegelian dialectic, has come round with Stalin to the view that the laboring man must have no intellectuals on his side. To suppress élites has become the cornerstone of the totalitarian theory of practical politics. That is why the peoples in chains retain their passions and their weaknesses, their hatreds and their greed, while those who might give them counsel or reasons for constraint are dead or silent.

Then, too, there was the presence and also the example of the Ghetto. Place of reputed ignominy, of poverty, of rasping and grasping humanity, it was nevertheless awesomely, breathtakingly beautiful when the Sabbath eve descended upon it. Prayer became not so much what was engaged in but rather that which swept the world aside and created a wonderland of peace and holiness. One knew that in all the shabby little rooms which sheltered human beings in their wretchedness a fire had been lighted which had gleamed for thousands of years—the same leaping flame which had set the bush ablaze for Moses and had kindled the light that danced before the Ark of the Covenant. And though the vision of sanctification which now held this poor, often stricken community in thrall was different from that which the Christian peasant nursed at his fireside, with his children and his beasts about him, the words with which it was conjured up were very often the same for both. Love the Lord, thy God; love thy neighbor as thou dost thyself —the affection so hard to find in the daily street, but longed for even more earnestly, desperately than a dear woman is desired, seemed for the moment to have been ushered in over the sagging thresholds. . . . And then, of course, the Sabbath would end and the bitterness would return, and Leah would stand in the street to see the Gentile curse her children. Yet even so there was a bond between the spurner and the spurned. They knew in their hearts that they were all God's children, dirty and dissolute children, but they were certain they had a place to go home to, come the eve of the Lord's Day.

In any event, the general character of the Church and its activities in Central and Eastern Europe was formed historically by the dramatic tension between mass tendencies and leadership. In Austria-Hungary religious institutions grew rich and powerful, sometimes paying for their prosperity with a measure of undue dependence on the Habsburg state. Even now, in a drab time, the traveler through Austria will look with admiration on the great monasteries—St. Peter in Salzburg, Melk on the Danube, St. Florian, Klosterneuburg on a hill above Vienna, and many others—which outdo in splendor manorial castles and are surrounded by rich lands. These were centers of humanistic education, and numerous merited tributes have been paid to them. And in many another place, urban or rural, the Church owned important properties amassed through the generosity of the faithful or received through royal donation. In every part of the Empire, church bells rang rich and deep, even when the piety to which they appealed was woefully superficial.

But in the end these possessions stirred the envy not merely of ambitious and worldly men but also of the land-hungry poor. To be sure the Abbot of a flourishing monastery might correctly point out that the revenues did not enrich the monks, who normally lived under his guidance by an austere religious rule. These religious in their bare cells did not taste the fine vintages pressed from monastery grapes carefully tended by brothers who rose at four for Matins and then expended themselves zealously for the cause of God. Nevertheless the critics were not by any means only emancipated spirits who found moral discipline irksome and the Church old-fashioned. They were also earnest, weather-beaten peasants, with no soil to till, and often desperately poor, who understandably looked upon Church estates with a covetous eye. And of course everywhere the well applauded and sharp-tongued ideologies of the time— Marxism, Nationalism, Nihilism—were allied against the Church, often looked upon by the seemingly more enlightened folk of those days as the heritor of a creed outworn. And it must be admitted that sometimes a segment of the clergy, grown comfortable and worldly, acted as if they thought so, too.

Protestantism inside the old Empire clung to the enclaves which had been established during the era of the Reformation and the Counter-Reformation. Despite the strife incident to the Thirty Years' War both Lutheranism and Calvinism maintained themselves resolutely in Hungary, for example, so that prior to the outbreak of World War II Catholics in that country constituted about 67 per cent of the population, while Protestants numbered nearly 27 per cent and adhered to both the Lutheran and the Calvinist tradition. In Czechoslovakia the situation was relatively the same, though the number of Protestant groups was greater. A considerable part of the population —6 per cent in 1932—professed no religion of any kind. Another characteristic of the old Empire was the presence of the

Greek Orthodox Church, which though united in its Uniate
form with Rome, preserved its old language and customs. This
Church became the target of special Russian propagandistic
and repressive efforts as soon as the Iron Curtain was established.

Elsewhere outside the former realm of the Habsburgs the
situation was comparable. In Poland a Catholic peasantry
whose loyalty was deeply moving lived confidently though
primitively in the light of a mystical faith, while worldliness
and skepticism were prevalent among the upper classes. It was
commonly said there, after World War I, that the most religious
of peoples was governed by the most morally lax of bureau-
crats; and that may well have been the case. Nor could the
coming of industrialism to such mushroom cities as Lodz, so
bitterly lamented by Ladislas Reymont, bring about the immediate solution of any grave social problem. Nevertheless,
as we shall see, there existed in Poland religious elites of extraordinary quality and dedication. In eastern Germany, over-
whelmingly Protestant despite certain vigorous centers of
Catholic activity such as the Ermland in East Prussia and the
border districts west of Poznan (Silesia was a province apart,
its culture having been developed under the Habsburgs), one
could go from the old conservative, rural Church communities
of the landed estates along the Baltic Sea to the liberal atmosphere of Saxony, where the social problems inherent in modern
industrial society dominated thought and action. Concerning
the Balkans one need say here only that, though they suffered
from the normal diseases of feudalism, they offered much of
vital and absorbing interest to the student of religious life.

These observations will help to explain the situation which
followed the First World War. The old Austro-Hungarian Empire was dissolved, and dissident nationalist sentiment, supported by the will of the victorious Allies, demanded the crea-

tion of separate states. Therewith a tide of Liberalism merged with the currents of upsurging tribal nationalism to create the pattern of conflict which was later to prove so advantageous to the totalitarians. Czech nationalism, having in Thomas Masaryk a brilliantly effective standard-bearer, seemed at first blush to usher in a new era of democratic and progressive social thought. It soon became obvious, however, that the autonomism of the Czechs—which led at the outset even to the establishment of a National Church—would of necessity engender comparable feelings in the breasts of the other peoples in the Czechoslovak Republic. The Slovaks rallied round their own traditions of language and culture, and swiftly but surely became committed to a quest for autonomy which found a temporary though unsatisfactory haven under Hitler. Among Sudeten Germans feeling was almost as strong and led ultimately to the fateful formation of a political party which advocated union with Germany. Nor was the situation different elsewhere. Yugoslavia was plagued from the beginning by deep and bitter conflict among the Serbs, the Croats, and the Slovenes.

In Hungary a violent Communist revolution, spearheaded in late 1918 by Béla Kun, ruled for a time by bloodshed. But ere long this uprising, which had very little popular support, was put down; reaction set in, and a dictatorial government was established after it had compiled its own catalogue of excesses. Here was made manifest, probably for the first time, how significant the stability of religious groups could prove to be. Not only did they temper noticeably the excesses of extremists, but under the leadership of great churchmen they began to build organizations dedicated to social improvement. It is also true that bitter experience under the Béla Kun regime made Hungary one of the most anti-Communist countries of Europe.

And so, as the turbulence engendered by the war apparently subsided, it seemed probable that a period of relative security and peace would ensue. In so far as Catholics were concerned, tactful Papal diplomacy insured the continuance of the work of the Church, under altered conditions. But the position of all religions in Eastern Europe was considerably improved. New currents of thought and new forms of group action strengthened Protestantism. Anticlericalism gave way in many quarters to a desire for cordial relationships with the churches. To a very considerable extent Eastern Europe profited by the extraordinary effectiveness and freshness of Christian theological and philosophical writing in France and Germany. But the strongest impetus came from the younger clergy, many of them veterans, who devised and directed new agencies to cope with social problems. It could no longer be said that Catholics, for example, were all bedfellows of special privilege. Confidence was nearly everywhere greater than it had been for generations. It is scarcely extravagant to say that if Hitler had not arisen to inflict doom and agony on countless millions, the great effort of Christian reconstruction in Eastern Europe might have succeeded.

The strangely magnetic and mentally diseased Austrian artist who became the dictator of Germany was the spokesman for a derouted, unhappy, and unsettled following. As his power was extended over Eastern Europe the Christian churches suffered only less horribly than Judaism. Priests were shot, sent to concentration camps, exiled from their parishes. Religious communities were suppressed, and their property and their schools were removed from under the jurisdiction of the Church; journals of religious opinion were silenced. The long catalogue of acts of oppression contains almost every kind of persecution save those spectacular mass executions by which the Jewish people were decimated. But at least it was made apparent that there was only one kind of opposition which the Nazis needed to fear—the refusal of faithful Christians, both

Catholic and Protestant, to accept one of the most flagrant heresies of all time.

There can be no doubt that Nazism dealt a crippling blow to religion, not only by reason of the attack on elites—men and women of intellectual status and forceful character, able to lead the people—but also because of the widespread perversion of youth which resulted from the activities of the Hitlerjugend and similar organizations. It is true that Hitler's attack on the Church lacked both the decisiveness and the skill which we have since come to identify with Communism. The Nazi intention was, however, to launch such an attack as soon as victory had been gained. Himmler's plans, as we study them in retrospect, bear the stamp of his diseased romantic imagination; but it may well be that in an hour of world-shattering victory he could have put them into effect. Fortunately there was no such triumph. Even so the scars left on the spirit of Europe by years of unrestrained and vicious Nazism will not be healed over for a long time to come. Thus, the Communist advance westward after the close of the war was aided on the one hand by the corrosion of spirit which was a bequest of Hitler, and on the other hand by the belief, prevalent in many quarters, that Sovietism was the opposite of German tyranny and was friendly to democratic institutions. This was unfortunately accepted as something close to self-evident truth in our own United States, so that there is little reason why we should wonder at the illusions of Europeans.

Stalin's road into one of the heartlands of the Christian faith was at all events open. The second stage in the passion of sorely tried peoples was to begin. How feeble the surviving elements of Liberalism, counted upon sometimes to impede the Russian dictator's progress, had become, is amply demonstrated by the fate of Eduard Beneš. Less imaginative and resourceful, less courageous or determined, few statesmen have seemed to be, though the verdict is not wholly just. There remained no intellectual obstacle save the stark Christian faith to one of the most ruthless powers humanity has known.

Accordingly we shall glance briefly at the historical relations between Church and State in Russia in order to gain insight into the formation of Soviet policy on the religious question. It is not easy to do so. Russia, which possesses a great literature, has had no school of cultural historians; and, though many noble refugee scholars—Berdyaev, Timasheff, Stepan, von Eckardt, Gurian among them—have written significantly on cultural topics, persons who do not know Russia are hard put to follow the convolutions of a history very different from that of our own peoples. There is, however, a line of development which one can observe with reasonable ease if one asks a few questions. What were the relations between Western Christianity and Russia? When and how did the Russian Church become subservient to the Czars? How did that Church confront the rising strength of Bolshevism? Did it make its peace with Stalin?

Christianity came to Kiev from Byzantium in the year 988. This does not, however, mean that the Russians were deeply committed to the Eastern Church in contradistinction to Rome. Missionaries came from both centers of Christendom, and there seems to have been little difference in the welcome accorded them; but at the time of the occupation of Constantinople by the Crusaders in 1204 a change had set in. Excesses committed by uproarious defenders of the Cross deeply embittered the Greeks, and some of this feeling was communicated to the Russians. The charge that Rome was the seat of an archheretical Papacy, prevalent in Greek writing of the time, found an echo in Kiev. Then came the Mongol invasion of Russia, followed by a period of occupation lasting two hundred and fifty years. Autocratic rule by the Mongolian masters deepened the trend to absolutism among the Russian princes—a trend already implicit in Byzantine social and political practice. During the same time Russia was also obliged to fend off invasion from the West. An alliance between the Swedes and the Teutonic Knights loomed up as a dire threat, but the victory was won in battle by Prince Alexander, perhaps the most glamorous figure in Russian history. This victory was followed by a significant deepening of the rift between East and West.

Then at the beginning of the fifteenth century the hope of reuniting the Churches of the East and West burned bright. The Council of Ferrara, which convened in 1437 and then removed to Florence, brought distinguished Churchmen together. It was the last great conference of ecclesiastics that might conceivably have merged differences in a new unity. Russia was represented by Isidor, Metropolitan and monk, famed for his learning and zeal; but, although he and very probably the Russian Church generally favored reunion, Prince Basil II disapproved. Isidor could continue his journey to the Council only after he had escaped from prison. Some years later Basil appointed another Metropolitan and meted out heavy punishment on all that opposed him. It should also be noted that in the interim the Metropolitan See had been transferred from Kiev to Moscow.

Byzantium fell to the Turks in 1453, and this calamity was interpreted by Russia's rulers as a punishment inflicted by the Lord on the Eastern Church for having sought union with Rome.* When Ivan the Terrible ascended the Russian throne

---

* The siege of Constantinople, resulting from the desire of Sultan Mohammed II for possession of the city, was conducted by a huge army of Turks, supported by a navy of 150 vessels. The defending garrison at no time numbered more than 7,500 men—about one to every four of the Turks. Nevertheless the attackers were beaten off again and again, the city falling as the result of a curious mishap. An old gate, traditionally blocked up, had been opened to permit a sortie but was forgotten and not blocked up again. Fifty Turks managed to enter through it. They were discovered and dealt with, but a cry went up

in 1547, he declared that the Russian Church was dependent neither on Greece nor Rome. Relying on the sentiment of the people, freed at last from Mongol bondage, the Russian ruler proclaimed the religious autonomy of Russia. Moscow was now become the "Third Rome," to which spiritual dominion over the world had been transferred. The Edler Philatheus ("God lover") declared in a letter to Basil III, that "this third Rome, the Holy Church of the Apostles, is more resplendent under thy mighty rule than is the sun . . . All Christian states will be united by you . . . Two Romes have fallen, but the third is firmly established. No fourth can ever come to be." This concept Ivan imposed upon the Russian Church.

After this ruler's death, the influence of one who may no doubt be termed the greatest of Russian churchmen made itself felt. The Patriarch Nikhon deplored the subjection of the Church to the secular authority and the consequent loss both of independence and of influence. He sought to sever religion from blind national ambitions and to recover an international ecclesiastical outlook. But seldom has a man had to reckon with more determined opposition. A large number of Russian clergymen had become satisfied with their lot, and they preferred custom and inherited practice to fundamental religious values. They accused the Patriarch of favoring the West. He was deposed by the Czar, but not before he had introduced important reforms. His last action was a vain appeal to the Pope for unity. Now there was dominant in ecclesiastical circles a "zoological nationalism" (one of blood and soil, in Hitler's words) of which the great philosopher Vladimir Soloviëv wrote in anxious criticism.

The princes and czars of whom we have spoken were reli-

---

that the enemy had entered the city. The garrison gave way to panic, the walls were left undefended, and Mohammed had his victory. These strange events could therefore easily enough be attributed to supernatural intervention.

gious men. There now arose two monarchs whom the Church interested very little. Peter the Great scoffed at an independent clergy, and Catherine the Great followed in his footsteps. While Peter not only deposed the Patriarch and appointed in his stead an official responsible to the Crown, Catherine confiscated the properties of the Church and conferred upon the clergy the status of civil servants with appropriate salaries. It seems wholly probable that for both monarchs religion was merely a nuisance which interfered with the authority of the civil ruler; but commitment to Christianity was the most signal characteristic of the Russian people, and nothing could be done to obliterate the "superstition" entirely. Nevertheless the period during which these autocrats ruled brought about a considerable loss of confidence in the Church. Visionary mystical sects arose on the soil of Russia, undermining irretrievably the solidarity of religious institutions.

Then came the great war against Napoleon. This not only deepened the spiritual convictions of the Russian people but also renewed their associations with the West. In Germany particularly, soldiers of the Czar gained a knowledge of idealistic movements then afoot; German culture was then perhaps at its height as an exponent of universal ethical principles, and many Russians returned home determined to revitalize the intellectual and spiritual life of their country. They failed in large measure. Suppression fell heavily upon them, but in spite of this there ensued a great ferment which remained vigorous throughout the century. On the one hand this took the form of criticizing the Russian Church for its subservience to the Russian rulers. On the other, it gave rise to a movement for the reunion of the religious forces of East and West. Soloviëv became the protagonist of union with Rome. Others strove to deepen the theology of the East.

Czarism perished in the aftermath of the bloody battles of

World War I, for reasons not the least of which was the obsession of the ruling house for a morbid spiritualistic cult. The revolutionary government organized by Kerenski proclaimed freedom of religion, and won applause throughout the world for this reason among others. The Patriarchate was restored. These noble ambitions were rudely ended by Lenin, who had been transported to the Russian scene through the courtesy of General Ludendorff, then all-powerful in Germany. For Lenin, the dialectical materialist,* the Russian Church was as old-fashioned as the Ptolemaic theory and as corrupt as a rotten apricot. It was expected that a single order would demolish the moribund institution once for all. But instead the resistance of the faithful was moving and breath-taking. The Russian people, for all its weaknesses and sins, its subservience to the czars, and its dissatisfaction with a clergy too often supinely dependent upon the state, proved itself to be a profoundly religious folk.

The Communists attacked with blind fury. Church property was taken away, the priests were left without any means of subsistence. Houses of worship were profaned. A few excerpts from the Pastoral Letter issued by Patriarch Tikhon on January 18, 1918, summarize the situation at that time: "Daily we are in receipt of letters reporting the horrible, bestial murders of quite innocent and bedridden people . . . All these things are done not at nighttime only, but in the light of day. There are no hearings, all rights and laws have been abrogated. The holy edifices are targets for gunfire, or are subject to looting, ridicule, and degradation. Venerable persons residing in monasteries and honored by the faithful are seized by the dark, ungodly powers of this age. Schools supported by the Orthodox Church for the education of priests are turned into institutions

* Dialectical materialism, the doctrine of Marx and his followers, changed the idealistic religious pantheism of Hegel into a form of materialism, but retained Hegel's theory of "dialectic."

of nonbelievers or are made into houses of prostitution."

Rigorously the Communists continued their efforts. The Metropolitan of St. Petersburg, the Metropolitan of Kiev, and the chief representative of the Roman Catholic Church in Russia were tried and executed. How many others suffered a like fate, no one knows. Many were exiled to Siberia, and not a few fled to other lands. Then there took place an incident which was indicative of the future. During June, 1923, the Communist newspaper *Izvestia* published the "confession" of Patriarch Tikhon. The case against him was dropped. How many times subsequently were we to read of trials and "confessions," and led to wonder through what horrible means these words of renegation were extracted!

Up and down went the tide of Russian persecution, reaching a climax of vehemence after the purges of 1936 and 1937, through which Stalin conferred absolute power upon himself. All, whether of the clergy or of the laity, who had attracted attention as devout Christians were dealt with as accomplices of the "Old Bolsheviks" and of army officers upon whom the full fury of the repression descended. Whole throngs were arrested. The resistance, however, was far more vigorous than had been anticipated. Elderly men and women took upon themselves the duties of the imprisoned priests, and services were held in private homes, in ruined buildings, and in the forests.

Then in 1939 the government altered its policy and eased considerably the restrictions upon the Church. The outbreak of the war brought further improvement. Both government and army looked benevolently on religion as a source of consolation and hope for the average soldier. Churchmen responded by supporting resistance to Hitler, though to be sure they had been decimated since the previous clash at arms between Russians and Germans. According to official Russian sources the churches were fewer than one-tenth of the number which had served the faithful in 1917, and the Orthodox clergy had dwindled comparably. On September 3, 1943, Stalin had a conference with the Metropolitans Sergius and Nicholas; and it was thereupon announced that Sergius had been elected Patriarch of Moscow and of all Russia. Many have criticized the Orthodox Church for agreeing to collaborate with the dictator, but it is clear that any other course was impossible. How could the Russian faithful have understood an action which would have been interpreted as a departure from age-old patriotic tradition?

But one must admit that the subsequent subservience of the Orthodox Church cannot easily be condoned. After 1945 the Patriarch broke off all ties with the West, repudiating the Vatican and the Protestant Ecumenical Movement alike, both of which had not only opposed Nazism but used every available resource to mitigate the persecution of the Russian Church. The Ecclesiastical Assembly which convened in Moscow during July, 1948, did little except to subscribe without a quaver to Stalin's peace propaganda. The resolutions adopted accused Western Catholicism and Protestantism of fomenting war, and called upon them to emulate the conduct of the Moscow Patriarch.

The trend thus inaugurated has continued. A "Peace Conference" of the Russian churches, held in a seminary near Moscow during May, 1952, strove to mobilize ecclesiastical opinion both in Russia and abroad for the "peace" objectives dear to Stalin. The Metropolitan Nicholas described the world as being divided into two camps—one bent on war and the other seraphically concerned with peace. This time the onus did not rest solely on the Orthodox Church. For example, Canon Strode of the Roman Catholic clergy of Riga assailed the "gold-greedy multimillionaires of the United States" as the abettors of "the bacteriological weapon of warfare." And Zhidhov, chief Baptist minister in Russia, called upon his fellow Baptists in other countries to "become active fighters for peace." This "Peace Conference" opened with the singing of the Russian national anthem, and a huge portrait of Stalin loomed behind the speakers' table.

Meanwhile, however, the Communist Party has by no means abandoned its militant advocacy of the godless view of life. Official speakers and writers in dense array continue to express the view that "the Communist education of the working people is inconceivable without a vigorous struggle against all remnants of the old society, including religious superstition and prejudice." Nevertheless there is insistence upon the freedom of all to practice religion. For example, on April 25, 1951, an article in *Komsomolskaya Pravda,* organ of the Communist youth movement, stated: "In our country the Church is disestablished from the state. For a Soviet citizen religion is a private affair. But it is not a private affair for the Bolshevist Party, which continues to educate the worker in the spirit of the only true scientific, materialistic world outlook." It would be pointless to multiply this quotation here. Official Soviet publications, in the U.S.S.R. and outside, duplicate it with a regularity which may be dialectical materialism's substitute for infinity. Conclusions are difficult to draw when they can be no more than inferences from sources only partly subject to control. There are, however, observers who think that dialectical materialism may be maintaining its position in the Russian scheme of things with some difficulty. Religion has become its rival, because religion has agreed to serve as an instrument of foreign policy. Who can say? For though it is conceivable that the Orthodox Church, were it able to find many abroad ready to credit its version of the "peace" propaganda, might supplant Leninism, such a Church would be the abject slave of the State, to an extent undreamed of in Czarist Russia. We were wont, many of us, to make uncomplimentary references to the clergy of the old regime. Some of the strictures were too sweeping. But, alas, what we must be prepared to say about the Russian Church under the Soviets is far more devastating. It has become an institution which all but blesses the concentration camp system, and escorts slave labor to its doom with a kind of liturgical brass band.

The Soviet objective is to reduce religious organizations outside Russia to the status of the Orthodox Church at home. The formula is always and everywhere the same, though it may be applied with greater or lesser rigor. Therefore inevitably the Vatican becomes the great antagonist, to be fought with every means. The Holy See, pledged to the profession of the Christian Gospels without dilution of the ethical obligations which they impose upon everyone who accepts them in the Catholic sense, cannot agree that the Church is to be an instrument of the State —even, indeed, a benign and merciful instrument. The Vatican is therefore the ignoble Fascist Beast of the Bolshevik Apocalypse. Upon the heads of persons who remain loyal to the ancient See of Catholic Christendom, blows have rained in constant succession. This is the direst persecution the Church has suffered since the days of the Caesars.

Because most of what may be reported concerns the Catholic Church, a brief review of its history and endeavors in Eastern Europe will help to bring events into perspective. The cleavage of the Roman Empire, establishing the rivalry between the emperors of Rome and Byzantium, begot two Churches also, each claiming for itself the charisma of Apostolic Christianity. With the passing of time, profound differences of a dogmatic, moral, and canonical kind developed. The organizational character of religion was also modified radically, so that, while in the East the ties binding the religious nations to the historic patriarchal See of Constantinople were either broken completely or allowed to become loose and tenuous, in the West the structure of the Roman Catholic Church became more monolithic in fact, if not in theory. No doubt this divergence was rooted partly in theology, but one cause was the decline of Constantinople as an important Christian center and its subjection to Turkish rule.

Yet there could never be any doubt that both Churches were intensely and ardently Catholic. They kept the tradition of the priesthood as a sacramental ordination administered by bishops whose authority had been handed down in direct line of succession from the Apostles. Both retained the Mass as that in which the Sacrifice of Christ was reenacted so that His body and blood might be with the Church always. Devotion to the Virgin Mary, so long a thorn in the flesh of Western Protestantism, was a common heritage and treasure, however different the conceptions of Mary's personality and presence or the liturgies in which her praise was spelled out in prayer. Therefore efforts to effect reunion have never flagged since the Middle Ages. The fact that they have failed may well be, as many writers have thought, one of the great tragedies of history.

For every thoughtful Western Catholic the virtues and attitudes cherished in the East are precious because they reflect mystical prayer and thought and often the vital, profound humility of the human sinner who does not lose himself in "personalism": the personalism which in the West has so often favored the delusion that the rights and righteousness of man are pearls grown within himself through the practice of religion or morality, independent of the sacred order which is in God and which, when he is sometimes devout and submissive, he may possess in the deepest core of his being. On the other hand the West, unlike the East, has an illustrious tradition of endeavor to permeate the speculative and practical intelligence by holiness, so that the other human being, the brother, with his needs, fears, and failings as well as his innate good qualities, may be brought into a community of charity and justice. The great Saints of Roman Catholicism are not seldom found among men who, like Francis, Dominic, Benedict, and Ignatius, were builders of communities that sought the fullest possible human expression of man's sense of union with God and with his fellows upon the earth.

Yet it is over the question of authority that the contest between East and West has been most keen. In Western eyes the great failure of the Orthodox Church has been its inability to disassociate itself from the control of the secular state. We see, for example, in Communist Russia today as well as we seem to see in czarist history, a religion which does what it is told to do, which lulls the consciences of men into obedience to tyranny. But if I understand such writers as Berdyaev correctly, freedom to find Christ in the Church is all that matters to the Russian Christian, and any authoritatively formulated faith is in his eyes a serious denial of a cardinal rule by which the soul must live. This philosophical restatement of the remarks concerning the Grand Inquisitor which are familiar to readers of Dostoievski's *Brothers Karamazov* is, of course, a valid critique of those moments in the history of Western Catholicism when force was used to insure men's allegiance to the Church; but it does not deal at all with the central and abiding doctrines of Western Catholicism on authority. The Papacy is not, in the view of those who recognize it, an institution with the purpose of driving people into the Church and holding them there, but is rather the sublime instrumentality through which Divine Grace wards off from the Catholic communion all that, whatever its source, was not present from the beginning in Christ's teaching, literally or implicitly. For this reason Western Catholics have loved it, died for it, borne persecution for its sake, and reverenced those who, however worthily or unworthily, represented it to the world. The Western Catholic is as free as anyone else to come to his insight into the fullness of the meaning of Christianity but he has a certainty held with profound gratitude that when he is in his Church he will not unwittingly find strange gods upon the altars.

In any event, the quest for reunion continued and reached, as has been indicated, an initial nadir during the period of the Crusades and a moment of optimistic hopefulness at the Councils of Ferrara and Florence during the fifteenth century. Only a brief reference to either is possible here. The Crusaders, who were roused by eloquent preachers like St. Bernard to take up arms and make the long journey eastward to wrest the Holy Places associated with the life and death of Our Lord from the Turks, served a consecrated cause; but many of them were very human, indeed. Some historians conclude from the sermons of St. Bernard and other preachers of the time that the purely mundane benefits which accrued to the men who took up the Cross were so great that many ruffians (contrary to romantic historians, the Middle Ages had their share of them) embarked on the adventure. It is also evident that although the Crusades owed their origin to an appeal for help from the Byzantine Emperor, to which the monks of Cluny responded as best they could, the net cultural result was that the East was not only disappointed in what the West could achieve but disgusted with the conduct of the armies, even as since that time many another occupied country has been with foreign soldiers who have been billeted on its soil. On the other hand, the West heard many a report about the corruption and venality of the East, even as the home people in this our day have listened to shocking stories of lands which their soldier sons have seen. It must be added that the subsequent continued dominion of the Turks likewise dampened the ardor of friendship.

The great Councils to which we have referred opened in a spirit of optimism, despite the nationalistic bickering to which Europe was then subject. The Greeks were in a conciliatory mood, due largely to their need of Western allies against the followers of Mohammed, but they arrived in Europe at a time of bitter conflict over whether a Council took precedence over the Pope. The Decree of Union did not satisfy the great mass of the Greeks, even though the overwhelming majority of their ecclesiastical representatives assented to it in accordance with the wishes of the Emperor. The only positive result was the formation of the Greek Churches in union with Rome, usually called the Uniate Churches. In Russia, as we have seen, the Czar vetoed any plan of reunion.

But the great dream of reunion did not die, and after World War I it was revived especially by Pope Pius XI, who had intimate personal knowledge of conditions in Eastern Europe from the high vantage point of the Holy See. Institutions under the auspices of the Papacy were established to promote the achievement of One Fold and One Shepherd. At the same time the Protestant Ecumenical Council likewise began to search for ways in which to draw the Eastern Churches into union, with the Churches bound together under its roof. These efforts were not wholly useless, but it was again obvious that the disunity of the Christian West had puzzled and confused rather than attracted the East.

Meanwhile great changes had taken place. The Papacy was compelled to reckon with the rise of secularism, which swept across Eastern Europe from the West during the nineteenth century. Medieval ecclesiastical institutions were widely identified with feudalism; and in addition new intellectual and scientific movements gave rise to a widespread conviction that religion was in itself a barrier to the development of the good, or at least the prosperous, society. The attack on feudalism which became the great French Revolution of 1789 was also a rebellion against the privileged Church; and after the rise of a capitalistic society the estrangement of the poor from religion became the dominant fact in the cultural history of Western Europe. Hegelian philosophy—combining a doctrine of the constantly mobile and shifting Mind with a theory of the State as the sole primordially ordained center of permanence in an otherwise impermanent world—came to prominence at a time when dissatisfaction with Liberalism (in the continental sense) was breeding myths of political utopianism among the masses. Of these myths the strongest, temporarily at least, was the Marxist faith, rooted in a class-conscious usurpation of Hegelian thought. Yet observers who looked deeply into the well-springs from which the intellectual behavior of the time was fed could see that a creed drastically counter to Marxism was arising in many different places, almost spontaneously. This might be termed dynamic traditionalism—that is, investing the past of man with sacredness and subsequently selecting from it forces and figures that could be made objects of the cult, in which the concept of human sacrality might receive a quasi-liturgical form. Perhaps such a force might be race, or classical antiquity, or one of the urges which some historians read into the Renaissance. To the exponents of dynamic traditionalism, the Catholic Church often seemed to be one great force among many others. For did it not have discipline, as Charles Maurras observed, and a heritage of beauty ranging all the way from the austerity of Cluny to the gorgeous splendor of St. Peter's?

This traditionalism tempted many Catholics—was indeed a far greater peril to orthodoxy than even the antecedent, all-pervading Liberalism. That no doubt had led not a few to believe that the Christian creed was outmoded and so could be made serviceable only by adapting it, more or less subtly, to the assumptions of modern scientific and philosophical thought; but dynamic traditionalism transformed the Church of the Master into a genteel and eminently historical institution, with the role of conferring the august dignity of an assumed other world upon the power politics of the here-and-now. The robes of prelates fitted very well into the pageantry of the State, and so there were not a few who thought that a benediction might well be expended upon Nazis and Fascists, to the accompaniment of incense and carefully selected items of Gregorian chant, if only their grandiose parades would include a section devoted exclusively to the clergy. It may be said parenthetically that today no one knows whether the Russia of Stalin was a devotee of Marxism or of dynamic traditionalism. Had Stalin donned the robes of Ivan, who could have told which heresy he was espousing?

A succession of great Popes, possibly the most remarkable in the long annals of the Church, accepted the challenge. Leo XIII, intellectual and aristocratic, recognized the necessity for demonstrating to the workers that they were not at present inside the realms of a Christian civilization that doomed them to a condition of perennial peonage. His successor, Pope Pius X, left to the world the conviction that the Church is the servant of peace; and Benedict XV committed all Catholics to the support of an international order. In 1922 began the vigorous pontificate of Pius XI, distinguished for the world-wide scope of his interests and sympathies. Whereas during several centuries the See of Rome had worn an air of Roman provincialism, the tireless leadership of this learned, mountain-climbing North Italian imparted to it a new tinge of contemporaneousness and cosmopolitanism. The Vatican ended its old quarrel with the Italian State over the Papal territories, even though at some risk of seeming to assent to the dictatorship of Mussolini. It acquired a radio station, an Americanized library system, and even a scientific academy. Through adroit and conciliatory diplomatic activity agreements were reached with the new states of Europe as well as with many countries overseas concerning relationships between Church and State. In ways which were often startlingly new, the laity was associated with the clergy in the work of the Church; and social reform was advocated, in the spirit of a great Encyclical letter restating and re-forming the principles of the moral teaching concerning society which are implicit in the Catholic tradition. All these things were then kept alive under the next Pope, Pius XII.

It is part of the universal tragedy of our time that so very much of what seemed so promising should have been engulfed by the fearful upheavals which, originating in Europe, for a time threatened to shatter the foundations of human society everywhere. In Adolf Hitler appeared the demagogic voluntarist who gave the heresy of dynamic traditionalism its most drastic and frightening formulation. Meanwhile, in nearly every other country Marxism became the gospel of the dissident intellectuals, who often were able to commit to their view sections of the working population, indeed not infrequently unwilling sections. Yet Pius XI had felt, almost from the moment he assumed Pontificate, that a great and shattering storm was brewing in Europe. That is why he labored so vigorously for the development of the Church in other parts of the world, including Africa and Asia. He took steps to forestall the disaster, opposing the mighty heresies whenever he could even though sometimes the infection had spread so far among Catholics themselves that—as in the case of the *Action française*— Princes of the Church did not concur with him.

In Eastern Europe the position of the Church was inevitably and critically affected by inability to arrive at a *modus vivendi* with the Bolshevik government. The lengthy story of efforts to reach an agreement cannot be told here; but it may be recalled that until the summer of 1924 a Papal Relief Mission was active in Russia at the request of the government, bringing food, clothing, and medicine to many tens of thousands. Yet even while this work of charity was in progress, priests and prelates were sentenced to death and executed, churches were looted and closed, and many of the faithful were exiled. The Bolsheviks insisted that, until the Vatican recognized the regime as a lawfully constituted government, clergymen professing allegiance to Rome must be regarded as enemies; Russian émigré circles were just as vehement in demanding that no such recognition be accorded; and circles representative of the Orthodox Church opposed even the Papal Relief Mission, on the ground that its directors were in reality proselytizers. In the circumstances, the Vatican tried to carry on its relief work as long as possible, and to use whatever influence it could muster to save the persecuted bishops and priests. In the end, however, the isolated remnants of Roman Catholicism in Russia lost even the remotest hope that Rome could do anything for them.

The countries west of Russia, most of them newly established, presented less formidable obstacles to the mission of the Church; but in not a few of them conditions were turbulent enough. In Czechoslovakia, for example, insurgent nationalism combined with anticlericalism to create within the Catholic clergy a sizable group who not only wished to rid the Church of every vestige of association with the Habsburgs but also strove to "reform" the ecclesiastical organization itself and to do away with such constraints as celibacy. However, the secession and subsequent excommunication of this group led to a great strengthening of the loyal majority. Catholics were collectively more resolute, and by 1925 the fever had abated, and relations between Church and State were established on a solid foundation. Elsewhere the story was similar, though perhaps less stormy and tawdry.

In attempting to visualize the complex continuous effort by

the Church in these lands to educate the people and to meet their physical and spiritual needs we deal not with an island in the stream of modern life—as we should if, for example, we set out to evaluate the influence of religion on the art, music, and architecture of present-day America—but verily with that stream itself. For example, the press that appeared under Catholic auspices in Poland, Hungary, and Czechoslovakia was a mighty force, in all its ramifications from the daily newspaper to the monthly periodical, for the shaping of public opinion. On the other hand, hospitals and refuges, schools and day nurseries, conducted for the most part under the supervision of religious orders, were almost the only institutions of such character to be found in some countries. Therefore the Communist onslaught upon this manifold activity was not merely against tradition but verily against action. It could not have succeeded unless its directors were safely established behind a dense array of Russian machine guns. It was an invasion resembling in some respects the earlier inroads from the East under which all these lands had suffered not once but many times. Assuredly the men in the Vatican, pondering the news each day, must often have let their thought return to times when Turk and Tartar bombarded the ancient citadels of once Christian Europe.

We shall now summarize, though of necessity far too briefly, Protestant efforts to establish ecumenical union with the Russian Orthodox Church. On the one hand they resulted to some extent from the failure during the Pontificate of Pope Leo XIII to prepare the way for the union of the Anglican Church with Rome. This failure, it will be recalled, was in large measure due to Rome's decision that Anglican Orders were not valid. On the other hand, Protestant Churches in Eastern Europe often felt that the attitude of Russian Orthodoxy toward the State was more compatible with the traditional views of

Protestantism than were those of Roman Catholicism. Lutherans, for example, were not averse to identifying their Church
with a political power; but their belief that the Kingdom of God
and the kingdoms of this world are radically different also led
to the conclusion that the Church could accept responsibility
for approving or opposing actions by the State only when these
controverted directly the moral and religious truths which had
been made explicit in the teachings of the Lord Jesus. Thus a
section of the German Lutheran Church opposed Nazism with
sublime courage because Hitler had repudiated in principle
such central teachings as that of the validity of Christian bap-
tism when administered to persons of Jewish origin.

But Protestants viewed with uneasiness the Catholic practice
of creating organizations of the faithful for political and social
action—which led in Germany to the creation of the Center
Party on the basis of organizational efforts that had their origin
in 1840. This was by no means merely an opportunistic reaction, even though upon occasion ecclesiastical rivalry may have
played a part. While some loyal Protestants cooperated with
and even voted for the Center Party, even as did a number of
Jews, the great majority felt—no doubt, upon occasion, quite
properly—that partisan activity brought the Church into realms
where religious teaching was compromised for the sake of political expediency. This cleavage was intensified after Karl
Barth and his associates formulated a neo-orthodox theology
whose profound influence extended beyond Germany to Calvinism and Lutheranism in the whole of Eastern Europe. How
strongly this criticism affected Catholic practice cannot be discussed here; but it may be pointed out that, during much of the
Pontificate of Pius XI, Rome contemplated withdrawing the
faithful completely from organizations of a political and social
character, and building up instead the groups which received
the generic name Catholic Action. Only toward the close of his

Pontificate did Pius XI reaffirm the desirability of the more secular associations. And in Germany after World War II Catholics elected to create an interconfessional party, the Christian Democratic Union, instead of resurrecting the old Center Party (which emerged as a small minority movement only).

In any event, wide circles of the clergy and the laity looked upon the Russian Church with deep if sometimes nostalgic respect, particularly when the yearning for the reunion of Christendom was spiritually motivated and sincere. Despite many efforts, the outlook for an eventual peace with the Roman See which would obliterate the divisive past seemed to be unpromising. And on the other hand the "Social Christianity" to which American Protestantism appeared to be irretrievably committed impressed the more traditional European theologians as being thin and relatively mundane. There remained the hope that by forging a bond with the Orthodox East a new Christian community, transcending national boundaries, could be established. The writings of Russian exiles were read with avidity; and the authors were of such talent, insight, and sometimes genius that they exerted a great influence. There can be no doubt that, if after victory in 1945 Stalin had adopted a conciliatory policy and had conceded genuine religious and social freedom, Central and Eastern Europe would have become strongly, even ardently pro-Russian. The response in Protestant communities would have been particularly sincere.

The hope for such a policy was at times as fervent as a messianic dream, and it died hard. Pastor Martin Niemoeller has perhaps been its most eloquent exponent, but there have been many others. It is not possible to understand fully the situation that developed unless one bears these things in mind. Only with great difficulty could Europe resign itself to accepting the intellectual and cultural leadership of the United States. This sobering thought may also be a healing one.

2 THE SITUATION IN EASTERN GERMANY

═══

THE PROVINCES OF Eastern Germany which at present constitute the Russian Zone of Occupation no doubt afford
the most advantageous point of departure for an inquiry into
religious life behind the Iron Curtain. Not a little is known
about conditions prevailing there; and for a variety of reasons
the Soviet authorities have on the whole laid down policies
which are in some respects more moderate than are those in
force elsewhere. The beleaguered island of Berlin remains, to
an even greater extent than Vienna, a point of exodus and in-
gress between West and East. It should be borne in mind that
the Zone is merely the torso of prewar eastern Germany. The
great agricultural regions of East Prussia, Pomerania, and
Silesia were detached from Germany in 1945. Of the five remaining states, Brandenburg, Saxony, and Thuringia are the
most important, and are in part highly industrialized.

When the Russian armies first marched in, ruthless violence
was the order of the day. Some idea of the lawlessness which
prevailed is given by the fact that more than half the Catholic

clergy in the area were put to death in varying ways, and that the losses suffered by the Protestant clergy were also great. Gradually order was restored under a puppet German government to which at first all political parties were contributors. Soon, however, the Unity Party in which Socialists and Communists were merged gained complete control. Sizable police forces were created, and recruits were sought in both the East and the West. Economic conditions have on the whole remained primitive. Food resources have never been adequate, and in years of poor harvests (for example, 1952, when early frosts spoiled a large part of the potato crop) the plight of the population has been dire indeed. As a matter of fact, widespread famine would have decimated the population had it not been for relief shipments of foodstuffs from the West. The great religious eleemosynary organizations have siphoned more than a third of all supplies from outside Germany into the Eastern Zone; and in addition giving by West Germans has continued on a notable scale. Industrial production by nationalized mines and factories has, however, steadily increased, though wages are low and the working groups disgruntled.

The Constitution under which the East German government presumably functions is so similar to the basic written law elsewhere in the Russian sphere of influence that the provisions which govern religious activity will serve to illustrate rather well what the over-all juridical framework is. The exercise of religious beliefs shall not (we read) be curtailed. This is in accordance with the Soviet contention that full religious liberty is guaranteed by the Soviet Constitution. Church and State are declared wholly separate, so that the independence of religious organizations is formally recognized. To be sure, this recognition is subject to the whimsical impulses as well as to the over-all political strategy of the Communists. When parents give their consent, religious instruction may be imparted to chil-

dren under fourteen years of age. After that age they are pre-
sumed to be their own masters, so that they themselves must
decide whether they desire any additional religious indoctrination. The Constitution further provides that anyone who wishes
to withdraw from the Church shall be able to do so without
incurring any social stigma. A number of specific prohibitions
are also included in the fundamental law; but these are quite
like the caveats established by the Nazis. Thus any action by
a religious association which is deemed to be in violation of
the principles of the Constitution, or which may be interpreted
as having a partisan political character, is subject to censure
and punishment.* It is likewise unlawful to impose an obligation to attend religious services—an obligation which the German *Wehrmacht* had traditionally made a part of military
training. Private or parochial schools were forbidden, although
until recently it was possible to send children residing in East
Berlin to religious schools situated in the Western part of the
city. Finally, no one can be made subject to a demand that he
manifest a religious faith in public.

So much for the law. The pro-Soviet Unity Party has, however, its own code of conduct in so far as religion is concerned,
resembling in this respect Communist parties in power elsewhere. A good deal of experience with this code has been accumulated, and religious leaders have commented on various
aspects of it. The cardinal principle is that while open, full-
scale onslaughts on religion are to be avoided, Communists
must do everything in their power to spread the Gospel of dialectical materialism. A highly significant practical corollary
is that since service to the Russian state is the major business
of Communist parties, everything possible must be done to

---

* Under Hitler, action was based not on the Constitution but on the decree
against pro-Communist activities which had been signed by President von Hin-
denburg. This decree was made applicable to statements by the Protestant Confessional Church, the Catholic Bishops, etc.

form a group of "democratic" or "patriotic" clergymen, so that after they have been wholly won over they can be appointed to positions of power and influence within the Church, thus curbing or if need be liquidating the "reactionary" and "imperialistic" clergy. This is the standard method of infiltrating religious organizations. Lay people, too, are subjected to the same pressures. If a number of them can be found who are willing to form a "progressive movement" designed to demonstrate that true religion is wholly in favor of the Communist system, the seeds of disunion can be planted. Some who join such groups are dupes, others are subject to intimidation for reasons ranging all the way from fear of public exposure of some weakness to dread of losing a position. In Eastern Germany there are also quite a number of truly religious persons who feel that the Church should disassociate itself from all worldly affairs, and avoid either support of or opposition to the civil government. For all such governments are, in their view, purely mundane and therefore evil—or at least necessary evils. The "neutralists," as they are familiarly called, are above all anxious to avoid any commitment which would align the Church with military effort and therefore with potential war. Such persons are not pro-Russian, but they are likely to be anti-Western.

Two statements by Communists prominent in the Unity Party may be cited as typical of the views prevailing in such circles. During January, 1950, a prominent Thuringian leader, speaking for internal Party consumption, stated frankly:

We Marxists-Leninists are aware of the fact that religion is merely the opium of the people. We will always maintain this Communist principle, but the situation requires that we deal with the problem as such as diplomatically as possible. It may sound strange, but it is true that we must protect religion even while we are keeping a close watch on the clergy. Should any one among them become dangerous to us, he must be removed. Every district chairman must report priests to us who seem to be reactionary, so that the necessary further steps can be taken by the Land Board.

During June, 1949, the same policy had been formulated more bluntly at a meeting of officials responsible for the security of the East German State:

Since the Church in the Greater German Republic [the official Communist label for the government of the Russian Zone] is beginning to allow itself to be exploited as a trumpet by the Western Imperialists, we must see to it that these comedians of Heaven lose all interest in such activities. Enough room is still available in our camps for additional labor companies composed of these black brethren. Physical work will persuade them once and for all to quit inciting against us the people who are still gullible enough to listen to them.

To date, however, neither the Lutheran Church, to which the great majority of Germans in the Russian Zone of Occupation belong, nor the Catholic Church * has felt the full impact of the threats implied in such utterances. It may be added that, although the whole of Eastern Germany north of Silesia has long been strongly Protestant, displaced persons from the territories taken over by Poland have for the first time raised the number of Catholics in Thuringia, Anhalt, and Mecklenburg to more than 10 per cent. The initial step taken by the Communist-dominated government was to establish an Office for Religious Affairs. This is a part of standard Russian procedure, but in East Germany the agency, strikingly like the bureaus created by the Nazis for the regulation of religious affairs, ostensibly

---

* There are four major Churches in Eastern Europe to which the word "Catholic" is applied. Roman Catholics—that is, Catholics who acknowledge the Pope as their Supreme Head—follow either the Latin or the Greek rite. Those who follow the second are usually referred to as Uniates. Orthodox Catholicism does not assent to the primacy of the See of Rome. It may be either Greek Orthodoxy, which implies affiliation with the Patriarchate of Constantinople, or Russian Orthodoxy, presided over by the Patriarch of Moscow.

had for its primary purpose the consideration of complaints voiced by responsible ecclesiastical leaders. Some such protests were formulated in a letter addressed, on April 23, 1950, by Bishop Otto Dibelius to the Lutheran clergy and faithful. He listed as the principal objects of concern: the teaching of a materialistic philosophy of life as a substitute for religion in the schools and youth organizations; the pressure methods used to weaken the consciences of Church members; and the refusal of legal counsel to persons brought to trial on charges of opposition to the government. It soon became obvious, however, that the real task assigned to the Office for Religious Affairs was to recruit clergymen willing to serve the Communist State and to support any propagandistic efforts which it considered particularly worth while. The recruits were approvingly labeled "national," "patriotic," or "democratic," in accordance with the estimated local popularity of any such adjective. Those who remained aloof or critical were of course called "reactionary" or "imperialist." Wherever and whenever the number of recruits became sizable, the fortunes of the "reactionaries" declined. These were attacked in the official press, and their views were grossly misrepresented. Eventually some of them were brought to trial on charges of having succumbed to the lures of Wall Street, and upon occasion sentenced for espionage activities.

Still another phenomenon is worthy of note. Normally the Communists will treat with special consideration the representatives of a religious minority, particularly one which has suffered at the hands of the majority group. The purpose is to elicit a statement that all is well with the minority, which can be used propagandistically as evidence that only the larger "reactionary" Church is indulging in unwarranted criticism and opposition. Fortunately relations between Lutherans and Catholics in eastern Germany had improved very remarkably during the Nazi period, as a result of hardship and persecution both groups suffered. The younger clergy in particular had shared moving and harrowing experiences. Accordingly the Catholic minority was proof against party blandishments.

Oddly enough, therefore, the full weight of Communist opposition fell on Jehovah's Witnesses, a sect which has long had a following in Eastern Europe and so was well known in some sections of the expellee population. The Witnesses had also been a target for Nazi hostility, and many hundreds of them perished in Dachau and other concentration camps. During 1950, the Communists banned the sect in eastern Germany, on the ground that it was a branch of the American "espionage system," even though specially favorable treatment had been accorded to it in Poland. It is believed that by the close of the year nearly eight hundred Witnesses were serving terms in prisons and labor camps, and that life sentences had been imposed on thirteen of its principal advocates.

It has been surmised that all this happened because some prominent German Communists profess to be masters of "astrological science," and indeed several had been initiated into the recondite subject by no less a master than Rudolf Hess. Jehovah's Witnesses believe that the end of the world is rapidly approaching, on the basis of their deductions from Holy Writ, and therefore indulge in prophecies concerning the impending demise of our world, due to human sin and frailty. Communism believes in prophecy, too, but holds that the sole reliable form of soothsaying is that outlined by Marxist philosophy as a corollary of "natural science." This "science" enabled Stalin to predict the future of human society with complete accuracy. Communist literature is therefore rich in attacks on "bourgeois" and "mystical" soothsayers, and in equally savory eulogies of Stalin as a social-scientific fortune teller. But Jehovah's Witnesses, confident that the Word of God had been vouchsafed to them, are incorrigible. No "patriots" or "democrats" have been reported from their ranks.

Thus far the major denominations have fared less badly; but heavy blows have been struck at their influence. Many of them have fallen in the field of education. All private schools have been closed; only the unified educational system survives, and religious instruction is no longer a part of the normal academic curriculum. Recently most of the kindergartens have been placed under the control of the state. In order to understand how revolutionary these various actions are, one must call to mind certain interesting facts about German social history. Traditionally German schools provided for religious instruction, regardless of whether they were organized in accordance with the denominational affiliations of the pupils or were attended jointly by Catholic, Protestant, and other children. Even Socialist and Communist parents, who themselves seldom if ever entered a church, often insisted that their children receive religious instruction, either because they deemed it ethically beneficial or because they wanted their youngsters to profit by whatever modicum of prestige might later result from Church membership. In Germany prior to 1933, it was hardly possible to persuade even Communist parents to leave their young children in nurseries not supervised by Catholic or Protestant religious. I myself have seen workingmen in the "red" districts of Berlin greet the nuns to whom they entrusted their little ones with a clenched fist and a hearty smile. Moreover, eastern Germany had a number of excellent private schools which were conducted under Protestant auspices; and one or another of them was held in as high esteem as Eton or Andover. I think that it is not an exaggeration to say that Count Schwerin von Krosigk remained in Hitler's Cabinet, to which the Conservatives named him in 1933, solely because membership in it enabled him to save the school of which he was a director.

Today education is exclusively the business of the state, and the materialistic philosophy is taught—even as the tenets of Nazism were a few years ago—in all courses bearing on contemporary life. Marxist indoctrination is insisted upon at all levels, from the elementary school to the university. There is a great wealth of evidence on the subject, all indicating that (as one would expect) efforts to counteract it are out of the question. Yet it does not follow that the results are by any means what the Communist leaders desire. There is, to be sure, a complex and sometimes fantastically lavish plan for winning over youth. It involves on the one hand setting up at regular intervals grandiose youth rallies, such as the one staged annually in Berlin during the Pentecostal season, and on the other appointing very young people to important offices—so that boys of eighteen have served as mayors of cities. Literature of all kinds is made available in the quantity desired. A German can buy for the equivalent of about one dollar two fat volumes of the works of Lenin bound in full morocco. All this does unquestionably generate a great deal of intellectual and emotional fog, but no one of my acquaintance who knows eastern Germany thinks that the Communists have as yet succeeded in winning over German youth. If one bears in mind how many Communists have long lived there the reports are all the more astonishing.

Just as 1953 was drawing to a close Marianne and Egon Erwin Mueller, in behalf of the students of the Free University of Berlin and of West German student organizations generally, published an absorbing if harrowing analysis of the academic situation in the Russian Zone, on the basis of reports supplied by all the major universities and technical institutes in East

Germany. This indicated how thoroughly the subordination of instruction to political purpose has been fostered. The right to determine the methods and the content of instruction has been taken from the professorate; the election of students to office in student councils and similar organizations is under rigid Party control; the admission of students is now almost everywhere determined by examinations given in political orthodoxy; and the academic institutions themselves have taken on the character of strictly regulated barracks, in which even recreational activities are decreed. The book (". . . *stürmt die Festung Wissenschaft*") reveals also how courageous and tenacious the opposition has been. A roster of hundreds of names of persons arrested, tried, and often imprisoned for activities looked upon with disfavor by the regime will give even the casual reader some insight into how costly and bitter the struggle was.

It may be observed at this point that a vital part of the Communist propaganda effort in this region is currying favor with former Nazis. Much of the effort is of long standing; but it was the Soviet note of March 10, 1952, to the Western Powers on German unification, that gave official confirmation of its existence. The note proposed that Germany be evacuated by all the Powers within a year, that the State then created be permitted to create a national army of its own, and that all former German soldiers and all erstwhile members of the Nazi Party receive full rights and privileges. The pertinent section of this document reads:

All former members of the German Army, including officers and generals, except those who are serving sentences imposed by the courts for the commission of crimes, shall be accorded civil and political rights on a par with all other German citizens so that they may participate in the building of a peace-loving, democratic Germany.

Apparently the practice of welcoming them into the police forces and other branches of the East German civil service is already well established.

At any rate, the lot of the Christian clergy is a difficult one, exacting exemplary heroism. Intellectually they are isolated, because more and more of East Germany's well trained professional men have sought refuge in the West. They are under constant pressure to sponsor causes in which their Communist masters are particularly interested—the Stockholm peace petition, the abolition of the atom bomb, the return to the United States of every American soldier. On the other hand, they and the Christian Church they serve are continuously and vigorously attacked for indulging in "political activities," which include criticism of the wholly secularist educational system and of the materialistic philosophy. Their financial resources have been curtailed, though not so drastically as elsewhere. They may receive financial gifts from the West, even if the rate of exchange offered by the banks is so catastrophically bad that the money is virtually wasted. After 1949 clergymen were dropped from the category of intellectuals, and so could not claim the somewhat ameliorated rations made available to this group. Moreover, the number of pastors and curates is far smaller than that needed; and many now stationed in the Russian Zone have been overworked to the point of exhaustion. Hundreds of thousands of expellees have come from regions which were once German, and it is only too obvious that many believers of both confessions are not ministered unto. Inevitably there have also been some unavoidable transfers of specially endangered clerics to the West; but such shifts are fewer than might have been anticipated. In summary, one may end with an estimate made during the year 1950 that some nine hundred Lutheran parishes were without pastors, and that there was dire need of at least two hundred fifty Catholic priests.

Theoretically there is no dearth of theological faculties serving the Protestant churches, because formal action to close them in the six major universities of the Zone has not been taken. However, the requirement of political indoctrination is now rigidly enforced, so that it is out of the question to expect the training of a well instructed or devoted clergy in such institutions. The aim has been therefore to educate young men and women in the West and then somehow to arrange for their admission into the Russian Zone. This has grown steadily more difficult, not merely because of opposition from the Communist Government but also because of the candidates' need for unusual heroism and ability to adapt themselves to a course of training which alone will equip them for their almost superhuman tasks. Most of these young people come from escapee backgrounds, and are therefore in a sense preparing to go back to their places of origin. One cannot talk with them without feeling almost overawed in their presence. Yet they are usually quite simple and matter-of-fact. If there was a cloud of glory somewhere about them, they concealed it admirably. The Lutheran Church is permitting trained deacons to act temporarily as pastors, and has permitted laymen to preach while exercising their normal callings. One may say without hesitation that many of these lay people are devoted and exemplary. Both Lutherans and Catholics have also found it necessary to recruit catechists in order to provide religious instruction for children after school hours. The training given is hard and modern in every sense of the term.

Catholic and Protestant welfare agencies have not been suppressed, though there exists an official Government welfare agency. The Inner Mission and the Evangelisches Hilfswerk are Protestant; Caritas is Catholic. Through these are channeled most of the donations received from the West. This freedom is in marked contrast with the situation in Czechoslovakia and Hungary, not to mention Albania and the Balkan countries. Hospitals, homes for orphaned or sick children, and refuges for the aged and the crippled are still conducted under religious auspices, though there has been some curtailment of the training afforded to nurses and social workers at such institutions. No doubt this relative freedom has been strengthened by the poverty and dissatisfaction of the German worker in the Zone, who must contend not only with deteriorating standards of living but also with the abolition of all the freedoms implicit in collective bargaining, which his trade unions had won for him over a period of generations.

It has also proved possible to conserve some religious youth organizations, even if these may now be only local in character. Government-sponsored activities alone are sanctioned on a Zone-wide basis. Societies formed to rally university students still carry on their work. In so far as the press is concerned, Protestants are considerably better off than Catholics. There are a Lutheran press service, a newspaper (*Die Kirche*), and a number of local weeklies published in small editions. Catholics, however, have not been able to secure permission to set up a publishing house or to import printed matter from the West.* Such reading materials as they distribute are more or less covertly smuggled into the Zone. Some cultural activities are likewise carried on under religious auspices, but these are overshadowed by the program of the government-sponsored Kulturbund, which at times receives lavish support.

Very noteworthy is the fact that the Lutheran Church has managed to arrange for periodic synodal conferences, attended by leaders from every part of the Eastern Zone. That which convened in East Berlin during April, 1950, was inspiring and impressive, but was overshadowed by the Kirchentag in the

---

* Early in 1954 it was announced that permission to publish one Catholic journal had been granted.

same place a year later. This was undoubtedly one of the most significant events in recent German spiritual history. More than a hundred thousand persons attended; and the wise, frank, and deeply Christian discussion profoundly moved persons from the West who were fortunate enough to participate. In all probability, no event of the postwar era has been more indicative of what religious faith can mean to sorely tried men and women. Some observers believe that it is in Eastern Germany, under constant threat of persecution, that the Christian Church has grown genuinely strong. It is unquestionably true that contact with the elite fashioned there on the anvil of ordeal is a humbling and strangely strengthening experience that makes one wonder whether the mantle of Western prosperity hides comparable religious treasure.

Nevertheless it is realistic to conclude that organized religion has lost some ground in the Eastern Zone even though the core may be sounder. The fact that so much influence was recovered, despite prewar weakness and the inroads of Nazism, is truly extraordinary; but the young had received very little sound training, and so, when the Communists insulated many of them against even conventional religious instruction, it was only natural that many should at least pay lip service to the Communist cause. Nor have efforts to recruit "patriotic" and "democratic" clergymen been wholly unavailing. Some Catholic priests and Protestant pastors alike have professed to see no reason why an agreement could not be reached between a socially oriented Christianity and Communism. The official propaganda, stressing peace and anti-imperialism, also made at least a temporary impression; and of course it has not been too difficult for some who once were Nazis, despite their clerical garb, to persuade themselves that Stalin is only a *Führer* in a somewhat unusual disguise.

What is the greatest impediment to the open profession of

religious principles in Eastern Germany? No doubt it is the Communist system of justice. Whereas one can only tentatively evaluate the practice of the courts in the satellite countries proper, the relative freedom in Eastern Germany makes it possible to observe rather closely the course of legal procedure there. Basically the system is not very different from that established by the Nazis. Once it has been laid down as a principle that "the healthy feelings of the people" have priority over codified legislation, and once it has been made self-evident that the welfare of the community takes precedence over the rights of the individual, it is easy for a judge to hand down any decision which his political superiors desire. And while the Communists pay less attention than the Nazis to "healthy feelings" their addiction to the welfare of the State is no less ardent and complete. One case may be adduced here by way of illustration. On January 5, 1950, three young men were arrested because they had painted the word *Freiheit* (freedom) on house walls. Two of them had also passed round some pamphlets of Western origin, picked up during a trip to Berlin. The lower court found all three guilty and imposed sentences of three months in jail. But when the prosecutor appealed the case to a higher court the verdicts were revised to read ten years, five years, and two years respectively.

It was argued, and the court agreed, that these young men sought to create in the minds of East Germans the impression that they were not free. "This," said the court, "is gossip which in the most serious possible manner endangers the peace of the German people." For was it not true that the laboring masses of Eastern Germany had freed themselves from the enslaving chains of the lords of finance and industry? Indeed, the court went on to declare, one of the pamphlets which the defendants had circulated urged the population to resist the Communist occupation authorities. Because the ultimate consequence of taking such hate-mongering documents at their face value could only be a new war, the principal defendant, a boy of eighteen— was clearly guilty of having attempted to incite the nation to armed conflict. Of special interest is the sentence imposed upon the third defendant, aged twenty-two. He had not wished to distribute the pamphlets but had permitted himself to be talked into doing so once only. After that he had refused. Nevertheless he was sentenced to two years in prison because in the court's opinion he, as a member of the FDJ (the Communist youth organization, Freie deutsche Jugend), should have known better.

Under such a system of justice, which considers even the mildest form of propaganda against the government to be an action "inciting to war" or "undermining the peace," it is extremely dangerous to indulge in any form of criticism. On May 9, 1951, the Minister of Justice of the Eastern Zone issued a proclamation which reads in part as follows:

The fascist tyrants who ruled over Germany threw tens of thousands of honest anti-fascists into prisons, houses of correction, and concentration camps. It was enough to have been a member of or an official in the labor movement to make one a victim of persecution, maltreatment and loss of freedom. We refer to these victims of Fascism with the term "political prisoners."

Today no one is arrested because of his opinions. Anyone who attacks our anti-fascist democratic order, or who hampers the building up of our peace industry, commits a punishable offense and is penalized because of his criminal actions. Prisoners of this character are therefore to be called not "political prisoners" but just plain criminals. It is as a consequence forbidden to refer to them as "political prisoners." If in an individual case some more accurate description is desired, one should employ a concrete term, such as for example "criminal in accordance with Article 8 of the Constitution," "criminal in accordance with Article 6," etc.

Add to all this the characters of many persons entrusted with the administration of justice, and the maintenance of national security. The Investigating Committee of Freedom-Loving Lawyers in the Soviet Zone (Untersuchungsausschuss der freiheitlichen Juristen der Sowjetzone) has published a series of short biographies, in many cases fully documented, which reveal with startling clarity what kind of person has been recruited for the bench in the Russian Zone. Thus Bernhard Bechler, a Nazi who was for some time Minister of the Interior in the State of Brandenburg and was later Chief Inspector of the People's Police, had been assigned to the Eastern Front during the war, and was captured by the Russians. Soon thereafter he joined the Moscow-sponsored National Committee for a Free Germany, and was utilized in broadcasts to Germany. His wife, also an ardent Nazi, was thereupon visited by a stranger who told her of having listened to her husband's speeches. She took this as an insult, denounced the man to the police, and refused to ask clemency for him. As a result she was interned first by the Americans and then by the Russians. Meanwhile Bechler decided to marry his secretary, and persuaded the court to declare his wife dead, even though it was well known in which camp she was being detained. She was released unexpectedly during 1948 and returned home to see her children. Bechler managed to have her arrested once more, and this time the death sentence was imposed. To his great annoyance, however, the penalty was commuted to life imprisonment. Evidently some one higher up was playing grim jokes on the Chief Inspector!

It is no wonder that under such a system of jurisprudence security and freedom should seem very frail and unpredictable. Countless thousands of refugees have come into the Western Zone through the "open door" of Berlin, and others have

crossed the frontiers to the south and west, taxing all the resources of the reception agencies.

Conditions in the Russian Zone have been relatively so tol-
erable, despite all that has been or could be adduced to make
evident the callous tyranny which prevails,* that many people,
churchmen as well as men of affairs, argue that everything
possible must be done to dissuade the Communists from adopt-
ing more ruthless policies and thus duplicating the situation
which exists in Czechoslovakia. This point of view is not restricted to the "neutralists." It is held that the Church should
scrupulously refrain from taking sides in the great debate between East and West, and even avoid being drawn into the discussion of Germany's own future. The exponents of this policy
would do everything, even at the constant risk of martyrdom, to
preach the Gospel of Christ. Some may dismiss the reasoning
as fatuous, but it seems to me that it is tenable, at least for the
very few who can live in the spirit of pre-Apocalyptic Christianity even during Apocalyptic times.

Would it be possible for the great majority of both the clergy
and the laity to preach and practice the Christian faith without
at the same time making concessions to the Communist philosophy? Nowhere else under the Russian tyranny has it been
possible to do so. If it is difficult enough in the Western world
to live as a Christian without making concessions to the all-
pervading secularism, what must happen when the dictator is
able to curb the apologist for the Scriptures by suppressing his
independence? Nevertheless, if one responds to these questions

* Thus *Osservatore Romano*, March 2, 1950, reported Cardinal Frings, Archbishop of Cologne and Primate of Germany, as saying: The goal of education in
the Russian Zone "is atheism. It is taught in the schools that Jesus Christ did not
exist. There is no possibility to establish a Catholic press. Catholic newspapers,
even ecclesiastical bulletins, are not permitted. . . . There is no Catholic Youth
Movement in the Soviet Zone, which is very dangerous. Youth is admitted only
to the organization of 'Young Pioneers,' which exercises a baneful influence."

pessimistically, the practical course to be taken by the Church is far from clear. Were the impression given that the Christian conscience favored the use of force in order to end the terror of Communist rule, the enemy would pillory it for having fomented war with all its unspeakable consequences. On the other hand, supine and hopeless conformity with the decrees of the Kremlin and its henchmen could result only in the gradual desiccation of orthodoxy. Of course it is true that Christianity can always survive in the Catacombs; but as it does so it will cry out in anguish, and sometimes (as we know from history) it will be anguish that those who hearken cannot distinguish from despair.

It is at this point that the great decision as to whether only the remaining free areas of the world can be protected only by effecting a coalition between the NATO Powers and Western Germany can be seen in the right perspective. Would such an alliance automatically seal the fate of Eastern Germany and at the same time render hopeless the situation of West Berlin, so brave and imperiled an island in the sea of Communism? Anyone who has seen with his own eyes the infinitely moving antitotalitarian crowds of that drab but still pulsing city, or who knows how many of them bear on their bodies and their souls not merely the scars of Hitlerism gone mad but also the deep and bitter wounds inflicted by the Cromwellian fanaticism of the East, knows that West Berlin has become the vital symbol of all the values for which men and women have lived and died on the soil of Europe; and the loss of it cannot for an instant be contemplated because the darkness which would ensue after the putting out of that fire would be contagious. It is not easy to refute the reasoning of persons who on such grounds have opposed the entry of Western Germany into a military alliance, for they have on their side all who plead in the East that the little of liberty they still possess be not taken away from them. Nevertheless I think that it was incumbent upon us, in view of the extremely ominous threat which lies upon our time —in which mighty and insignificant events alike are pushing us all forward to ultimate dramatic decisions the results of which only Infinite Wisdom can foresee—to make the choice for weal or woe in favor of bastions that can be defended, even as in battle outposts are endangered reluctantly. I say these things with a heavy heart, not knowing whether they be right or wrong, merely hoping that they may be right.

At any rate, the drawing up of an agreement between the NATO Powers and Western Germany and its discussion in the Bonn Parliament aroused fears that Communist policy would be altered. To some extent it was. A "strip of no man's land" was created along the borders of the Zone, and in various ways freedom of movement was curtailed. At the same time efforts were redoubled to make the youth organizations effective instruments of Communist propaganda. Loyalty tests for admission to the institutions of higher learning were administered with increased rigor, and forms of military drill were introduced for both boys and girls. Target practice in particular was ordained. But it appeared that Russia still hoped that a settlement of the crucial German problem that served its own best interests could be reached, and therefore preferred diplomatic and propagandistic maneuvers to drastic suppression. Open conflict over religious matters was therefore avoided, even though the noose around the throat of the Church was tightened.

This period of waiting with bated breath was marked by three assemblies of dramatic interest and importance. The world watched anxiously to see how the Russians would react to them. The first was the Lutheran World Federation meeting in Hanover, the See of Bishop Lilje, no doubt one of the ablest theologians and churchmen of our time. Many thousands of clerics and laymen, young and old, gathered in the heavily bombed city to discuss the challenge to the Christian conscience presented by the time in which we all live. There was not much allusion to political questions, although Bishop Berggrav of Norway, once a doughty antagonist of Nazism, declared firmly that it was the Church's duty to condemn vigorously the injustices of which governments are guilty. The Soviet Zone authorities had withdrawn their offer to make interzonal passes available in number, but did finally permit eight persons to attend.

Subsequently another great Protestant conference met in Berlin. And finally, during August, the Catholic Day brought together in the same city a crowd estimated at more than 200,000 persons, half of whom came from the East. The government did not hamper the travel of this mighty throng, although an earlier offer to make excursion tickets available was canceled. Here again, political topics were avoided, even if the newly appointed and very able Bishop of Berlin, Monsignor Wilhelm Weiskamm, assured the audience that "God also lives in a land where there are said to be no more crosses"—an allusion to government orders which had removed crucifixes from classrooms. These gatherings were major topics of conversation in all parts of Germany.

More controversial was an exchange of views between Bishop Otto Dibelius and the East German government. The Bishop addressed a Pastoral Letter to the faithful after permission to travel in the eastern part of his diocese had been refused to him. This document was an eloquent plea for pastoral unity, far more outspoken than anything he had previously uttered. It urged the clergy to remain in close association with the bishops, and made some acrid comparisons between Nazi and Communist attitudes toward the Church; and it declared any pastor influenced by a political power rather than by the leadership of the Church was a disloyal shepherd of his flock. His criticism evoked a response, but one more moderate than had been foreseen. Communist spokesmen declared that there was no conflict between Church and State in the Eastern Zone, and that none was desired. They added that the Bishop had permitted himself to become a mouthpiece for Western Imperialism.

That is the story to 1953. What are the outlines of the perceptible future? I shall try to reflect the spirit of answers to this query that have come from a number of people who are very close to the situation, and to refrain from expressing any opinion of my own. Negatively, many speak with foreboding about youth. Education, which teaches Marxism according to Lenin and Stalin at every available opportunity, and the endless waves of propaganda that inundate in particular members of youth organizations which are transmission belts for Communist doctrine, unquestionably have had a considerable influence. Many of these young people have no personal knowledge of a social order devoted to political and cultural freedom. How could they have any? They went from Nazism to Communism; and for many the difference is scarcely perceptible save in the fact that the influences to which they are now subjected are alien. Nevertheless this foreign character of the Russian control is at the same time for not a few the only bridge that connects them with the outside world. Communism sells its own brand of internationalism. Life that is steeped in dour poverty can acquire a vestige of glamour if one follows the brass bands and the parades. To be sure there are not a few who believe that the impression left on German youth is only skin-deep. They point to the rapidity with which the Nazi veneer could be rubbed off. They think that the Communist variety is even less adhesive. If only, they say, the dominion of this dictatorship does not last too long!

And what of religious faith, hearth from which the fire of

devotion to inner freedom (which alone can insure the permanence of outer liberty) is lighted? These are the words of an East German storekeeper, a Lutheran from Thuringia, who came West to attend a conference:

When one lives where I do, one comes to believe that Europe can be saved only by the power of prayer and the rediscovery of prayer. This I believe because only so can man renew the bonds which link him to the Source of Goodness, moral courage, and holiness. Perhaps the requests for aid which are on the lips of so many who have suffered under tyranny, and suffered so long, will help to regenerate society. One can only hope so. One can only pray that it may be so!

The man cited is neither a simpleton nor what is termed a mystic. You would find him a little chary of speech. He received a good education. He got no thanks from anybody for having refused to shout for Hitler. He expects none from anyone for now remaining loyal to his creed. His is the kind of bravery which would rather not be applauded.

The burden of his remarks is repeated over and over again by persons in every walk of life. There is no doubt, they say, that Europe and indeed the whole world of the West suffers from a deep-seated spiritual malady, perhaps the ultimate spiritual malady: loss of belief that God, even if He be assumed to exist, answers the petitions of men. Even as the exploration of the mighty forces of nature proceeds apace, and men grow able to behold with their eyes the rhythmic swimming in space of almost innumerable great stars, to alter verily at will the life processes of animals and plants, and to break apart with instruments the secret embrace which makes the atom the creature of elemental union, there is no feeling among them that the nearing forge of the Creator puts forth any warmth for human beings, or that the spiritual friendship, intimate and personal, which the saints have always contended was possible with God, is either practicable or potentially interesting, heart-warming for us. Europe has moved out of a time which unfortunately spawned various forms of pseudo-Christian magic, through a sort of competition with paganism, into an era when large multitudes of people can no longer distinguish between wholly illicit and banal echoes of totemism and the sublime, life-illuminating words of Jesus: "Seek, and you shall find." For what was thus said is a mystery, but a verifiable truth as well. Alas (I heard it repeated often), what many of us now call religion has become something like the patina on old pewter bequeathed by our ancestors. Or it has become a syrup, very sweet still but not life-sustaining, which flavors many a man's longing for the past when he is no longer transiently young enough to feel a craving for the future.

On the other hand there are everywhere about us remnants of organized materialistic naïveté, bred like Nazism by the first vulgar shock produced during the nineteenth century by Darwinism—a simplified though cumbersome and therefore curiously imposing dialectic claiming for itself all the discoveries and achievements of natural science, as if these were not the products of meditation and intellectual experience. "When Soviet propaganda tells us," some one remarked, "that nearly every great contribution to the exploration of the laws of nature was made by a Russian we may well think it preposterous; but we must bear in mind that what we are listening to is only a consequence of Communist logic. For, if bourgeois society is responsible for all evil, how can it have produced any sizable amount of that which is good—namely, scientific and technological knowledge?" And it can be asked also, supposing that religion is the implacable foe of all science and so merely a chain of vague imaginings generated by vitalistic anxiety, how shall one account for Pascal, Mendel, and Pasteur? These questions suggest their own answers. But when Communism uncompromisingly proclaims that all truth is scientific and all science materialistic it lames the will of the working masses, who have no deep personal reason for not agreeing, and are in addition the heritors of Marxism. In Germany, as elsewhere, some naturalists are among the most vigorous opponents of Communism; but it may be feared that their deepest reason is ineradicably professorial—bound up with their own strong desire constantly to be heard—and can appeal very little to the great majority of men who do not covet the privilege of oratory or the lesser delights of literary composition, but who wonder how much they can crowd into a week end, including young men whose thoughts are on girls, bicycles, automobile races, and fresh air.

At any rate, during the final months of Stalin's lifetime the pressure mounted. After all propaganda and counterpropaganda had been discounted, two facts remained: religious leadership became more and more difficult to provide; and readiness to follow such leadership increased notably. Catholic authorities estimate that death, imprisonment, and exile have reduced the number of priests, secular or monastic, stationed in the European territories now occupied by Russia at least one-half from the thirty thousand who were there before the war. Apostasy, too, has taken its toll. Even if in most satellite countries Bishops can be found who will ordain young men trained in seminaries which are virtually institutions for the inculcation of Communism, the Orders they receive will be mere mockeries of Catholic dedication to the sacred ministry. Accordingly it is not hard to predict the date on which there will be no more priests in Eastern Europe. Granted that tyranny should through some unforeseeable development cease at that time, whence would the Church derive its clerical leadership? West German Catholics have been trying to find the answer to this question. Young men, culled from refugee and escapee groups, are being trained for the mission.

Meanwhile the major spokesman for the Protestant cause, Bishop Dibelius, was being equally realistic and resourceful. This imperturbable prelate, for all the world like a theological counterpart of General von Seeckt, went on predicting that faith in God would not merely enable its protagonists to endure but guarantee their triumph. Therewith was ushered in evidence that the followers are ready. As part of a general attack on all remnants of the bourgeois order, the Communists loosed an assault on the Junge Gemeinde, the organization of Lutheran youth which was not so much an organization as a sort of outcropping, everywhere spontaneous, of boys and girls who wanted religious tradition rather than the Leninist utopia. It held no meetings, staged no rallies. The members gathered for the study of religion. Now suddenly it was called a "terroristic group" dedicated to the advocacy of the political goals of the West. Every device known to totalitarianism was applied to break the fidelity of these young people to their religious faith. Often in the gymnasia, which are equivalent to advanced high schools, pupils were assembled and asked to sign a pledge that they would resign from the Junge Gemeinde. Failure to comply meant immediate expulsion from school; and yet hundreds of young people did not hesitate. It has been reported that during weeks the headmistress of a school in the Russian Zone said at a general assembly of her charges: "Present today are x many pupils and one saboteur." This horrendous individual was a girl of fifteen who refused to resign from the Junge Gemeinde. At least equally harassed was the organization of Christian university students.

As a matter of course the heavy hand of suppression fell on the clergy who were closely identified with the activities of the Junge Gemeinde. More than fifty Protestant ministers and their co-workers were arrested and imprisoned during the first five months of 1953. Heavy sentences, comparable to those handed down in the satellite countries proper, were meted out. The Reverend Werner Gestrich of Heinersdorf was condemned to twelve years in prison for hostile remarks about the State. The Reverend Karl A. Brandt of Lohmen received six years on a similar charge. A court ruled that Pastor Albin Drechsler of Chemnitz was a "Fascist provocateur" and sentenced him to ten years in prison. In all these instances the real crime was identification with the Junge Gemeinde.

Equally ruthless was the action taken against religious institutions. Dramatic in a terrifying way was the closing of the old Lutheran school at Schloss Mansfeld in Saxony. Pupils were sent home, the headmaster was clapped into jail. The leader of Protestant youth in the province went to remonstrate. He has disappeared without a trace. A home for boys in Neinstedt, where some four hundred persons were lodged, was charged with the heinous crime of ignoring Soviet educational methods. Everywhere the story was the same. Meanwhile the tramp of countless thousands westward to liberty continued, despite all hardships and sacrifices. Refugees assembled in West Berlin in such numbers that international relief action became unavoidable. Every day and night peasant and intellectual, civil servant and even politician, sought refuge. It certainly looked as if the Russians had decided to carry out the Sovietization of Eastern Germany as uncompromisingly as they had destroyed their opponents in the satellite States. The Church remained steadfast. Bishop Dibelius, preaching in East Berlin, declared: "We shall not answer with counterpropaganda. We shall simply stick to the truth. The truth may be buried for some time, but in the end it always wins."

A word about the fate of Catholics is now in order. Priests have been imprisoned, and institutions have been closed. Father Friedrich Hildebrandt, pastor of a parish near Magdeburg, received a prison sentence of more than four years.

Father Franz Busch of Kelten was doomed to five years of confinement. The Bishop of Berlin engaged in debate with East German authorities concerning the fate of religious institutions. Though relatively few, Catholics were resolute. Bishop Wilhelm Weiskamm proved himself a worthy confrère of the unwavering prelate who guided the Lutheran Church.

Then on June 10, 1953, in a startling moment of deviation from previous commitments, the East German government announced that the attack on the Churches had been abrogated. This declaration was part of a general statement to the effect that "a series of mistakes" had been made by those in authority. In the interest of "German unity" concessions were offered to private industry and the peasantry. Keenest of the severance swords employed was undoubtedly that which now professedly distanced the rulers of East Germany from any desire to hamper the teaching and the exercise of religion. The reasons why it was resorted to are of course impossible to fathom. We can only guess that the barometer of public opinion had fallen so sharply that for the moment at least the Kremlin was in no need of martyrs.

Almost immediately thereafter came the uprising of workers in East Berlin and other parts of East Germany: a heartrending and yet stirring manifestation of popular sentiment. It was almost entirely spontaneous. On the lips of poor people coming out of hovels and cellars there was an awesome request for the rights of man, for liberty, for human dignity. Driven these masses may have been by hunger, despair, and a detestation of perfidy and injustice. For the first time since the war, a people behind the Iron Curtain held out its hands to the people of the United States; for the first time there was uttered a new demand for the great declaration. We can never forget that men and women died with words about these things spilling from their hearts.

There was little the people of America could do in response. Perhaps through their official representatives they did too little. It was feared that, in the nebulous period after the death of Stalin, any overt expression of support and sympathy might usher in forces bent on Armageddon. Was not the West still too weak to court any such danger? At all events, we showed no mighty resolution in those days. The uprising died as so much that is comparable has died under tyranny. But in the West Konrad Adenauer mustered an overwhelming vote for liberty.

3 THE FATE OF CZECHOSLOVAKIA

WHILE CZECHOSLOVAKIA WAS SUBJECTED to Communism more recently than some other countries we shall consider, it is in several respects the most dramatic and (in a sinister sense) instructive example. A great deal of what happened there could also be observed, day in and day out, by representatives of foreign governments, so that we have at least some reliable information on nearly every aspect of the transformation of what was once no doubt the most democratic of East European states into an exploited Russian colony. Noteworthy also is the high level of culture which once flourished here, not merely as a legacy from the past but as a continuous creative movement in literature, the arts, and productive scholarship. The Charles University was one of the great European seats of higher learning; and the level of popular education was high.

In all probability historians will some day be impressed—if perchance they are still allowed to arrive at independent conclusions—by certain lessons of great importance which are implicit in the tragedy of the Czechoslovak state:

First, as Ivo Duchacek has observed, the aftereffects of a

diplomatic disaster are long-lived. The Republic was established, under Czech leadership, primarily because of the adroit
and persistent appeal by Thomas G. Masaryk to the sentiment
of the Allied Powers during World War I. Mr. Wilson and M.
Clemenceau in particular manifested a maximum of good will,
by incorporating into the new state territories which had traditionally belonged to Poland, Hungary, and Germany. And so
when, at the climax of Hitler's gamble for world power, the
successors to these statesmen concluded not only that the claim
of the German-speaking minority to secession should be recognized, but also that a "war over Czechoslovakia" was not
worth while, the diplomatic edifice so elaborately constructed
by Masaryk and Beneš began to totter. From this collapse, as
we shall see, was derived the later temptation to preserve freedom in the future by relying on Russia rather than on the
Western Powers.

Second, it has been clearly shown that President Wilson's
plan to reorganize Central Europe according to the principle
that the old Austro-Hungarian imperial organization was evil
because it ignored the peoples' right to self-determination was
itself subject to revision; for the extent to which further efforts
to effect tribal independence could be fanned into being was
unlimited unless one placed in the foreground of discussion
regional traditions of cooperation and the economic and political realities of the Danube Basin as a whole. By 1938 Czechoslovakia had become an ironical caricature of the old Empire.
Some 3,000,000 Sudeten Germans, living in the western areas,
had waged a ceaseless struggle for autonomy. In Slovakia and
Ruthenia, the territories annexed from Hungary, the sense of
group solidarity also grew stronger year by year. Most Slovaks
in particular insisted on what they termed equal rights, and on
complete cultural independence. After the establishment of
Nazi rule in Germany, and in particular after Hitler seized

Austria during March of 1938, a strong Sudeten German political party began to demand incorporation of the German-speaking area into the Third Reich. An international commission headed by Lord Runciman supported the demand. Then Slovak separatism intensified, and the Czechs were isolated.

Third, the lack of cultural cohesion which characterized Czechoslovak democracy became increasingly manifest. The liberalism of Masaryk and his associates had derived a measure of strength from the hostility to the Catholic Church of some Czech nationalists and idealists, who held that it had been favored during centuries of subservience to the Habsburgs. Their view was not unsupported by evidence. There were many reasons why the Church and the Empire were intertwined, for good and evil, and they cannot be discussed here. It will suffice to note that the Czechs, who numbered John Huss among their national heroes and had in part espoused the Protestant cause during the era of the Reformation, made an attempt to establish a dissident National Catholic Church at the close of World War I. While the attempt mustered some strength from the clergy and the laity alike, the great majority of the people supported union with the Holy See, at least nominally. We may conclude that the Church was far weaker than the statistics indicated, and that strong secularistic tendencies made Czechoslovakia seem upon occasion to be a center of organized agnosticism and a breeding ground for various sorts of neo-Communist fellow travelers. The fact that this was far less true in Slovakia, where the people were neither sophisticated nor "emancipated," was another source of tension.

The situation which existed in 1945, when Nazism was battered into submission, mirrored all the facts and trends which have been indicated. The Czechoslovak government-in-exile, seated in London under the presidency of Dr. Beneš, was preparing for the peace which would follow the defeat of Hitler.

I participated in discussion with this government, and can say that at least until the close of 1941 it was primarily concerned, apart from the restoration of its own sovereignty, with how a federation of liberated East European states could be formed. In so far as the Sudeten German problem entered into the discussion, the official view was: "In some cases local transfers of population may be desirable, but such transfers should never mean expelling total populations from their ancestral homeland. Czechoslovakia seeks a truly humane solution of the Sudeten problem, a solution which can be acceptable to the majority of the Sudeten Germans." But as the war progressed President Beneš evidently came to feel that only the expulsion of the Sudeten population and an alliance with Russia could insure the solidarity and independence of his country. When it seemed likely that the Soviet armies would march into Prague, a secret treaty was signed which gave expression to his skepticism concerning the West and his fear of a possible German recovery. Indeed, on his own responsibility he indicated to the Kremlin that Ruthenia could be ceded to Russia with the approval of his government. No acknowledgment of this offer is known to have been received; but as a matter of fact the Russians proceeded unilaterally with the annexation during 1944, despite vigorous Czech protests. When all this then became known, and a Russian army of occupation began to terrorize the country almost more than Nazi rule had oppressed it, the average citizen decided to resign himself to possum playing.

Meanwhile American army units under the command of General George Patton had occupied southwestern Czechoslovakia and could without difficulty have taken Prague. But the ratification of the Potsdam Agreement, and ill-fated haste to bring the troops home, caused the withdrawal of the United States Army from the strategic key to Central Europe after it had witnessed the expulsion of vast numbers of Sudeten Germans. In all some 2,500,000 men, women, and children were driven from their homes; and many of them were compelled to walk without food, drink, or shelter over countless miles of hot and dusty roads to the Austrian and German frontiers, where no provision had been made to receive them. The shocking and brutal spectacle aroused the pity and indignation of many Czechs; but when it was followed by the withdrawal of American troops under what could only be interpreted to be Russian pressure it was bound to mean to them that the West had once more decided that Czechoslovakia lay outside the sphere of its vital interest. Approval of such a policy by the government of the United States, in violation of every canon of historical reflection, of political acumen and simple humanitarianism, was unquestionably due to ignorance in the men to whom the destiny of our country, and indeed of the world, was entrusted.*

In any event, the reorganization of political life in Czechoslovakia was inaugurated. Answering a desire entertained by many pro-democrats, the government decided that local autonomy should be fostered, and so a series of new units of local government, called "National Committees," were established. But no sooner did these "committees" emerge from their chrysalises, than it became apparent that Communists who had been in the resistance movement or had been trained in Russian indoctrination centers stood ready to take them over. These Communists were knitted into a solid organization subject to orders from Moscow, whereas the opposition was pathetically

---

* It is fair to say that the judgments expressed here are not *ex post facto.* Prior to the close of the war, I made as many speeches as I could stressing the imperative necessity of maintaining the freedom of Czechoslovakia; and after victory I pointed out how in this respect particularly the Yalta and Potsdam agreements imperiled the security of Europe and of the United States. The sole consequence was to attract to myself all the barbs which all the sellers-out of American sagacity and honor, from Gerhard Eisler to the littlest Communist on Park Avenue, were able to fling.

inchoate. Naturally the Communists accentuated cleavages and took advantage of every democratic inability to arrive at a decision.

After the era of Nazi occupation, the question of "war crimes" and "collaborationism" was very much in the foreground. Czech Communists were able, as their counterparts in France were not, to stage a reign of terror under which anybody who had not actually been in a concentration camp was hard pressed to demonstrate his innocence. Some of the trials —for example, that which resulted in the imposition of a death sentence on Monsignor Josef Tiso, head of the government of Slovakia while it was a republic under Nazi domination—were spectacular, but most were drab little partisan courts-martial manifesting not a trace of impartiality.

Because of the great role such trials played in the drama of Czechoslovak subjugation, a word must be said here about war-crimes trials in general. Necessarily criminals of such barbaric magnitude as the Nazi leaders were had to be brought to book. But the association of the free world with Russia in the trials conducted at Nuremberg and elsewhere unwittingly but none the less really placed a stamp of approval on an integral part of the Communist judicial system.

For while, in courts established in accordance with the traditions of the West, it has always been essential that the allegedly guilty shall be tried only by impartial judges on the basis of previously established laws, the Russian tribunal—like the Nazi tribunal—is by its very nature a board of inquiry bound by the objective to be reached, and not by law either written or unwritten.

Under a totalitarian system like that established by the Nazis, actions involving a measure of conformity are inevitable. Only the very heroic and, perhaps, the very intellectual will become martyrs. And so the war-crimes procedure could be used and was widely used to bring to the dock a variety of "reactionaries" and "collaborators" objectionable for one reason or another to Communists and their friends. Nowhere, probably, was it employed more effectively and arbitrarily than in Czechoslovakia. That the war-crimes trial is an integral part of the Russian juridical system is demonstrated anew each day, and finds its present affirmation in the widely propagandized statement that in the event of a new war Western leaders and military men will be tried in Moscow for "their crimes against peace."

All this does not mean that the heinous offenses committed by a number of Nazi leaders should have gone unpunished. It was possible to mete out justice either through quick and effective courts-martial or through the establishment of neutral courts. Nor can we in any manner infer that those who were servants of the legal procedures followed at Nuremberg and elsewhere wished in the slightest way to aid the Communist cause. Most of them were men of probity and righteous indignation. But it must always be remembered that the line of demarcation between the Free World and the Enslaved World is not miles wide but as keen and narrow as a razor's edge. When we said that it was meet and just for the victor to sit in judgment over the vanquished *in accordance with the long tradition of the West,* and when we agreed to sit side by side with the Russian victor despite the multitudinous crimes he had committed and concerning which we had full knowledge, we assented without being aware of what we were doing to a cardinal principle of Soviet justice. It is true that we mean by justice something entirely different from what Moscow means. We should have made that clear.

At any rate, matters went from bad to worse. A hastily recruited militia was soon dominated by Communists, who enlisted hundreds of young men in quest of careers of lawlessness and banditry. Moreover, after the nationalization of industry the Central Labor Union, dominated by Communists, became the strongest single body in the country. Nevertheless in the elections of 1946 the Communists mustered only 38 per cent of the vote. This was to be sure a great victory, in the light of the traditions and the real sentiment of the nation—achieved through pressure on the individual citizen by the Ministry of the Interior, which controlled the police power, and the Ministry of Agriculture, to which was entrusted a "land reform" consisting primarily in the transfer of properties once owned by Sudeten Germans to worthy souls who professed to gaze upon the hammer and sickle with ecstasy, and in the distribution to equally unexceptionable mortals of tractors, other machines, and fertilizers. In the circumstances, granted so large a multitude of timeservers and profiteers, it is almost a miracle that the pro-democratic forces reacted with any spirit and success. Duchacek says that the eclipse of the old Social Democratic Party by its traditional Leftist rival made the surviving remnants of this party the principal political target, with the result that when a move to the Right was discernible in these groups the Communists had to fear the defection of large numbers of workers and so to abandon every pretense of fidelity to democratic principles; and his opinion is reiterated by others.

Slovak writers interpret the course of events in their area somewhat differently, on the whole. The established Catholic Party in Slovakia, vigorously led by Monsignor Hlinka, who died in 1938, less than a year after Masaryk, was committed to an autonomist policy likely to please an observer who is influenced by Slovak opinion and to displease one who is not. It will suffice to say that the establishment of a Slovak Republic by Hitler, and the at least alleged collaboration of Monsignor Tiso, Hlinka's successor, caused this Party to be considered as

Fascist when the war ended. Therefore its followers rallied to the support of the newly established Democratic Party, only to find that the Protestant population of the region, a strong minority, did not join forces with them. Even so the manifest survival of a large and disciplined voting public in Slovakia seriously interfered with the Communist timetable, although confessional differences helped to create a paralyzing disunity in the pro-Democratic camp.

The Communist decision to stage the *coup d'état* of February, 1948, was carefully planned during the late summer of 1947. Orders had previously come from Moscow that Czechoslovakia was to withdraw from the list of countries to which assistance under the Marshall Plan would be given; and they implied that, regardless of how the majority of the Czechoslovak people might feel, there was no way out of bowing to the threat of the Red Army. On February 20, President Beneš took official cognizance of a crisis in the government. Almost immediately thereafter, the Central Labor Union was mobilized, and a general strike for the period of one hour was ordered. Then bands of workers' militia, armed with weapons seized from the depots of the nationalized armament industry, took over the streets of Prague. They were opposed only by some few thousands of university students who staged a counterdemonstration. These were set upon and suffered severe casualties. A few hours later, the Communist Minister of the Interior dispatched to the capital city several regiments of well organized and thoroughly indoctrinated police. On February 25, President Beneš, old, ill, and utterly bewildered, assented to the formation of a new government formed and controlled by the Communists. "It has not been an easy decision for me to make," he wrote to their leader Gottwald. "It has, indeed, been very difficult for me to make. I have given long and earnest thought to the crisis, and have come to the conclusion that your proposal ought to be accepted." That was the end of freedom in Czechoslovakia.

It is vain to inquire what would have happened if Beneš had decided to resist the demands of the Communists. Well informed observers who were in Prague at the time answer in conflicting ways the question whether an appeal to the army, then not yet completely infiltrated, would have been obeyed. The weight of the evidence seems to favor the view that the President could have evoked at best a token resistance. In short, the pattern of the coup followed almost to the letter that of the Anschluss of Austria in 1938, with a difference of dramatic effect. Then the battalions were all on the side of Hitler; now they all marched according to the bidding of Stalin. But in Austria the last pre-Hitler Chancellor, Dr. Kurt von Schuschnigg, acting on a heroic though wholly quixotic resolve, ordered a free election and therewith compelled the Nazi dictator to march in.

The coup meant that the leaders of the Christian Churches, now the sole potential spokesmen for decency and freedom, had to confront alone the menace to their integrity, their mission, and their existence. We shall review their history summarily on the basis of such a prodigal wealth of data that only a small part of it can be adduced here. The confusion which followed the First World War and which involved efforts to establish a Czech national church has already been described. Relative calm followed that storm. A *modus vivendi*, dated February 2, 1928, led to the stabilization of relations between the Vatican and the Czechoslovak State; there was an exchange of diplomatic representatives, and Catholics not only participated in the life of the country but sponsored a vigorous program of religious and social action. Although the trend toward secularism and away from religious commitment was more pronounced, the Catholic population in the country as a whole was large: 76.85 per cent in 1930. Protestant minorities were specially important in Slovakia; and though the Jews constituted only about 2 per cent of the population they enjoyed every right and privilege.

When the Nazis occupied the country after Hitler's flagrant breach of his promises to Chamberlain, the clergymen of all denominations were (if one excepts Slovakia) among the foremost sufferers from a persecution which was primarily an attack on the intellectual leadership of the Czech people. Hundreds were arrested, held in prison, sent to concentration camps, and many died in captivity. When the United States Army liberated Dachau in 1945, only a remnant of the Czech priests interned there remained alive. These survivors were enthusiastically welcomed upon their return to Czechoslovakia, and it seemed for a time as if these words of cheer indicated that Moscow would welcome the cooperation of the Church. But few were under any illusion that this glistering was truly gold.

The government-in-exile returned from London via Moscow early in 1945 and convened in Košice, a Slovakian town. It then took office in accordance with a Program of Action proclaimed on April 5, 1945. The program began with a declaration that punishment would be meted out to all who had collaborated with the Nazis. It went on to decree the nationalization of the "monetary and credit system," of key industries, and of "natural and power resources." Czechoslovakia therewith became a socialist state.

From London the government had approached the Vatican with a view to resuming diplomatic relations once the war was over. However, when the time came for a Papal Nuncio to be appointed, the Communist members of the Cabinet objected on the ground that the Russians would protest if the representative of the Vatican were dean of the diplomatic corps. Rome solved the problem by sending an "internuncio," with the rank of minister. Various important bishoprics had become vacant during the war. Very able new prelates were named to these sees. Archbishop Josef Beran brought prestige to the See of Prague as a courageous priest who had survived the ordeal of Dachau. One of the foremost theologians of Czechoslovakia, he had been rector of the major seminary and professor in the Charles University. The new Bishop of Brno, Dr. Karel Skoupý, also had been a professor of theology. Unquestionably one of the ablest, most farsighted priests in the province of Moravia, he enjoyed a wide following among both the clergy and the people. A third bishop, Joseph Hlouch, had taught in the University of Olomouc and was a pulpit orator of renown.

The attitude of the Church toward the trend of events was at first one of anxious waiting. Conflicts arose, it is true, over ecclesiastical properties and the conduct of schools. Yet these were minor, compared with the plight of the Greek Catholic or Uniate, Church, in union with Rome but observant of the rites of the East. After the annexation of the Ruthenian district of Czechoslovakia, unceasing pressure was applied to the Greek Catholic Church with a view to subjecting it to Russian Orthodoxy. A tense and unequal struggle followed; priests were imprisoned or exiled, and churches were closed. Greek Catholics, however, had a doughty and imperturbable leader in the aged Bishop Paul Gojdič, who was of the stuff out of which martyrs are hewn. His resistance was ended only by his imprisonment during 1951. The Greek Catholics, though few, proved to be extraordinarily stanch in the defense of their traditions and beliefs.

In Slovakia tension between the pro-Communist government and the Catholics (as distinguished from Protestants, for the time being) was strong almost from the beginning. The National Council, in whose hands authority over the region had

been placed, issued a decree on May 16, 1946, transferring
from the jurisdiction of the Church to the State nearly 1,900
schools—70 per cent of the Church total. Additional regulations curbed the activities of religious organizations and the
religious press. Meanwhile the war-crimes trials took their
grim toll in a land deemed to have cooperated with National
Socialism. The Slovakian Hierarchy, led by Archbishop Karol
Kmeťko, appealed to the President of the Republic in a memo-
randum dated January 10, 1946, that set forth the major aspects of the situation. The Bishops stated that nearly three-
fourths of the Slovak people were stanchly Catholic, and protested against the arbitrary steps taken by a tiny minority of
pro-Communists against the clearly expressed will of the
people. They pleaded for the restoration of the schools to their
Catholic owners, and urged that the crucifix be suffered to remain in schools wherever the parents and the children so requested. They asked further that the confiscated property of
the Catholic Youth Organization be restored, and that expropriated charitable institutions, many of them erected with the
help of benefactions from Catholics in the United States, be
given back to their rightful owners.

When none of the desired results was obtained, efforts were
made to rally popular support for the Slovak Democratic
Party. The government countered by denouncing what it termed
"a huge Fascist plot" and arresting on October 16, 1947, more
than 200 persons, among them many of the most prominent
Catholic intellectuals in Slovakia. A month later the Minister
of the Interior published a commentary on the "plot," entitled
"Conspiracy Against the Government." Some days after this
the whole Catholic Episcopate of Czechoslovakia met for the
first time after the war. It decided to send a delegation to see
the President. To this Dr. Beneš reiterated his desire to preserve religious freedom and amity, and observed that the prac-

tice of religion was clearly growing more fervent and wide-spread. But he was powerless to alter the situation, which was of course soon affected radically by the coup of 1948.

Immediately after the seizure of power, the Central Action Committee of the National Front—the central organ of the Communist Party—sent Dr. Čepička, then Minister of Justice, to the Archbishop of Prague in order to assure him that Catholics had nothing to fear from the new regime. In acknowledgment of this visit the Bishops once more addressed the government, professing indifference to the form of the State or to its political tinge but insisting anew on what they held to be the rights of the Church. The reply came in a letter inviting every priest in the country to join the Communist Party, and containing a compliment for Archbishop Beran. He responded in a lengthy epistle to the Minister of the Interior, two paragraphs of which are quoted here in order to indicate the state of affairs during the tense days of April:

It has been stated that the Catholic Church has not clearly defined its attitude toward the program of the government now in power. But, Mr. Minister, the letter which was directed to you bearing the date of March 4th of this year, as a result of the conference of all Catholic ordinaries at Brno, made the attitude of the Catholic Church quite clear. I can assure you that none of us who are Catholic bishops and priests will betray his State and Nation. None of us, however, can endorse a political program which at many points is adverse to the rights of God and the precepts of the Canon Law. These divergencies cannot be approved either by the Catholic Church or by any Church which believes in the God we worship.

We shall never betray the State or the Nation. But on the other hand we shall also not be traitorous to God and the Church. The new Education Bill violates the natural right of parents to decide freely what kind of education their children are to receive. It prescribes an education subservient to one ideology. Thereby it nullifies the right of the Church to provide religious education for the faithful, in the spirit of a supernatural religion. Religious training dominated by an ideology which denies the existence of God and the fact of human survival after death is not a religious education in any sense. The proposed two hours of religious instruction are therefore only a mask behind which the annihilation of all religious freedom in education is to be carried out.

The new Czechoslovak Constitution was presented to the National Assembly which convened in Hradčany Castle, shrine of the nation's traditions, on May 9, 1948. It conforms closely with the pattern of Communist basic law already discussed in the chapter on Eastern Germany. Defining the freedom conferred on the individual citizen, it ordains that education is the exclusive prerogative of the State, that liberty of conscience is guaranteed, that while freedom to practice a religion is assured it is not "advisable to misuse this right for non-religious purposes," that the press is free although further legislation will determine who is "authorized to edit and print newspapers and periodicals," and that the "right to hold meetings and establish associations is guaranteed in so far as these are not a menace to the people's democratic institutions and to the public order." It would be impossible to devise a Constitution which more effectively gives and takes at the same time.

The President of the Republic, before he died, sent to some of his friends abroad a parting message which shows clearly what was happening behind this façade of words:

The Ministers are accusing me of failure, and I am accusing them of failing to help me at the critical moment. Without their intervention, which was promised to me, I was helpless. When Gottwald gathered hordes of bloodthirsty militia in the old Town Square, I expected that other crowds would gather in Wenceslaus Square. I could not have imagined that readiness and organization were lacking to such an extent when action was imperative. I believed that the demonstration of unarmed students would prove a summons to a general uprising. But when nobody made a move, I could not permit Gott-wald's belligerent mob to inflict wholesale massacre on the defenseless people of Prague. There were no limits to the threats they uttered.

There was no one to sound the alarm, and few were ready to respond. Czechoslovakia was prepared to lay its head on the block. The general election on the 30th of May presented a single list of candidates and resulted in an overwhelming Communist victory. Nearly nine-tenths of a cowed population voted as they were told to vote, thus reiterating the standard procedure under totalitarian regimes. In so far as religion was concerned, the shadow of things to come could be discerned some days earlier when, in violation of an order given to all the clergy by the whole Hierarchy, three priests were listed among the candidates recommended for election. The most impressive and ever since the most notorious of these disobedient clerics was the Reverend Josef Plojhar, who was immediately suspended from his priestly office by Archbishop Beran. The government protested to the Vatican about this disciplinary action. "The Constitution guarantees not only the right to vote, but also the right to be elected to public office," said the newly elected Prime Minister, Antonín Zápotocký. "No one, not even a Church, is entitled to render impossible what has been assured by the Constitution. Therefore we are determined to defend the right to vote and the right to be elected against all efforts to undermine these rights or to make their exercise impossible." Thus there was begun the process of dividing the clergy from the bishops, and as a consequence subordinating the Church to the State.

Soon after the adoption of the Constitution, steps were taken to secularize Church property, the effective agency being the Ministry of Agriculture. All the estates belonging to the Archbishopric of Prague were sequestrated, and expropriations of properties owned by monastic orders followed. Thus there came into the foreground of the struggle a highly controversial issue. The Church in Czechoslovakia, resembling in this respect its sister Churches in States carved out of the old Austro-Hungarian Empire, owned considerable property. Its holdings amounted to somewhat more than 400,000 acres, and in addition there were many utility buildings. It has frequently been contended, by Catholic students of the question as well as by others, that the Church should of its own initiative have dispossessed itself of landed properties. It must, however, be borne in mind that by far the largest number of such properties were to be found in Slovakia, where the income was reasonably well expended for religious and caritative purposes, and where there was relatively little demand for a change.

Confiscation continued, so that by the close of the year 1950 the Church was almost denuded of its financial resources. Despite a measure of vandalism, which now and then recalled the mood of the French Revolution, the actual expropriation was carried out with the implacable, and indeed inexplicable, calm which seems to characterize Communist rule. Consider, for example, the fate of the Home for the Crippled in Prague, which was from time immemorial supported with the profits accruing from the sale of rosary beads. The structure was taken over by the government, which offered instead a dilapidated house on the western border of the Republic. This the religious were invited to repair at their own expense. In all such matters, chivalry and benevolence are outmoded. The very Communist government which has so far not permitted the expatriation to Germany of able-bodied nursing sisters of Sudeten German origin has nevertheless taken from the communities to which they belong everything they possess. But the loss of Church property could be relegated to the periphery of religious interest, were the question merely one of the loss of material possessions. Indeed, it may well be that some of the clergy of Central Europe needed a lesson in the nature and meaning of poverty. But whether an established faith can carry out its mission if all the physical and financial instrumentalities upon which it must rely are owned by a hostile state is another question; and precisely this was being raised in all its stark simplicity in Czechoslovakia.

The dawn of the year 1949 found the Communists in complete possession of all the powers of the State. A network of "Action Committees" had been formed throughout the country. Every organ of propaganda was in the hands of the government, and the only channel through which protests could be made was the reading from the pulpits of the Pastoral Letters of the Hierarchy. It is against this background that the financial dependence of the clergy on the government must be considered. During October, 1948, decrees had been issued "to provide for the economic security of the Churches and Religious Associations." They established a salary scale according to which the clergy were to be paid—an arrangement wholly without precedent in Czechoslovakia, where previously clerical salaries had been supplemented with subsidies from state funds. Now the confiscation of property made the ecclesiastical organization totally dependent upon the government, and subject to conditions which one need only to cite in order to perceive their ominousness. One condition was that only such persons might function as ministers of religion as had obtained the consent of the government in advance; another was that such persons might be appointed to posts only after the government had approved both the person and the post. To enforce these conditions, a rather elaborate bureaucratic apparatus was created.

During January, 1949, representatives of Church and State conferred, with a view to resolving the most vital differences.

By the beginning of March it was apparent that the negotiations had been fruitless, and Archbishop Beran said as much in an interview. The Bishops met again, only to discover that a secret listening device had been installed in the conference room; and the courageous Archbishop made the fact public. By this time, however, it had become exceedingly difficult for even so widely known and respected a prelate to obtain a public hearing for what he had to say. Meanwhile the government, through the Ministry of Culture, announced that it would commence publishing a Bulletin to furnish priests and religious with information of interest to them. The Archbishop protested anew. He observed that while the official publications of the Church had been suspended by reason of a "dearth of paper," there appeared to be an ample supply for the Bulletin.

This publication, when it appeared, manifestly had for its purpose widening the breach between the Bishops and the lower clergy which had been opened by the defection of the Reverend Josef Plojhar. It professed to be the organ of a "Catholic Action Movement" sponsored by the State and organized without the sanction of the Hierarchy. It should be borne in mind that while Papal Encyclicals leave Catholics entirely free to join and work for political parties of their choosing, provided these are not professionally antichristian, Catholic Action is by definition an organization of laymen interested in the defense of Catholic doctrine and the development of Catholic religious activity *under the direction of the Bishops*. Therefore the government's Catholic Action Movement could only be organized secession from the Church's authority. Following the receipt of directives from Moscow, the first meeting of the Catholic Action Movement was held in Prague on June 17. It was addressed by Father Plojhar and others. The results of the conference were announced with a great flurry of newspaper articles and radio commentaries. Yet hardly more than a dozen of the 6,600 priests who lived in Czechoslovakia at the time attended; and not all these were aware of what the objective really was. What difference did this make? On June 20, the head of the legitimate Catholic Action, the Reverend Antonín Mandl, was arrested and jailed. Meanwhile the police had occupied the Archbishop's palace. He countered valiantly by preaching in the Abbey of Strahov a sermon which was reported in part throughout the free world. "No doubt," he said, "you will soon hear all sorts of things about me over the radio. You may hear that I have confessed . . . And if some day you learn that an agreement has been concluded between Church and State, you will know that I would never underwrite an agreement which curtailed the rights of the Church and of the Bishops." Shortly after the sermon was reported, the Abbot of the monastery in which it was preached was arrested.

The most important endeavor of the Catholic Action Movement was to collect signatures endorsing the resolutions passed at the Prague convention. The most significant of them contained a veiled allusion to the Vatican as an "outside power" which sought to interfere in the affairs of the Czechoslovak people, and absolved the government from all responsibility for the tension which now marked Church-State relations. An exiled priest who was an eyewitness described the signature collection as follows:

All the automobiles at the disposition of the Communist secretariats, the labor councils and the factories were made available to the "Church." A whole army of officials drove through the country, speeding to one rectory after another, announcing that they were good Catholics who had only the interests of religion at heart. The petition was presented to the clergy as a quite innocent expression of a desire to bring about harmonious cooperation between the Church and the government. Some older priests, poorly informed and perhaps intimi-

dated by the thought of being sent to a concentration camp if they refused to sign, succumbed to the lure. The laity also were importuned,
but the great majority of them did not waver.

Meanwhile Father Plojhar was described in the government
press as a veteran of Dachau who had discovered the pro-
Fascist sentiments of the Vatican when he reluctantly had to
admit that nothing whatever was done by Rome to aid the unfortunate victims of Hitler. The disciplinary action taken
against him by Archbishop Beran was therefore an indication
that Rome had not abjured its diabolical tactics. The Archbishop replied in a letter which, though it was not given to the
press, is of great interest because it sets forth the career of an
unfortunate priest.

[Father] Plojhar was suspended solely because he had refused to
obey the authority of the Church. As a priest he must have known the
law of the Church, and he had taken an oath of loyalty to his bishop.
When he was warned in advance of the danger of suspension, he merely
replied that he would not withdraw his candidacy and that he merely
took note of his suspension.

To the criticism that the Vatican did nothing to ease his lot while
he was in a concentration camp, I can only state that Plojhar was
ordained in České Budějovice as a priest of German nationality, and
that when he arrived in Dachau he was assigned to Block 26, a barracks for German priests.

The Vatican did everything it could for all the incarcerated priests
and sent them all needed supplies. Himmler, however, permitted only
German priests to receive these parcels. The priests in Block 26 also
enjoyed this privilege, although the rest of the camp protested this unjust treatment. Plojhar entered this block in 1942, when these privileges were being granted. Those who were in Dachau can testify to
these facts.

On June 14, 1949, the Archbishop was back in Prague to
officiate in the Cathedral of St. Vitus on the occasion of the

Feast of Corpus Christi. To understand the significance of the occasion, one must remember that this Feast and the processions which accompany it are among the most hallowed religious observances in many parts of Europe. The Archbishop, seeing the vast crowd, preached a sermon denouncing the Catholic Action Movement and all its works and pomps. A thousand catcalls interrupted him, rising from the throats of secret police and militiamen who had been planted in the Cathedral. The Archbishop left the pulpit, and the observance of the Feast of Corpus Christi came to an abrupt halt.

When Catholics arrived for Mass on the following Sunday, they listened to a Pastoral Letter signed in the name of all the Hierarchy by Archbishop Beran. In it he denounced the Catholic Action Movement sponsored by the government, and insisted upon the right of the Church to name its own representatives and spokesmen. This letter was followed by an announcement which made the deepest possible impression on the Catholic world. On June 20, 1949, the Sacred Congregation of the Holy Office issued a decree declaring the Catholic Action Movement schismatic and excommunicating in the most formal manner all those who continued to participate in it. Lifting of the ban was reserved to the Pope. Seldom in modern history had Rome issued so stern a decree. The Prime Minister of Czechoslovakia responded for the government. He declared that the State "would protect all those who conduct themselves in accordance with the principles of the people's democracy," and would not allow anyone "to violate the freedom of opinion of patriotic priests or to terrorize them."

There followed another Pastoral Letter, signed by the most prominent members of the Hierarchy, which was a lengthy recital of the ills which had befallen the Church. It asked questions and answered them. The following passages will indicate the tenor of the whole:

Could we, your bishops, accede to demands which are in defiance of the laws of God and man?

Could we approve, in the presence of our people and of the whole world, everything that has happened, even when it has not been in conformity with the teachings of Jesus Christ?

We shall, with cheerfulness, render unto Caesar the things which are Caesar's. But it is quite impossible to sacrifice unto him the things which are God's. For it behooves us to obey God rather than man.

It is not a question of favoring capitalism, for we know that not even a liberal capitalistic society fulfills all the ideals of Christianity. Indeed, capitalism has more than once been denounced by the Church.

You all know that the bishops who serve you are not capitalists. They assuredly would be better off than they are now if they came out for the cause of Judas.

The government reacted violently to this Pastoral Letter. After days of agitated demonstrations, the Archbishop was informed that a police guard was being assigned to insure his safety and protect his residence, and that the guard would accompany him wherever he went, to ward off likely attacks on his person. Archbishop Beran replied that under such conditions he would not leave his home. A similar guard was forced upon the Bishop of Hradec Králové, senior member of the Hierarchy. Archbishop Beran was also expelled from the Union of Warriors for Freedom, the official association of those who had been deported to concentration camps, or who had gone into exile during the period of Nazi rule. An intensive drive to recruit members of the Catholic Action Movement accompanied this personal campaign against the Archbishop.

Without ample or even limited opportunity to discover what was really going on, good priests and worthy laymen often came to the conclusion that Archbishop Beran was being unnecessarily belligerent and that, perhaps, this was due to unwise prodding from Monsignori in a far-distant Vatican. From this point of view the address delivered on May 18, 1949, by the Reverend Dr. Josef Fiala, then chairman of the Catholic Action Movement, is very illuminating. After expressing the hope that there would be no duplication of the *Kulturkampf* Bismarck had waged against the Catholic Church, he presented the views of St. Thomas Aquinas on the value of harmonious cooperation between Church and State, and compared the situation which had existed in his native country after 1918 with that which had obtained since 1945. Was it not true that the present government had assured full religious liberty, that members of the Cabinet had been present when the Archbishop was enthroned in 1946, and that Gottwald, after his election to the presidency of the Republic, had done what no other head of the Republic had thought of doing—repaired to the Cathedral, where a "Te Deum" was sung and solemn Benediction given? Why then, asked the somewhat naïve but still thoroughly good and honest Dr. Fiala, was harmony so difficult to arrive at? "The faithful," he said, "cannot understand why harmonious relations have not been established, and they are interested in knowing who is at fault."

Dr. Fiala subsequently saw the error of his ways and went into exile. His address, which at the time created a considerable sensation, indicates clearly how tangled and beclouded the situation then was. First, the Czechs were so conscious of the suppression which they had endured under the Nazis and so accustomed to considering Germany as the great menace to their well-being that Dr. Fiala cited the *Kulturkampf* of Bismarck as the most striking illustration of religious persecution he could call to mind. Second, the various overt acts by which the Archbishop had given expression to his readiness to cooperate if the government manifested a measure of good will had a far greater symbolic value for the people than he had intended they should have; and conversely the acts of religious worship which Gottwald and others added to their chores—even as Henry IV of France had invested in a Mass— deluded the innocent who had had no previous experience with Communism. In the circumstances, one must respect the discipline which maintained to such a notable extent at least the outward unity of the clergy.

Then on July 1 a stern challenge came from the Vatican. A decree issued by the Sacred Congregation of the Holy Office excommunicated "the Christian faithful who profess the materialistic and anti-Christian doctrine of the Communists, and especially those who defend or propagate it . . . incur by that very fact, as apostates from the Catholic faith, excommunication reserved in a special manner to the Holy See." The decree likewise rendered it unlawful to support the Communist Party or to publish or read its literature. This solemn ban had, however, the result that a number of members of the government delivered addresses indicating that all those who obeyed the Vatican, a foreign power long since allied with Fascism, would be held guilty of high treason. All this meant that, on the one hand, all clergymen who had aligned themselves with the Catholic Action Movement and would not now retract were under sentence of excommunication and so unable to exercise lawfully their priestly offices, and that, on the other hand, the government had assured them of protection.

The Vatican did not withdraw its diplomatic representative, though both he and his co-workers were subjected to a number of indignities. On July 9 the Internuncio returned to Rome; and his successor was not permitted to enter Czechoslovakia. Simultaneously the government took steps to bring the clergy under complete control. But the action taken by the Vatican had made an impression, and many statements were read from parish pulpits during the summer, pledging loyalty to the Hierarchy and the Holy See. The Catholic Action Movement none the less made progress, even proceeding to organize pilgrimages to favorite shrines. Members of the Cabinet participated in some of these.

The government now played its trump card. It announced that a Bureau for Ecclesiastical Affairs would be established in the Ministry of Culture, to regulate all matters affecting the Church. A delegate from the Bureau was to be assigned to each Catholic consistory. Moreover, the State would henceforth guarantee the "economic security" of the clergy as a sort of generous reimbursement for the expropriated Church properties. Thus the chains of enslavement were forged. During the summer Alexej Čepička, Minister of Culture, delivered several addresses that made clear what was planned. He stated: "Anyone who executes on our territory the orders of an enemy of our State [that is, of the Pope] must realize that he therewith loses the right to call himself a good Czech or Slovak."

The Bureau for Ecclesiastical Affairs was established on October 14, but the definitive laws regulating it and fixing the salaries of the clergy were dated October 17 and November 4 respectively. What was it to accomplish? According to the text of the law the new bureau was to "see to it that church life and religious life develop in accordance with the constitution and the principles of the people's democratic order, and thus secure to everyone the right of freedom of religion based on the principle of religious tolerance and equal rights for all denominations, as guaranteed by the constitution." More specifically, it was to exercise supervision over such matters as "personnel and budgets relating to clergymen, teachers and members of the staffs of university theological schools, other theological schools and seminaries, and teachers of religion; the ecclesiastical press and the publications issued by it; the publication of an official journal for clergymen; and the charitable activities of the churches and the religious associations."

Salaries were to be paid "only to ministers of religion who are Czechoslovak citizens, are politically reliable, are of irreproachable conduct, and otherwise meet the general requirements of the civil service." Clergymen were also required, when assuming the obligation of teaching, to give religious instruction free of charge, "unless another arrangement has been made for the teaching of religion." No one was permitted to officiate as a clergyman unless he had obtained the consent of the government and had taken an oath of office. Concerning Church property, the legislation stipulated that "representatives of Churches . . . shall take inventory of all personal property, real property, and property rights of the Churches and religious associations," and that any disposition of or encumbrance upon such property should have the consent of the government.

A convention to which the majority of the Catholic dioceses sent delegates met in Prague on October 11 to discuss the restrictions thus placed upon religious activity; and a resolution was passed which stated in part that the measures taken signified "the complete subjugation of the Church and its misuse for political ends." There followed an appeal to the clergy which merits quotation in full:

We leave the final decision concerning the matter of increased salary and the oath which is to be demanded to the Very Reverend Ordinaries themselves. But it is clear from the manner in which the two issues are conjoined—that is, the compulsory acceptance of the salaries and the simultaneous taking of the oath—that the question is not merely whether the salary is to be accepted and the oath taken, but also whether the laws concerning the Church are to be approved. It is clear that no priest can reach a decision salutary to his conscience or avoid betraying the Church unless he follows exact directives given by his Ordinary.

We and His Excellency, the Archbishop of Prague, Josef Beran, wish to remind our brethren that they did not take orders so that they could enrich themselves or insure a good livelihood in this world, but so that they might minister unto souls and insure their eternal salvation. That is the basis on which the faithful will judge you; and in accordance with how you fulfill your duty Almighty God will reward or punish you. Giving priority to temporal rather than to spiritual interests in such a critical hour means sullying your priestly honor and confessing to the faithful that you are without a genuine calling to the priesthood and are a hireling rather than a shepherd.

Do not forget that hundreds of your brethren are in prisons and labor camps. If you accept material advantages at a time when so many of them are in duress you will sin grossly against brotherly love. Do not forget that every day there knock at your door many poor people who in spite of all the vaunted progress of Socialism are suffering horribly and cannot scrape together enough to keep themselves alive. If you permit yourself to gain advantages when so many of those entrusted to your care are suffering and are in spiritual as well as material need, you will bring down upon yourself the contempt and hatred of those who long to find in you a shining example, a source of moral support, and a reason for hope.

Among the hundreds "in prisons and labor camps" were the majority of Czechoslovakia's best known and most highly respected priests. They had been arrested for reading from their pulpits letters issued by the Hierarchy, insinuating that not all was well for the Church in the people's democracy, and for sundry other reasons. Thus, quite typically, *Osservatore Romano* of September 22, 1949, reported that all the Capuchins of the Monastery of Fulnek, Moravia, had been arrested; that priests in various towns of Slovakia had been sent to labor camps, regardless of whether or not their innocence had been upheld by the local tribunals; that Professor Čulík, the Counselor of the Archdiocese of Prague, had been arrested; and that a number of members of the staff of the Prague Seminary had been jailed. Similar actions had been taken throughout the summer, and other penal measures had been resorted to. Fines were levied; automobiles and motorcycles were confiscated.

The Bishops then indicated that they would not adopt an uncompromising attitude. A formula was devised in accordance with which the clergy might take the oath and accept the salaries, while making a mental reservation that the oath pledged them to no action contrary to the laws of God and the Church. The language of the oath as prepared by the government read as follows:

I promise on my honor and on my conscience to be faithful to the Czechoslovak Republic and to its People's Democratic Order. I will not undertake anything contrary to its interests, security and integrity. As a citizen of the Popular Democratic State, I shall perform conscientiously the duties associated with my office and will to the best of my ability support the constructive efforts which are directed to the advancement of the people's welfare.

As soon as the Bishops had agreed to permit the taking of this oath, President Gottwald declared that the struggle between Church and State had been resolved. An amnesty was declared, and many priests were liberated from prison. No official cognizance was taken of the reservations which the Bishops had instructed the clergy to keep in mind.

On December 6 the government published a volume entitled The Conspiracy Against the Republic which levelled a number of accusations at the Hierarchy. Archbishop Beran was declared guilty of high treason, and some of his fellow Bishops were described as accomplices. For all that the Archbishop had suffered in a German concentration camp, said the authors, he had nevertheless permitted himself to be carried down the path of treason by the Vatican. As a representative of the ecclesiastical aristocracy, he had forced the Bishops into a traitorous counterrevolution and compelled them to bid their priests to betray their fatherland. The Papal Internuncio, Mgr. Gennarro Verolino, was termed the Vatican's most astute spy. The incidents of the Corpus Christi observance of June 14 were used to expound the theory that the Archbishop had been anxious to buttress the cause of Rome by posing as a martyr. Publicity efforts to create a market for this book were on a vast scale, reminding the observer of the propaganda in Nazi Germany in behalf of Herr Rosenberg's *Mythus des zwanzigsten Jahrhunderts*.

The year 1950 hewed to the line adopted in the Conspiracy. During January one of the Slovak Bishops died. A successor was designated by the Cathedral Chapter; but the government refused to endorse the choice, and itself appointed the Reverend John Dechet administrator of the diocese. Though the Vatican promptly excommunicated this priest, he remained in office. Shortly thereafter the Communist press announced that a Father Horák, pastor in Bylnice, had agreed to make a thorough study of Marxist-Leninist teaching and would report the results of his research at a number of educational conferences. There followed an exchange of letters between the Hierarchy and the government on these matters. The most signal event of all was that toward the close of January the Auxiliary Bishop of Prague, Antonín Eltschkner, took the oath of allegiance in company with the Vicar General of the Diocese. A high churchman in Moravia followed their example. For all that Bishop Eltschkner was described as a weak and elderly man, government propagandists took into account his defection from the hitherto unbroken ranks of the Hierarchy. Obviously the defenses of the Church were crumbling.

During April the government seized monasteries throughout the country, on the ground that the "religious Orders have become instruments of the foreign enemies of the Republic." So that a halt might be called to these treasonable activities, the official report continued, "measures have been taken to restore such Orders to their original and genuinely religious purpose." Because it was evident that the larger monasteries housed only a few persons, "who did no work and spent their time primarily in arousing the people," the government was concentrating their inmates in a number of monasteries where they would be able "to concern themselves with the purely religious mission prescribed by the rules of their Orders." "The vacated buildings," said the report, "will serve the needs of Catholic charities, or general social and health purposes. Some will be converted into apartments, badly needed by the people of the country."

Thus there came into being the "concentration monasteries" of Pezinok, Jasov, and other places concerning which one can find no appreciable amount of information. Nor did the government fail to pounce upon the institutions for the training of the clergy. All Catholic seminaries were closed, and two new ones were created—one in Prague and the other in Bratislava. The training of clergymen for the Protestant and the Orthodox Churches was restricted in like manner. The Catholic Bishops were now confronted with the difficult problem of deciding whether it was proper to ordain young priests in the circumstances. They were of divided views on the matter. Meanwhile a considerable number of seminarians, unable to reconcile the nature of the training given with their consciences, withdrew. They were promptly drafted for duty with infantry regiments stationed in various parts of the country.

Late in the summer of 1950 Zdeněk Fierlinger was appointed Minister of Culture. He was destined to inaugurate the final stage in the liquidation of the Church. Every priest who had demonstrated his willingness to cooperate with the Catholic Action Movement as sponsored by the government was now appointed to a high ecclesiastical post. On August 1 a new penal code made it possible to try Christian clergymen loyal to their Churches for a number of crimes. None of the offenses was carefully defined. The code stipulated: "Whoever does not discharge his duties in the manner prescribed by the legal regulations pertaining to Churches and religious associations, and whoever, in particular, endangers or interferes with the exercise of supervision over the properties of Churches or religious associations, shall be punished by a fine not to exceed 100,000 crowns, or by confinement not to exceed three months." The arrests soon began. Priests beloved by their parishioners were the first to feel the impact of the law. Then it was the turn of vicars general and monsignori. Finally, a number of Bishops were taken into custody.

During December many who had been arrested were brought to trial. In most instances accusations were made of attempting to overthrow the people's democratic regime, of endeavoring to betray state secrets to foreign powers, and of collaborating with the Nazis. Heavy sentences were imposed. Thus Bishop Stanislav Zela was fined a huge sum and sentenced to a prison term of twenty-five years; a life sentence was imposed upon Abbot John Opasek; and a number of other priests and prelates (how reluctantly one uses the word "number" when each person merits a biographical sketch) received sentences ranging from ten to twenty years. Gestapo-like, the police meanwhile proceeded to file a detailed questionnaire about every cleric in the land.

The month of January, 1951, witnessed the arrest of more than 3,000 priests. Of these, 2,000 were placed in the "concentration monasteries." Many others were removed from their posts. As a consequence, nearly three-fourths of all parishes were bereft of pastors. The Bureau for Ecclesiastical Affairs proceeded to appoint "patriotic" priests to important positions in diocesan offices. New cathedral canons, for example, were installed in Prague and Brno. Bishop Eltschkner remained in office, but the courageous Archbishop was banished from Prague on March 10. It was reported that he was put under arrest in the Castle of Rozmítal, and subsequently transferred to another place of detention. Elsewhere members of the Hierarchy began to capitulate. Bishop Štěpan Trochta, of the diocese of Litoměřice, installed a canon who was a notorious "patriotic" priest. Once more the Sacred Congregation acted to excommunicate all who had in any manner been responsible for these various assaults upon the integrity of the Catholic Church. Yet by the end of the month the shocking news came that the most prominent members of the Czechoslovak Hierarchy still at liberty had taken the oath of allegiance. Shortly thereafter it was reported that Father Plojhar had been reinstated by his Ordinary, despite the ban of excommunication which had been issued against him.

Again the Vatican acted. The Bishops who had betrayed their trust were excommunicated, even though it was taken for granted in Rome that the concessions had been obtained through force. The situation was all the more painful because some of those involved had previously acted with great bravery. The Vatican Radio commented:

> Men of faith will remain loyal to their duly chosen ecclesiastical superiors, as is shown by Archbishop Beran who, having been exiled from his Archdiocese by reason of his fidelity to his Church, must now languish in prison. Beran belongs to the company of the illustrious in the history of the Church; and good priests will follow his heroic example.

Pope Pius XII spoke twice to the people of Czechoslovakia toward the close of 1951—on October 28, and on Christmas Eve. He said in part on the second occasion:

As the experiences of men indicate, the State and the association of States are necessary and appropriate forms of union and order among men, in view of the fact that human beings are by nature social. Only with them can humanity live. They help to make it more nearly perfect than it could otherwise be. No one can think of them without at the same time being conscious of the tranquillity of order, the *tranquillitas ordinis,* which according to St. Augustine is the definition of peace. These social ties exist by their very nature so that peace may be assured.

Since these things are so, Jesus Christ, the Prince of Peace, and His Church in which He continues to dwell, have entered into a new and intimate relationship with them, as being societies which exist for the maintenance of peace, so that human society may be lifted up and strengthened. This is the basis for the unique contribution which the Church by her very nature makes to the cause of peace—makes, that is, when her life and actions among men occupy the place that is their due.

And how will all this come about, save through the continuous enlightening and invigorating action of the Grace of God on the minds and hearts of citizens and statesmen, so that in every human relationship they perceive and conform with the purposes of the Creator, strive to enlist the common effort of individuals and nations for realizing those purposes, and practice social justice and charity within the nation as well as among the nations.

The 1951 message to the Czechoslovak people in honor of their Independence Day, October 28, reads in part as follows:

Even so, Venerable Brethren and beloved children, let no one lose heart because the difficulties of this kind are so extremely great. Above all consecrated pastors must not lose heart, they whose duty it is by reason of a special Divine appointment to nourish the faith of their flocks, to uphold their courage, and to strengthen the bond of union between them and this Holy See. Already over the course of centuries your people has overcome other and most dire ills. More than once in times past your ancestors have had to choose between martyrdom endured with fortitude, and treachery to the faith of their fathers. With unconquerable spirits they clung to their Catholic religion and sometimes professed it by shedding their very blood.

But neither the shame nor the glory of the Church in Czechoslovakia diminished, as the months passed. On November 1, Josef Plojhar, now become Minister of Health in the Cabinet, stated in a radio address:

In their anxiety, the Western imperialists do not shrink from laying hands on things which are sacred to everyone. They do not hesitate to abuse the religious convictions of the people. Capitalism recognizes the great moral strength of religious ties and therefore attempts to use the Christian and non-Christian faiths for its own ends. It wishes to employ the vast and intricate machinery at the disposal of churchmen for propaganda purposes and for the encouragement of espionage. We behold a truly un-Christian phenomenon in the association of the Vatican with the policies of the warmongers.

Therewith he disassociated himself as completely as possible from allegiance to his Church.

An official survey of the situation was issued by the government at the close of 1951. It declared that the Czechoslovak clergy had "clarified" its position in so far as the Vatican was concerned and went on to say:

The clergy, as they unanimously declared at the National Congress of September, 1951, recognize the Pope as their Head in religious matters, but repudiate the policies of the Vatican, which is our enemy. All the Bishops recognize the validity of the ecclesiastical laws and of all other measures taken to date; and they have solemnly sworn to contribute to the building of Socialism in Czechoslovakia, to support the peace movement, and to refuse to recognize or execute religious sanctions inflicted for political reasons.

Despite these words and their deceptive inlay of benevolence, the effort to eradicate religion from the hearts of the people was carried on relentlessly. It was not merely that the press and the radio ridiculed belief and practice incessantly and without rebuke. The faithful among the clergy were hunted down one by one. The following typical report is cited from ČTK, the Government News Service, of September 1, 1952:

Josef Maršálek, Catholic Priest and teacher of religion in Velké-Mezeříci, confessed his illegal activities to the Senate of the District Court of Iglau. The accused was brought to trial because of the hatred he had shown towards the peace efforts of the progressive populations of the world, and because of his faithful service to the war efforts of the Imperialistic Powers and the Vatican. . . . Maršálek approved of imperialist aggression in Korea and spread the war propaganda contained in foreign broadcasts. In conversations with his pupils and in his religion classes he systematically spread hatred against the people's democracy and chief personalities of our state. . . . He also tried to hamper the constructive efforts of the workers, and forbade his pupils to cooperate with working brigades on Sundays and Holydays. By his subtly clever inventiveness he sullied our economic and cultural expansion effort. Indeed, the evidence indicates that this reactionary slave of the Vatican strictly forbade his pupils to see the progressive films. . . . The accused Josef Maršálek was condemned to fifteen years in jail and to financial penalties. All his property was confiscated. The Court also deprived him of his civil rights and exiled him from County Iglau forever.

Two months later, Czechoslovakia was the scene of the sensational trials of Rudolf Slánský and his associates in the government. And perhaps no document in the history of the unfortunate country is more harrowing than the following, translated from the official Communist newspaper, *Rudé Právo*, of November 25, 1952. It is addressed by the son of one of the doomed men, Ludwig Frejka, to his judge:

Esteemed Comrade:

I ask that there be inflicted on my father the heaviest penalty—the penalty of death. I see only belatedly that this creature, who cannot be called a human being, did not possess a jot or tittle of feeling or human dignity. He was my greatest and most bitter enemy.

I pledge that wherever I may work I shall always work as a devoted Communist. And I know that the hatred I feel towards all our enemies, especially those who deliberately sought to destroy our life which grows steadily wealthier and happier, and especially also towards my father, will always strengthen my fight for the Communist future of our people.

I am asking that this letter be given to my father. If possible I desire to give it to him personally.

THOMAS FREJKA

No comment is required.

4 IN TITO'S LAND

YUGOSLAVIA, HAVING ACHIEVED nationhood at the close of
the First World War, was at one and the same time a ful-
fillment of ardent though varied aspirations to political and
cultural independence and a creature of social and strategic
necessity. It conjoined parts of the former Austro-Hungarian
Empire with the territory of that Empire's archfoe, the Kingdom of Serbia, responsible for the death of the Archduke
Ferdinand at Sarajevo. In terms of religious affiliation, the
disparity was equally marked. In the western areas of Croatia
and Slovenia, there were approximately 5,900,000 Catholics
in union with the See of Rome. Serbia, on the other hand, was
almost completely Greek Orthodox, 6,700,000 persons being
members of that Church. That a new nation culturally so
heterogeneous should find it easy to establish real unity was
not to be expected; and the deep, persistent cleavages engendered constant friction. A strong group of Croats in particular worked and, indeed, plotted unceasingly for independence.

The Croats could look back upon a long period of duress as
a result of service rendered to the Catholic faith and the Holy

See. During the early Middle Ages their ancestors had fought against the Mongols; and their steadfastness had earned the admiration of Dante Alighieri. Later they battled against the Turks during four hundred years. Chronicles relate that hundreds of thousands died in the struggle or were sold into slavery; and the cities of Western Europe at the time absorbed no end of refugees. The brave Croats could not ward off the Moslem attack fully, but they did manage unaided to hold Zagreb and the regions northwest of that city. Numerous are the praises which the Popes bestowed on their valor. This tradition of stubborn defense of their individuality made the Croats self-reliant, but it also enkindled an insatiable desire for cultural freedom.

The Slovenes, who were far less numerous than the Croats, also endured much at the hands of the Turks. Their country was devastated, and thousands were enslaved. During subsequent history Slovenia was under Bavarian or Austrian suzerainty most of the time, and so was drawn into the religious conflicts of Reformation times. But the Counter Reform prevailed, so that the people today are almost exclusively Catholic. During the nineteenth century, a Romantic movement greatly intensified interest in the Slovenian language and literature. A strong Catholic political party was formed after 1907, and gave rise to some talk of alleged clerical domination. After the First World War, clashes first with Austria and then with the Yugoslav monarchy manifested the strong nationalist feelings of the Slovene people.

The Serbs, a nation of great charm, tenacity, and ability, clung resolutely to their Greek Orthodox traditions during the period of Ottoman rule from 1389 to 1878, when independence was achieved. The strength of Serbia lay in its sturdy peasantry and in competent, though ardently, sometimes fanatically, nationalist leadership, and, as the most populous part of the new

Yugoslavia, it dominated the political scene after the new state was formed. Despite stormy periods of conflict with the Croats and Slovenes, the Serb monarchy must be credited with slow progress towards national solidarity. Poor and to some extent backward though the Yugoslavia of pre-Nazi days was, it is one of the most interesting and virile parts of Europe as seen in nostalgic retrospect. Culturally it combined an irritating staidness of bureaucratic procedure with a passionate zest for personal liberty. And what was ever more charming than any town in Dalmatia?

On April 6, 1941, the Germans and Italians invaded Yugoslavia. Later they were joined by Hungarian and Bulgarian troops. Within ten days the attacking forces won an overwhelming victory, and British armies moving up through Greece were thrown back to the sea. Units of the regular Yugoslav army continued to fight in some areas, and the struggle was grim. On the other hand, scattered bands of "partisans" were reenforced by Communist sympathizers, under a variety of disguises, after Hitler attacked Russia. Retaliation by the invaders was swift and brutal. Slovenia in particular was terrorized, no doubt because Hitler had vowed to incorporate it in the "East County" which was so vital to his dream of conquest. Many thousands of priests and people were executed or carted off to concentration camps.

To add to the sufferings of the population, warfare now broke out between antagonistic groups of resistance forces. For temporary advantage, each side would effect transitory alliances with the occupying armies, and sanguinary battles were then fought to a bloody finish. It has been estimated that as many as a million persons were slain during this weird and wavering struggle. Inevitably all religious and caritative institutions suffered grievously. Churches were destroyed, clergymen were slain, and all forms of normal living disappeared.

Among the more somber events of the time was the formation
in Croatia of Ustaša, an extreme nationalist movement formed
by Dr. Anton Pavelić according to the model of Fascism. As
soon as the Italian occupying armies designated Croatia an
independent country Pavelić attempted to rule it with his
"élite." He enlisted an odd array of extremists including two
Franciscan friars, one of whom even became the commandant
of a notorious Fascist concentration camp; but he could not
win the allegiance of the masses.

While these tragic events were occurring, the Catholic
Church in Yugoslavia had for its principal leader a man of
unusual ability and courage: Monsignor Aloysius Stepinac.
He had served during the First World War as an ordinary
soldier in the Austro-Hungarian army. Returning to civilian
life, he studied agriculture for a while and then decided to
prepare for the priesthood. After a period of training in Rome,
where he earned his doctorate in theology, he was ordained.
Soon he was consecrated a bishop; and subsequently he became Archbishop of Zagreb*—the largest and most opulent
diocese in Croatia, with 2,000,000 souls before Hitler's invasion. The new Archbishop was a man of warm sympathies
and great intelligence. When Austria and Czechoslovakia
were overrun by the Nazis, Zagreb became a haven for refugees. I was there in 1938 and saw a little of what was happening. The generosity of the Archbishop was notable.

Naturally the occupation and the political activities of
Pavelić brought the faithful of Archbishop Stepinac's diocese
face to face with momentous and troubling moral issues. He
himself was fully aware that Pavelić was the leader of a pro-
Fascist and therefore also a pro-Nazi political action group,

* It should be noted that as a Yugoslav patriot and an opponent of the Habs-
burgs, Monsignor Stepinac's elevation to a bishopric had the approval of the
Yugoslav Monarchy. His predecessor in the See of Zagreb had been loyal to
Austria and all else than friendly to the Serbs.

and he immediately opposed it with determination. During 1943 he said, on the anniversary of the coronation of Pope Pius XII:

It would be erroneous to suppose that the Catholic Church can ever approve of methods of action directed against the fundamental rights of man. The Christian way of life does not concede that the rights of any people may be violated, no matter how vast the territory of the aggressor or the size of his population.

He was especially outspoken on Nazi race theories. These he discussed frankly and frequently even while the Germans were patrolling the streets of the city and apprehending Jews and others deemed to be opponents of the Nazi regime. He said, for instance:

All people have their origins in God. There is only one race, which is His. The members of this human race may have an advanced culture or a retarded one. They may be white or black of color, they may dwell at the North Pole or the South Pole. All of them are nevertheless members of the same race, which has its origin in God. The nations and races of men share the right to life, to dignity and to the treatment which befits dignity. Europeans and Negroes, Jews and Aryans, have the same right to say, "Our Father, Who art in Heaven."

These utterances reflected, as a matter of course, the resolute stand which the Holy See had taken on the issues during the years which followed Hitler's rise to power. It was therefore one of Archbishop Stepinac's most important tasks to defend the Papacy against Nazi propaganda, in which the Pavelić group obediently reiterated whatever their masters in Berlin and Rome instructed them to say. The Archbishop dispatched note after note to them. Among his many tasks was that of opposing the persecution in Croatia of members of the Greek Orthodox Church on the ground that they had been abettors of Serbia. Thus when a number of Serbs residing in the town of

Glina were executed, the pretext being the proclamation of the independence of the Croat state, the Archbishop issued a stern rebuke:

It is my duty as your Archbishop to declare that such measures are forbidden by Catholic moral teaching. I demand that you take steps immediately to insure that not a single Serb will be executed until he has been tried and found guilty of a crime which deserves capital punishment.

Pavelić, to be sure, did not take kindly to this archiepiscopal advice. He accused the prelate of favoring Communism and of having acquired only a modicum of political experience. He also attempted to reach his goal with blandishments. But Dr. Stepinac, in all probability the only person in the country who could speak freely, was not to be assuaged. He forbade priests to join the Ustaša and excommunicated those who did. He refused to accompany Pavelić to Rome for the purpose of inducing Mussolini to make the Duke of Spoleto king of Croatia, and he was ostentatiously "not at home" when Pavelić called to pay his respects on the occasion of the burial of the Duke of Aosta. The pro-Fascist leader, understandably annoyed, then approached the Vatican in the hope of effecting the removal of the Archbishop from his see. This démarche naturally failed, because Dr. Stepinac was merely carrying out the firm wishes of his Roman superiors. The Croat people in their overwhelming majority remained loyal to the moderate antitotalitarian political movement headed by Dr. Vladimir Maček.

Meanwhile storm clouds of varying hues rose over Yugoslavia. The Communist Party, repressed and camouflaged during the period when the Stalin-Hitler Pact was in force, quickly emerged after the Nazi victory. It had a hard and disciplined core, made up in part of veterans of the Spanish Civil War. In

Josip Broz (known as Tito) the Communists had a sturdy, self-willed, and unflinching leader. Born in a small village near the Austrian border, of mixed Croatian and Slovenian ancestry, Tito had served with gusto and loyalty in the cavalry of the Habsburg armies. Captured by the Russians, apparently as early as 1915, he was imprisoned in Siberia. When the war ended, he joined the Red army and soon became an officer. This change in his rank and station persuaded Tito to throw in his lot with the Communists. He finished a course of indoctrination in Moscow, and returned to his native country as an agent of the Party.

There, after the German conquest of Yugoslavia, General Draža Mihajlović rallied the traditional guerrilla forces of the nation against the conquerors. He was a hard-fisted Serb officer who knew every mountain pass and counted on every device for rallying the peasantry. But he was as devoid of political and diplomatic skill as could well be imagined. Despite feats of heroism he and his men were soon isolated from the only foreign contact which mattered; namely, Great Britain and the Yugoslav government-in-exile which it harbored. He tried in vain to arrive at a *modus vivendi* with Tito, who had begun to assemble followers under the Communist banner. Fatefully the British decided to support the vigorous and talkative Communist leader rather than the difficult, indeed sometimes recalcitrant, Serb commander.

Tito, for his part, was a wolf clad in several varieties of sheep's clothing. The partisans under his command vociferously denied that they were affiliated with the Kremlin. He himself declared on December 29, 1943, to the Anti-Fascist Council at Jajce, Bosnia:

Slanders have been spread about us on all sides. Even now it is being said that our struggle for the liberation of Yugoslavia is Communist-inspired. We are accused of plotting to bolshevize the country, of wishing to place all power in Communist hands, of planning the abolition of private property and the destruction of the Church, religion and culture. These are old and badly battered tales. Few believe such lies, and the people of Yugoslavia certainly do not.

Although there were gruesome incidents—such as the slaying of priests and laymen by partisans—much was done towards proving the veracity of Tito. Partisan banners often bore as a legend the ancient Croatian motto, "Jesus and Mary be praised"; and it was not at all unusual to hear a soldier piously repeat those words. Partisan troops were sometimes detailed to keep watch at the replica of the Holy Sepulcher during Passion Week, and they often volunteered to act as escorts for Corpus Christi processions. Once partisan troops raided the farms of the Archbishop and took away twelve horses. But their leader was careful to explain that the theft was due to urgent necessity, and that compensation in full would be made later.

Nevertheless the Archbishop was much too realistic and well informed to become a victim of illusions. He wrote early in 1943, in a letter adduced afterwards as testimony against him: "Today the people believe that the 'partisans' are the least of the dangers we confront. They use shrewd tactics until the time when they take over has arrived." And a year later he wrote in the same vein: "The partisans are destroying all buildings in which state offices are housed. Until now they have nowhere touched churches, but of course we have no illusions about the future." It was not difficult to secure a good deal of information about the kind of discipline to which the partisans were subjected or about the ease with which the life of a dissenter in their ranks could be snuffed out.

The future towards which Dr. Stepinac looked with foreboding came to Zagreb on May 11, 1945, when the city was liberated. Immediately the war-crimes trials got under way,

and a few days later a Communist speaker branded him a war
criminal. One week later he was confined to his residence by
the OZNA (Department for the Defense of the People). Shortly
thereafter Marshal Tito arrived in the city, and expressed a
desire to confer with the clergy. The published text of his remarks included the following reflections on policy:

As far as I am concerned, I would say that our Church should be a
national institution, since this would be best suited to the needs of
the people. Perhaps you will be surprised to hear me stress nationality, but I am moved by the fact that we have shed so much blood for
our country. I have seen too much suffering not to wish that the Catholic clergy were more closely linked to the people than is the case
today. I should like to state publicly that I am not claiming the privilege of judging Rome, your supreme authority. I do not do so, but I
must say that my attitude is critical because this authority has already
been more favorable to Italy than to our people. I should like the
Catholic Church in Croatia to become more independent now, when
all the necessary conditions are present. That is my desire. That is the
basic question—the one we must solve. All other questions are of
minor importance and can easily be dealt with.

At this point a brief review of the political situation is in
order. According to Marshal Tito the meeting of the Anti-
Fascist Council at Jajce in 1943 was the prelude to a bid for
international recognition. The Yugoslav government-in-exile
in London had supported Mihajlović, leader of the irregular
army known as the Chetniks; but Tito had persuaded first the
British and then the Americans that his own was the genuinely
popular movement, as indeed it undoubtedly was. The point
at issue was the restoration of the Yugoslav monarchy. During
June, 1944, Ivan Subašić, prime minister of the government-
in-exile, was flown into partisan-held territory, to work out a
modus vivendi with Tito. This led to an agreement that
Mihajlović was to be dropped, and that the question of restor-

ing the monarchy was to be decided by free plebiscite once the war was over. It was further stipulated that a provisional government would be formed to rule until the result of the plebiscite were known, and that, in order to establish such a government, elections would be held to form a Constituent Assembly. These elections were to be conducted on a basis of freedom of assembly, speech, and balloting.

On March 5, 1945, Marshal Tito formed the provisional government, and it was announced that elections would be held on November 11. But there was no freedom of any kind whatever, and only candidates for the pro-government parties appeared on the ballot. It was announced on November 24 that 90 per cent of the voters had declared in favor of the government slate. The Constituent Assembly convened five days later and unanimously approved the Marshal's proclamation that a Federal People's Republic of Yugoslavia had been formed. On December 25, Great Britain and the United States informed Marshal Tito that they were according recognition to his government. This was done despite the fact that it had not been established in accordance with the pledges given.

On September 20 and 21, prior to the elections, the Catholic Hierarchy of Croatia had issued two Pastoral Letters, addressed respectively to the laity and to the clergy. The first of the letters is a document of great importance because it throws light on the situation at the time. After reviewing the grievous losses suffered by the nation during the war and the fratricidal struggles between Yugoslavs themselves, it welcomes the coming of peace and observes that wholly new conditions now prevail, and continues:

It does not appertain to the Catholic Church to prescribe to its faithful in what manner they shall resolve their political problems, provided that such solutions are in accordance with universally binding moral principles. . . . Prior to the cessation of hostilities, the

Federal Government in Belgrade pledged its solemn word to respect freedom of worship and of conscience, as well as private property. These principles were, from the outset, accepted by the Government of Croatia, but with the additional remark that the character of the Catholic Church here was not deemed satisfactory. In the very first days when we were able to contact the new Government we attempted to expound to its officials the needs and points of view of the Catholic Church. As many things in the State Administration created in the new spirit were at variance with the position and acquired rights of the Church, and as a consequence were detrimental to your spiritual good, our beloved brethren, we pointed out to and admonished those in power that questions bearing on the relationship between Church and State should be settled in an atmosphere of mutual understanding.

The Bishops then turn to the war-crimes procedures:

When the war operations were over, the infliction of capital punishment on Catholic priests did not cease. The number of priest victims is, as far as we know, this: 243 are dead, 169 are imprisoned in jails or concentration camps, 89 are missing. . . . To that number there must be added 19 seminarists, 3 lay brothers, and 4 nuns. For many a century Balkan history has witnessed no comparable slaughter. What is most especially and grievously painful is that all these, like hundreds and thousands of other Catholic faithful, are denied the Sacraments in their last hours, though all civilized nations permit them to be administered even to the most depraved criminals. Capital punishment was decreed by the courts summarily and quickly. The accused generally had no inkling of what crime they were charged with until the trial began, and then they were oftentimes deprived of the right of defense. . . .

Who can prove that so many priests upon whom the death penalty was inflicted were actually criminals deserving such punishment? For example, all Franciscans who were at their Monastery at Siroki Brijeg —28 all together—were put to death without judicial procedure. Not one of them took up arms, much less fought against the National Army of Liberation, as the Communists calumniously charged. Furthermore all of them were well known for their opposition to the Fascist ideology.

The Pastoral Letter goes on to deplore the suppression of the Catholic press, ostensibly due to the lack of paper; the closing and confiscation of the seminaries; the curtailment or suppression of religious instruction in the schools; the campaign of calumny waged in the Communist press; the closing of Catholic private schools, many of them famous; the encouragement given to looseness of morals among young people; and the placing of marriage under civilian control. In addition, it points out that the unjust manner in which land reform has been carried out has not only deprived the Church of property legitimately held, but will render the upkeep of the ecclesiastical establishment impossible.

Then come some very frank words of attack on the spirit and principles of the Communist Party:

There is something more which especially grieves us. It is the materialistic and godless spirit which is today being openly and secretly, officially and unofficially, propagated throughout our country. We, the Catholic Bishops of Yugoslavia . . . unreservedly condemn this materialistic spirit, from which no good can be hoped for for mankind. Likewise we condemn all ideologies and all social systems which are based not on eternal principles of Revelation and Christianity but on shallow foundations called materialistic and therefore philosophically atheistic.

All we have said has been pondered very carefully. And from all that has been said it is abundantly evident that the Catholic Church in Federal Democratic Yugoslavia is in a different situation and is faced with other difficulties than it has known until now. The present situation of the Catholic Church in Yugoslavia is separated only in name from open persecution.

As could have been expected, Communist reaction to this Pastoral Letter was violent. Marshal Tito dealt with it in a public address. He accused the Bishops of having remained silent while Pavelič and his Ustaša were committing depredations, and said that the schools conducted by Franciscans and other monks incited hatred against other groups than Catholics, and were therefore the breeding grounds on which Fascism was born in its various forms. Then followed a very characteristic declaration:

I do not believe that the lower part of the clergy will follow the appeal to oppose the Government in power. I know that there are many priests in Croatia, Bosnia, Herzegovina, Slovenia, etc., who do not think in terms of this letter. I know they are conscious of the horrible mistakes committed in the past and believe that the Church should now more than ever before become the bearer of peace and brotherhood among the peoples. I know that many priests and monks are deeply moved by the tragedy which has befallen our nation and that they now desire to go forward with the people. The declaration by Mister Archbishop Stepinac and some other Church dignitaries that they are ready to endure the struggle regardless of personal sacrifices leads me to conclude that they reached an agreement with the State under Pavelič not because of fear but for political reasons, and that they are now taking up the struggle against the new Federal Democratic Yugoslavia because they have a common plan with the rest of the reactionary groups in Yugoslavia.

In evaluating this exchange of views, one must bear in mind that the "liberation" was probably more sanguinary and repressive in Yugoslavia than elsewhere, for the reason that the old scores which were settled were so numerous and varied. It was not merely that Communist was pitted against Monarchist and collaborator. Earlier differences, such as that between Serb and Croat, also came to the fore, and political alignments which had been kept relatively intact during the occupation period were now summarily curbed. From the beginning, no one had the slightest chance to express an opinion other than that declared official by the Titoists. So abrupt and summary a seizure of power had not been possible in Hungary, Poland, and Czechoslovakia. From the outset Tito permitted neither political campaigning nor propaganda. And justice was whatever Communist courts decreed.

The Constitution of the Federal People's Republic of Yugoslavia, as adopted and then proclaimed on January 31, 1946, does not differ materially from the constitutions of the other satellite states, though there are divergencies. Thus "private property and private incentive in economic matters are guaranteed," and "citizens are guaranteed freedom of the press, of speech, of association, of meeting, of public assembly and manifestations." Nothing could sound freer or more democratic. The Constitution was, perhaps, a bit frank on marital relations, pointing out that all matrimonial disputes fall within the jurisdiction of the civil courts, and that parents are as responsible for children born outside wedlock as for children born in it.

However, before proclaiming the Constitution, the government began to consider ways and means of bringing Archbishop Stepinac to trial. It must be conceded that he did nothing to make the idea less attractive to them. On November 1, 1945, the Feast of All Saints, OZNA agents approached him as he was robing for Mass and warned him that if he did not desist from critical references to the government in his sermon a tumult would break out in the congregation. The Archbishop nevertheless delivered the sermon and closed with an account of the threat. Three days later, partisans ambushed him while he was on his way to the little town of Zaprešić to officiate at the dedication of a church; but he managed to escape. As might have been anticipated, attacks on him in the press and on the radio increased in violence. However, the government was far from anxious to proceed with the trial, because it was bound to raise an international furore. Efforts were made to secure the Archbishop's removal from his See by the Vatican. Marshal Tito himself said to Monsignor Hurley, the Papal Nuncio: "Take him away and relieve him of his duties. Otherwise we shall arrest him."

The immediate occasion for the trial was government action against the Kriźari (Crusaders), a diehard anti-Communist group who fought guerrilla-wise in the hills. Some priests were indicted as having been members, and one of them was alleged to have confessed that the Archbishop had given the movement his blessing. On the night of September 17, 1946, agents of the OZNA surrounded the archiepiscopal residence; and on the following morning Dr. Stepinac was arrested and indicted. Much has been said and written about the trial which followed, but some aspects of it still merit attention—much more, indeed, than can be given them here.

Since the liberation, the People's Courts had functioned as they usually do in crass revolutionary times. Presiding judges as well as juries were without legal training, being for the most part workingmen, sometimes waitresses and housemaids, whose sole qualification was membership in the Party. There was no legal code by which their actions could be circumscribed, the sole recognized principle being, "Whatever is against the People's Democracy is wrong." The decrees governing the protection of the State, nationalization of property, and taxation were grants of power to the authorities and not legislation on which anyone could base an appeal. Gradually some semblance of order was brought in; but the order was almost worse than the preceding chaos, for now the Public Prosecutor possessed unlimited power: he determined what crime had been committed, and then decided whether the sentence handed down by the court was sufficiently heavy. Woe betide a judge who erred on the side of mercy! He was simply fired from his job. And of course the Prosecutor had the right not only to select the jurors but to determine the desirability of the defense attorney, if indeed he permitted one to function.

Many appalling illustrations of these methods of securing justice have been reported. Thus the County Court of Zagreb heard the case of a well known specialist in nervous diseases, Dr. Vranešić, who was accused of collaborating with the enemy and of favoring racist theories. Dr. Znidaršić, a Communist intellectual, presided over the court, which acquitted the physician on the basis of a unanimous vote of the jury. But the Public Prosecutor took the case to the "Supreme Court" and compelled that Court to pass a death sentence. The physician was shot. The Zagreb "judge" was then tried in turn for having sinned against the People's liberation movement and sentenced to a year of forced labor. Hundreds of similar cases have been described in detail by witnesses.

Add that the Public Prosecutor had an espionage system which he could use as he wished. Every citizen was bound to "exercise vigilance" in the defense of the People, and could be called upon to serve as a witness whether or not he desired to do so. Evidence secured through wire tapping and similar means was naturally admissible, and it was rarely necessary for the Prosecutor to indicate how the evidence had been secured. In short everything which constitutes legal justice in the Western world was discarded in favor of a form of police rule which none could question or gainsay.

The trial of the Archbishop was preceded by a popular emotional struggle of great and moving interest. On the one hand, Communist meetings and demonstrations were organized to demand dire punishment. On the other, so many people crowded into the churches to pray for the Archbishop—despite the police ban of the Auxiliary Bishop's appeal for such prayers—that a command was issued limiting to five the number of persons allowed to congregate in front of a church. Throngs went in and out, none the less. The repercussions in the free countries of the world were naturally great. Nor was there lacking in American liberal circles a tendency to rejoice that a "reactionary" Archbishop had been brought to book by "progressive" justice.

Archbishop Stepinac was ably defended by two good and courageous attorneys. To be sure, they had little opportunity to confer with their client, only one hour being permitted. The Prosecutor presented the lengthy indictment in an address lasting forty-eight hours. It consisted of three groups of charges: first, that Dr. Stepinac had collaborated with the enemies of the people and had fomented divisive actions which undermined the unity of the resistance; second, that he had invited Western imperialists to occupy the country when the war was over; and third, that he had conspired against the People's authorities, leading "the whole Church and all the clergy in a struggle against the people and their State." These allegations were presented in an atmosphere of intense hostility, before a courtroom audience consisting for the most part of Communists.

The accusation of collaborating with the enemy could be refuted easily. So widely known and illustrious a record did the Archbishop have as a patriot, a repudiator of totalitarian theories, and a friend of the oppressed, that the Prosecutor could do nothing more than charge him with responsibility for every aberration of which scattered clerics, most of whom had never been under his jurisdiction, were guilty. His luminously clear and strikingly heroic behavior during the occupation will remain for all time an example of what the conduct of a priest in high station should be in such tragic circumstances. The charge of divisive endeavors, based upon an action taken by Ustaša fanatics against Orthodox Serbs, was so remote from anything Dr. Stepinac could conceive of as desirable that it, too, could be dismissed as a figment of the imagination. The second group of charges, having to do with Western imperialist powers, is ironic in view of what has happened to Marshal Tito himself; but it was intended as an assault upon the Vatican, which the Prosecutor was indicting through the Archbishop as its utterly loyal representative. The third group was undoubtedly well founded, and here Dr. Stepinac could have said, had he so desired, that it was necessary for a priest to preach the word of God, no matter what the cost to him personally might be; but his opponents did not recognize God, and there could be no doubt that he was guilty of opposition to the only power which had being in their eyes—namely, the Communist State they had created.

I think that one passage from the brief of Dr. Ivo Politoe, who at great risk to himself volunteered to defend the Archbishop, deserves remembrance as a tribute to the eminent Christian lawyers of his native Croatia, beautiful and unhappy land:

Sixteen years ago, at a time when Fascism was at the height of its power, and our Rijeka [Fiume] belonged to Italy, the Italian police there arrested a young Croat engineer on the suspicion that he had committed a political offense. After his arrest, he was conducted to the Regina Coeli prison in Rome. His old father, also a Croat from Rijeka, came to me and requested that I go to Rome and make such inquiries as a foreign lawyer might be able to do, and help in every way I could. Accordingly I went as a foreign lawyer, not knowing the local conditions prevailing in Rome, and requested an attorney there to help me and to associate himself with me as counsel for this particular case. This Italian attorney replied, "Dear colleague, I am a Fascist, and according to Fascist principles I am not allowed to assist anyone who is suspected of a crime against the state and the Fascist Government." Such were the conditions in Italy at that time. But the like does not exist and must not exist in Yugoslavia today. If we make daily use of the slogan, "Death to Fascism," then we must mean also death to all Fascist actions and to such attitudes as that of the Italian attorney to whom I have referred.

Surely, braver and truer words no man had spoken in Yugoslavia.

During the trial the Archbishop refused to reply to any of the questions and taunts of the Prosecutor, because he was convinced that sentence had been passed in advance of the hearings. The Court was incensed, and once said to the prisoner, "You are taking the attitude here that you are Jesus before the Court of Pilate." Sentence was passed on October 11, 1946. The prisoner was condemned to sixteen years at forced labor and to the loss of civil rights for five years. He did not appeal the verdict.

Thus, in a somber drama played on a stage which had the world as its audience, the Archbishop joined hands with all those humbler priests and laymen who had to bear the full brunt of fanaticism. It is nauseating to read report after report of torture and injustice, of barbarity and illiterate suffocation of evidence, which comes from survivors of Yugoslav justice. And it must be confessed that, since the rise of Communism, Nazism, and Fascism, we have become so accustomed to the scornful, utterly irrational degradation of human dignity that few have the stomach to wallow further in this morass of infamy. Let it merely be said that a great deal is known about the interrogation prisons which have existed in Tito's country and still exist there: prisons in which Catholic priests and laymen have been beaten, tortured, starved, and reviled for days until, reduced to utter exhaustion, they could be brought to trial and made to confess the "crimes" for which they were sentenced to concentration camps. Hundreds upon hundreds, thousands upon thousands, of these phantoms of the iron heel of Communism parade unseen before the conscience of the world.

The trial of Archbishop Stepinac was so spectacular that few people have even heard of the trial of Bishop Gregor Rozman, of Ljubljana, Slovenia, who was sentenced to prison *in absentia* for eighteen years on charges very similar to those preferred against Dr. Stepinac. Bishop Rozman was accused of collaboration with the Italians, and of having favored groups hostile to the "People's Democracy." These he was able to refute. But to the allegation that he as a Bishop had defended the rights of the Church and spoken in criticism of the atheistic doctrines of the Communist Party he had of course no response to make, other than this:

I publicly recognize that I saw in atheistic Communism, in the sense of the Encyclical *Divini Redemptoris,* the greatest menace to the Christian religion and to the Christian way of life of my people. Accordingly I considered it my pastoral duty to warn the faithful of this danger. . . . I did my duty notwithstanding the possibility that many of my actions would be wrongly interpreted by the Communists as implying collaboration with the Occupying Powers. When I reflect upon all these things now, in the presence of God, the only conclusion I can reach is, in the main I would do the same again.

Then on June 28, 1948, the U.S.S.R. and Marshal Tito came to a parting of the ways. Henceforth Yugoslavia would continue to be a Communist-dominated country but would become increasingly dependent upon what the Marshal had often referred to as the "Western Imperialist Powers."

We shall therefore briefly review the religious situation prior to and after those days. During 1946 and 1947 the Communists were omnipotent. Any opposition at all was designated high treason. Perhaps the greatest fire-eater among them was the President of the "Croatian Republic," Vladimir Bakarić. The Croats, a spirited and lovable people, have the misfortune of producing extremists of varied hues. On September 29, 1946, Bakarić addressed the students of Zagreb University.

He declared that the attitude of the government towards religion was that of Marx and Lenin. The Church must therefore be annihilated, but in a calm and peaceful way. Bakarić's most extreme displeasure was occasioned by reports that the Blessed Virgin had appeared in Fatima, Portugal. He spoke as if he were about to issue a decree forbidding any such apparitions in the future. Bakarić, however, was only a symbol. Books, pamphlets, broadsides ridiculed and denounced the clergy. They were molested if they ventured in public; and if they remained at home grammar-school children would march past their windows, singing insulting songs.

During 1947 a well informed observer described very graphically in *Civilta Catolica* the existing situation. Freedom of worship? Yes, but, as in Nazi Germany, every subterfuge was used to prevent the faithful from attending divine services. Persons coming in and out of church were noted by the secret police; and any man in the uniform of the civil service was liable to suspension if he was reported. The young were summoned to work duty or to meetings on Sunday morning. The content of sermons was reported by appointed observers, and a priest who sinned against what the regime considered decorum was summoned for a hearing. The dying could have a priest only if they specially requested that he come; and even then, in the case of State employees, the favor might not be granted.

As for the schools, the illusory character of the freedom guaranteed by the Constitution became increasingly evident. Every possible form of chicanery was resorted to in order to prevent the limited amount of religious instruction which was permitted under the law. Young Communists were sent into religion classes to provoke a tumult; and very often, especially in smaller towns, the rooms in which such classes were to be held proved to be non-existent. The poor priest who had sur-

vived the drive to decimate the clergy, and who had good
reason to fear that he might be dispatched to a concentration
camp the week following, had to face organized jeers and
taunts if he put in an appearance. Even parents who attempted
to give at home the instruction which was no longer possible
in the school, had to reckon with the fact that denunciation by
their children would mean the loss of the family livelihood.
Catholic schools as such had of course been taken over by the
government.

Textbooks were rewritten from the Marxist-Leninist point of
view. Christ was presented as a myth, and the Church as an
outmoded institution unaware of the onward march of science.
Songs were taught to the children so that, as they passed the
churches where their parents worshiped, they could vent on
them the spleen of the Communist ballad writers. Old Catholic
boarding schools were transformed into institutions for the
training of a Party élite, forbidden to visit a house of worship
or to see a priest. Discrimination against students because
their parents were "reactionaries" was routine practice. And
of course teachers or professors who did not elect to praise the
new order wholeheartedly were dismissed from their posts, to
be replaced by persons who often lacked rudimentary academic
qualifications. Youth organizations took on more and more
an outright propagandistic character. They were mere instrumentalities for indoctrination into the Communist view of life.

Catholic publishing houses ceased to exist. In 1947 it was
not possible to print anywhere in Yugoslavia a Bible, a cat-
echism, or a prayer book. The few surviving religious periodicals were stifled by censorship. Catholic charities virtually
disappeared. Nursing sisters still worked in hospitals prior to
Tito's rupture with Moscow, but they were subject to a myriad
of forms of control and interference. They were menaced with
deportation to Siberia if they clung to their vows. They were

compelled to become members of the nurses' union. Orphanages and old people's homes were taken from the Church, to the tune of slanderous accusations against the priests and religious who conducted them. In the orphanages prayer was forbidden, and indeed the children were taught to repeat phrases which in Christian ears are sacrilegious.

There is no purpose to be served by continuing the revolting report. By the middle of 1947, it could be conservatively estimated that Tito's followers had executed 400,000 persons. Hundreds of priests had died; nuns and other religious languished in the prisons. Pillage of religiously held properties was the rule rather than the exception. And yet, breath-takingly enough, everybody who came out of Yugoslavia reported that the people showed devotion and fidelity to an extent never known before. Anyone who recalls Sunday morning in Croatia with crowds of peasants in colorful costumes moving across the fields to church while the bells rang from old churches, as I do, has sometimes wondered whether the spectacle was not a result of surviving convention rather than of firm spiritual purpose. It may well be that there was vastly more of the second than one fancied.

Thus ends the chronicle of the Roman Catholic Church in Yugoslavia, prior to 1948.

In so far as the Orthodox Church is concerned, observers generally conclude on the basis of reports received that it has proved far more resolute in Serbia than elsewhere. Patriarch Gabriel, who was noted as a vigorous opponent of Communism, had issued a strong Pastoral Letter from exile against Tito's persecution of the Church. He returned unexpectedly to Belgrade in 1946, and it is believed that the restoration of the Patriarch was due to the persistent endeavors of his friends in Czechoslovakia. Upon his arrival he received a delegation of priests belonging to the pro-Communist group in the clergy

and expressed the hope that it would be possible to make a
mutually satisfactory settlement of the relations between
Church and State. Some time later, speaking at the Pan-Slavic
Congress in the capital city, he deposited a small amount of
complimentary oratory at the shrine of Stalin, "Russia's
extraordinarily gifted leader."

These actions were preludes to the discussions which were
begun in 1947, in the hope of arriving at an agreement satisfactory to the Orthodox Church. Reports indicate that Tito
made many promises, and that the Patriarch was chagrined to
see how few were fulfilled. Cooperation between the Church
and the regime was approved in principle, but under the condition that the good name of the Church and the clergy must
not be tarnished. The priests were authorized to follow their
own consciences in the matter. At all events, the Patriarch had
by no means merely subordinated the Church to the policy of
the State.

On the whole the attitude of the Holy Synod of the Orthodox
Church and of the remaining bishops was even more steadfast.
A Pastoral Letter issued during the Easter season of 1946—
protesting against the curtailment of religious instruction, the
secularization of marriage, and the materialistic propaganda
of the Communist Party—reads in retrospect very much like
what the Hierarchy of the Roman Catholic Church told the
faithful in that time of dire stress. It is known that the Bishops
demanded the Patriarch's assurance that he would stand firm
in the struggle for the rights and the freedom of the Church.

The Orthodox Church can thankfully assert also that one of
its bishops was just as courageous as Archbishop Stepinac.
Barnabas, Bishop of Saravejo, was brought to trial during
February, 1948, for saying in his sermons that the enemies of
God would perish. His answer was unhesitating and unequiv-
ocal: that he had only said what all the people felt and desired.

A Roman Catholic observer, William de Vries, thus summarizes the position in which the Orthodox Church now finds itself:

> Only a minority of so-called "national" priests is on the side of the Government. This minority is, however, very active. It is organized in trade unions of priests and seeks to compel all priests to join these. These unions are conceived of by the Government as counterbalances to the Hierarchy. They are organized according to regions and there is a central organization for the whole of the Yugoslav Republic. In addition they are incorporated into the Communist national front and are subject to the authority of the Communist Party. The objective is to revamp the whole structure of the Church in accordance with democratic principles. . . . The Hierarchy is justly disturbed by the efforts of this "democratic" union of priests. But one may nevertheless conclude that the Serbian Orthodox Church as a whole has not yet capitulated.

No one should fancy that the break with Moscow—perhaps more difficult to comprehend than any other episode in the long history of Sovietism—meant the end then and there of religious intolerance. Marshal Tito continued to preach and practice Communist doctrine, tinted colorfully with Yugoslav nationalism. All the Party tricks were still in his repertory. The Society of Sts. Cyril and Methodius was the standard version of clerical organizations professing a pro-Communist platform. Addressing it, Marshal Tito asked why its members did not break with Rome, and so emulate his own rupture with Moscow. Nor did open and violent persecution of priests and laymen cease. As late as September 25, 1949, the Reverend Josef Vedrina of Labor was set upon by a group of Communists as he was returning from a burial service and slain. At the close of 1951, *Politika*, Yugoslav Communist organ, interviewed the prime ministers of the several Yugoslav republics. The prime minister of Slovenia denounced the Vatican as one of the "bulwarks of reaction," and as a "persistent meddler" in the affairs of all nations. He denounced the "persecution" inflicted upon priests who cooperated with the government and found themselves excommunicated. Bakarić, reviewing the situation in Croatia, noted with gratification that the membership in the Society of Sts. Cyril and Methodius had increased somewhat.

Nevertheless the consequence of the break with Moscow and of the attempt to arrive at an understanding with the West which inevitably followed slowly became manifest. Whereas the attitude towards the United States in particular had been unfriendly, Marshal Tito himself now sought out its diplomatic representatives. Interviews were freely accorded foreign journalists, and in April and May, 1952, *Life* published an autobiographical sketch "in Marshal Tito's own words." * Yugoslavia itself, suffering intensely both from drought and from faulty industrial reconstruction, was not pushed further into an all-out collectivist economy. The peasants had seemingly won a decisive victory against expropriation. Great stress was laid on modernizing the military establishment, and to accomplish this the good will of the American people had to be cultivated.

During April, 1951, Alex Singleton, correspondent for the Associated Press, was permitted to interview Archbishop Stepinac in Lepoglava Prison, where he had been confined during more than four years. The Archbishop seemed to be well informed concerning the trend of events, and expressed the opinion that relations between Church and State had improved since 1948, because the Communist Party had adopted a "more realistic approach to democracy." The Archbishop

* Interestingly and significantly enough, the official Yugoslav version of the Marshal's career differs in important respects from that prepared for the world at large.

declared that while a Concordat could be negotiated only with the Holy See, it was no doubt true that from the Catholic point of view what really mattered was the right to give religious instruction to children, to administer the Sacrament of Matrimony, to maintain a religious press, and to engage in charitable activities. When the news was received in Rome, the Vatican informally endorsed these views.

Eight months later, Archbishop Stepinac was released from prison and was "conditionally" permitted to exercise the duties of a priest in his native village of Krasic. The government's communiqué referred to him as the "former archbishop." Interviewed as he was returning from morning Mass, he refused to comment on any political issue but said firmly: "I was not released under any conditions. They released me of their own free will. . . . The reason I did not ask to be released is that I do not feel guilty." The comment in *Osservatore Romano* said in part: "Another Bishop, His Excellency, Monsignor Peter Cule of Mostar, is still held in prison unjustly." It then alluded to the two hundred priests and religious who were even then in custody, and to the "forms of discrimination against religion" practiced in Yugoslavia.

Yet there could be no doubt, and there is none now, that the situation had greatly changed. The official illusion that the masses of the people endorsed the Communist ideology had been dispelled. Every visitor reports that once the reign of terror visited upon the Churches had abated, the people flocked as always to the houses of worship. Much has been written about this in the press of France, Italy, Germany, and Great Britain. In the *New York Herald Tribune* of August 5, 1952, John K. Cooley reported *:

The Yugoslav Constitution of 1946 separates Church and State and scrupulously guarantees, on paper, the "freedom of exercise of all

* Reprinted by permission.

religions" to the Roman Catholics, various sects of the Greek, Serbian and Macedonian Orthodox Churches, Moslems and the tiny fraction of Protestants in the six Yugoslav republics. Piety is open and general in Zagreb, where there seems to be a church in every block, many members of monastic orders appear on the streets, and bells announce frequent masses during the day.

But a closer glance reveals the change. Church bulletin boards list only services and sparse items of parish news; no other activities exist. Gone are the Church schools which once, especially here in Croatia, exercised a guiding hand in the instruction of young people. Gone too are all traces of religious organizations for young people, women, veterans. The Party's present official attitude on the Church is perhaps best summed up by a quotation from Engels I saw beside a magnificently arranged collection of Croatian and German Gothic religious art in a Zagreb museum. "Every great religion is only a fantastic picture in men's heads, of such supernatural forces as make humdrum life easier; an earthly force which clothes itself in the guise of supra-earthly powers."

Whatever the case, a great many people in Yugoslavia today still cling to their "earthly forces."

This description is well corroborated and can be accepted as correct. There has recently been little overt persecution of the Church; but religious agencies are not free to develop any part of the many-sided program in which they normally engage. Party leaders continue to express their "new Yugoslav conception" of the Marxist gospel, but they cannot rid themselves of either the onus of heretical deviation from the teaching and leadership of Moscow, or reliance upon the credits and other assistance which the West provides. Daily, the official radio exchanges blows with Moscow; but everybody knows that if the country stood alone the Russian Army would end the debate in twenty-four hours. Whether this unstable stability can be maintained is a fateful question. Yugoslavia is desperately poor, ravaged by war, revolution, massacre, and collectivistic experimentation. The strength of Marshal Tito derives from his title and not at all from his ideology. He has proved himself to be a brave and able soldier. We should realize and respect this fact, just as we should never tire of asking why a man with so much native ability became a Communist in the first place. Nobody should indulge in idle fancies that the core of Communism, in Europe, is intellectual as it is in England and the United States. Every one of its important personages was once an embittered workman or peasant, or an opportunist to whom Communism was a gateway to power.

If Tito and his people should ever come to a parting of the ways—what then? Unless the men who took over were fully prepared and had the resolute support of the vast majority of the people, its armed forces, and its surviving intellectual leaders, the result would be still another period of upheaval fraught with the gravest national and international danger. This, all of us should reckon with in terms of the given international situation when we think of the "soft underbelly of Europe." It is not so soft any longer. Fleets and air forces of great power and mobility are stationed in the Mediterranean area. These provide, to be sure, no absolute guarantee that a reconciliation between Russian and Yugoslav versions of Communist doctrine will never be achieved.

Towards the close of 1952, Pope Pius XII announced that among the Cardinals Designate was Aloysius Stepinac. Official Yugoslavia professed to receive the news with great indignation. Diplomatic relations with the Holy See were broken off. Some days later, it was reported that Marshal Tito had invited the Yugoslav Bishops to confer with him about a possible settlement of the issues on which Church and State were divided. Reports indicate that those who responded said that, while a definitive settlement was reserved to the Holy See, they were prepared to discuss the situation with representatives of the government. Viewed realistically, this seemed to be a notable step forward. Some have contended, as a result, that if Cardinal Stepinac were appointed to an important post in Rome the way might be clear for a settlement of major difficulties, because Tito would not be required to lose face. Would such a move have been approved by the Society of Jesus, in the days of the high tide of its influence on the affairs of men? This query cannot be resolved.

Returning from a visit to the British Isles, where he had perforce to take notice of pointed public inquiries into the status of religion under his regime, the Marshal ordered a religious census of the population. This was widely looked upon as a device for exposing the secret creedal ties of persons in any way associated with the government, and as a spur to professed apostasy. If that was the intention, some of the results must have seemed a bit strange. On July 9, 1953, *Die Zeit,* of Hamburg, reprinted a letter which the Sarajevo Communist organ *Oslobojenje* had published on June 30, reading in part as follows:

In connection with a census of the population, I entered my name and the names of my children, and indicated the religious associations in which I hold membership by saying that I am an atheist. . . . The community secretary, Ljubo Zelenovic, who was in charge of the census, went through the whole village after he had left my house proclaiming that I was the only woman in the whole place who did not believe in God and who made infidels of her innocent children. At the same time he delivered a harangue about atheists, saying among other things that they approved of sisters and brothers living as husbands and wives. The women of the village made the sign of the Cross and refused to believe their ears. "God protect us!" they cried. "She ought to be driven out of town so that the people may not be corrupted." "God will punish her," said my aunt's husband. She urged him to throw me out of the house. . . . This mob was regrettably joined by several members of the Communist League. One of them,

Rajko Tadic, told my husband to his face that he ought to kick me out, because women who do not believe in God are immoral. Let me give you a still more deplorable example. The secretary of the Communist League, Petko Vukasinovic, gave my husband the same advice and added, "Women are in a class by themselves. We men can be accorded the right not to go to Church or to pray. But don't you realize, my friend, that my wife never misses Mass and that she goes to Confession regularly? Remember, such practices ought to be kept up for the children's welfare, if for no other reason. . . . Your wife, my friend, is a white crow in this town. If you want to get along with the people here, throw her out!" All this talk has been so widespread that my husband and I are seriously considering moving away from here. I am not a member of the Communist Party. The conditions I have described are responsible for the fact that only a very few women in the District of Zvornik are Communists. Are they not beyond the pale of democratic activity?

The town described is only a few miles from Belgrade. *Die Zeit* noted that such were the results of ten years of official Communist propaganda for atheism. While it would be very unwise to generalize on the basis of a report of this nature, it may be assumed that there are many similar villages in Yugoslavia.

Since this chapter was written the death of Stalin and the rise to power of Malenkov have apparently altered somewhat Tito's program for his government. First of all, the new Russian "peace offensive," directed primarily toward the Near East and the Balkans, met with some success; and a by-product was an increase of pro-Kremlin activity in Trieste, over which the Yugoslavs and the Italians were at odds. Communists there, many of whom had been ousted and exiled by Tito as pro-Stalin stooges, were now in a position to foment more trouble than their numbers warranted, particularly for the Allied Occupying Powers—a fact which incidentally leads to the conclusion that these agents should have been forced to move on when they sought asylum.

While Tito and the responsible Italian statesmen responded to nationalistic emotions aroused on both sides of the disputed city, Yugoslav interest in the Pact which bound the country together with Greece, Turkey, and Italy in a military alliance with the West waned. The Marshal himself did not formally withdraw from his commitments to this alliance, but organs of public opinion over which his Party has complete control ostentatiously did, giving rise to considerable speculation and some fear. United States diplomats thus inherited another conundrum from the immediate postwar period. On the one hand, it was not possible to deed Trieste over to Italy. On the other, the arrangements with the Yugoslav dictator, made at the cost of almost infinite pains, were in some jeopardy.

Acts reflecting hostility to the Church and its clergy increased. American observers reported a number of incidents troublingly reminiscent of the days prior to the Marshal's "conversion." Priests were attacked, and churches were pillaged. The motivation is impossible to determine. The hoodlums involved may have been venting their spleen on the Vatican, adjudged to be an ally of Italy; or they may have been carrying out orders of the Party, the nature and intent of which are veiled from view. One thing was made certain: the lot of a Church and its faithful under a dictatorship like Tito's is highly precarious, indeed.

5 POLAND AND RELIGION

POLAND, LARGEST AND MOST populous of the satellite countries, was also by all odds the most difficult morsel the Russians were to swallow and attempt to digest. This can best be realized if the problem is seen in its historical setting. The Polish State after its establishment at the close of the First World War was, as might easily have been anticipated, a product of strong nationalistic and irredentist emotions and a victim of grave economic and political weaknesses. Polish patriots, freed at long last from bondage, were eager to annex any territory which at some time had been under Polish sovereigns. Because a great part of the Ukraine, including Kiev, had been under such dominion, Polish forces battled against Bolshevik troops, who drove them back and were defeated only with great difficulty at the gates of Warsaw; and in the West sanguinary fighting took place between Polish "insurgents" and German veterans illegally mustered in to defend eastern Silesia. In like manner the Poles overran the southern part of the newly constituted Lithuanian State and took possession of the historic city of Vilna. It mattered little that the Victorious Powers had assigned to Poland boundaries which

conformed in most essentials with those fixed at the time of the
Second Partition of 1793, or had decreed that there should be
a Polish Corridor separating East Prussia from the rest of
Germany. Polish nationalists remained dissatisfied, and the
rights of minorities in the new State were seldom assured. As
a result it was embroiled in open or smoldering disputes with
all its neighbors; and during the twenty years after 1918 only
the might and prestige of the French army shielded it from
pressure or even attack.

At the same time the dire economic plight of large sections
of a predominatingly peasant population and a dearth of
experience with democratic political institutions created widespread domestic unrest and conflict. With the assistance of experts provided by the United States, the currency was stabilized
after 1920 and banking institutions were put on a firm foundation. The newly established port of Gdynia enabled the country
to establish a moderately profitable foreign trade. Upper
Silesian mines, taken from Germany by decree of the Allies,
were also sources of wealth. Nevertheless the masses remained
desperately poor. Meanwhile the form of government became
more and more authoritarian, and Marshal Pilsudski assumed
the role of dictator. After his death the nation was ruled by a
"government of colonels," who viewed the troubled international scene with shallow optimism, signed nonaggression
pacts with Russia and Nazi Germany, and sought to take advantage of Hitler's attack on Czechoslovakia by forcibly seizing
the area of Teschen. The Polish army, pride of the nation with
some of the best infantry divisions in Europe, remained anti-
quated in leadership, organization, and equipment.

The outcome was that one of the most romantic, appealing,
courageous, and gifted of peoples was plunged into pitiless
and awful tragedy such as history has seldom witnessed. After
the Stalin-Hitler Pact was signed, the German dictator struck

swiftly and savagely, while the Russians occupied the territory east of the Bug River, where the beaten Polish armies might conceivably have been redeployed. Subsequently another Russo-German agreement all but wiped Poland from the political map. The districts to the west came under German rule, while all territory east of the so-called Curzon Line were given to Russia in perpetuity. Lithuania also was ceded to Russia. Under Nazism the Poles suffered excruciatingly. Countless numbers were slain or deported. Major blows were also struck at religion. When the Second World War ended, Jewry in Poland had been almost completely destroyed, the few survivors having managed to hide in out-of-the-way places or miraculously survived the extermination camps. The Lutheran Church, which had served primarily Germans resident in Poland and was deemed by Hitler to have favored that country, was decimated. Scarcely less appalling was the persecution of the Catholic Church. Nearly two-fifths of all its clergy were imprisoned, and half of this number may well have died on the block or in concentration camps. The Russian occupation of eastern Poland was followed by almost equally barbarous treatment. Captured Polish officers were murdered in Katyn Forest. The Polish Catholic population which professed the Latin rite was ruthlessly deported and exterminated. Greek Catholics were the victims of unmitigated tyranny. Propagandists proclaimed the incompatibility of religion with the Communist view of life. By the close of the first brief period of Soviet occupation, more than 100,000 persons had disappeared, no one knows where. Then, as the tide of war moved to and fro across the stricken land, resistance forces battled first one side and then the other. The grimmest of these stories concerns the destruction of the Warsaw Ghetto; but there are many tales, and each is heartrending.

The Second World War ended, and the nation groped about

in its ruins. The loss of life, the destruction of public buildings and of private housing, the elemental plight of the population, all are beyond imagining. The Russians moved to take over control with mingled skill and brutality. By securing at Potsdam an agreement which took from Poland the district east of the Curzon Line and compensated it with territory traditionally and unmistakably German—Silesia in particular—they maneuvered the West into a position from which it cannot, seemingly, extricate itself by peaceful means. Thus the way was prepared for an irredentist *rapprochement* between Russia and Germany, should it prove desirable to the Kremlin; and no doubt this possibility today haunts the dreams of every chancellery in the free world. Stalin acceded, to be sure, to the principle that the government of Poland must be democratic, fashioned in accordance with the will of the people as ascertained in free and open elections. But the Russians soon snuffed out any hope that anti-Communist political groups would retain independence of action; indeed, they liquidated Social Democratic and other opponents with the utmost callousness when it seemed expedient. Far more quickly than had been anticipated, the pattern was traced in broad outline. All the freedoms existed on paper; but in bare and bald reality the Communist Party had acquired absolute mastery. A tragic byproduct was that Polish soldiers abroad, who had fought hard and courageously for victory at Monte Cassino and elsewhere, could not return to their native land.

We shall begin our review of the implications for religion with some data concerning religious affiliations in Poland. When Hitler declared war, Catholics worshiping according to the Latin rite constituted approximately three-fourths of the population. A tenth professed the Greek Orthodox faith, and the percentage of Jews was comparable. Protestants were a small minority, numbering about 842,000 in 1940. The Roman

Catholic Churches, of the Latin and Greek rites, sponsored a large number of activities and organizations. The Constitution recognized religion as an integral part of the educational curriculum and assigned a position of special privilege to the Roman Catholic Church as that of the vast majority, identified in a most intimate way with Poland's national history. The Concordat signed by the Holy See and the Polish government in February, 1925, accorded to the Church a measure of independence from the State which was, I think, not paralleled elsewhere in Europe. After it was ratified Pope Pius XI, who as Monsignor Achille Ratti had been Papal Nuncio to Poland, issued a Papal Bull entitled *Vixdum Poloniae Unitas* which gave formal expression to the Church's satisfaction and called attention to the close ties which had traditionally bound this imperiled country to the See of Rome.

The grant of so many notable privileges and the establishment of a large number of monastic institutions (for example, there were more than 18,000 professed nuns in Poland) aroused, to be sure, some opposition among the more discontented and anticlerical elements of the population. Prior to the Nazi invasion a not inconsiderable literature assailed the Church with varying degrees of bitterness and skill; much of it was of Leftist derivation, though there existed also a morally emancipated bourgeois anticlericalism. Accordingly the hostility which Catholicism encountered when the Russians assumed control was by no means wholly imported from the east. To offset diverse forms of animosity, there grew up in Poland after 1927 a powerful and effectively led Catholic Action Movement, specially suited to meet the conditions which obtained after the establishment of Marshal Pilsudski's quasi-dictatorship. It enlisted in the crusade for Catholic solidarity all groups of the population, young and old, peasant and worker, professional man and scholar.

Religious life in Poland had a special character. An intellectual élite, often marked by unusual insight into the values of humanism, was soundly trained in theology; but the poverty of the country outside the relatively few centers of commerce and culture was dire indeed, and left little leisure for intellectual pursuits. The vast throngs of peasants were just beginning to stir out of the passivity into which centuries of hopeless thralldom had plunged them. Nor was the lot of the average industrial worker much better. The quality of the wares offered to him for purchase was often so bad that I wondered why he bothered to buy them. Even the clergy were not infrequently uncultivated, caste-conscious, and bureaucratic. As a consequence there lay over much of the Polish landscape a recognizable, sometimes quite tangible sadness: the melancholy of the human being with a great and real endowment for poetry—as its writers and musicians bear witness—whose outer life was stark, unredeemed reality. Yet this mood was combined with a deep and imaginative introspection, so that religious mysticism, whether it was the Sabbath-day brooding of the Jewish Ghetto or the ecstasy of the Catholic pilgrimage, was deeper and stronger than it probably was elsewhere in the Western world.

No doubt hearts and minds are more easily kindled by ideas when they are not so cluttered up with extraneous concerns that no path to the hearth of the soul can be found. The oldest preserved fragment of Polish literature is a "Hymn to the Blessed Virgin." The great Russian philosopher Vladimir Soloviëv was wont to say that his own country and Poland would eventually arrive at concord through a common dedication to Mary. At any rate, a profound and no doubt Eastern concern with what is peculiarly dear and mystical alike in Catholic theology (which can to be sure also be conceived of purely emotionally, and indeed merely credulously) is the treasure garnered from the innermost core of religious experience for the preservation of which a struggle is now in progress in Poland. All else is of secondary significance. And it must always be borne in mind that what relatively uneducated men term "science"—the lightening of burdens as a result of the harnessing of nature to technological tasks—may prove to be the inspiration of mystical beliefs which can tease almost to the verge of delirium the feelings of those who have lived so long in a world in which the tyrant State merely mirrors the tyrant Nature.

We should never deal lightly or superficially with the ideology of the Communists. Observing the attitude of people not previously acquainted with machines towards these incredibly beneficent behemoths wearing seven-league boots and able to do in an hour what the arms and hands of many men could not accomplish in a day, one knows that initial feelings of fear, resentment, and an odd kind of envy soon give way to moods of deliverance and of enjoyment of fancied freedom which can induce a violent intoxication of the spirit. In this pseudo trance, people are likely to accept the conclusion that the human intelligence expended on creating these things, earthly though it be, is as near to Divinity as man can hope to come. Not until human beings rediscover the cruelty which is inherent in this intelligence when it is left alone to deal with the power urges implicit in its very nature, do they begin to realize once again that unless there be another Power, sempiternal, immutable, and inexhaustibly good, life cannot be loved or even endured.

We should remember also that rabid, uncompromising nationalist sentiment can corrode a society almost to the verge of spiritual extinction. Such sentiment was the grievous, if from some points of view explicable, sin of modern Poland. It was nowhere more manifest than in religious relations. Tension between Christian and Jew was constant, resembling that which existed between whites and Negroes in the United States at the close of the First World War. But it was often to be discerned in the relations among Christians as well. A distinguished Polish scholar writes:

Due to the steady increase of nationalist feeling, the area of co-operation between Latin and Eastern Catholics grew progressively smaller. Nationalists living in the southeastern territories of the country, where animosity between Poles and Ukrainians had increased considerably during the nineteenth century, did not hesitate to make use of religion as an instrument of political machination. Even some of the clergy who were active in nationalist movements misused the Church and organizations associated with it for purposes alien to the Church's mission. The successes of Hitler and Mussolini then made such nationalists feel surer of themselves and more persuaded of the correctness of their ideas. Though not very numerous, the followers of such leaders were unusually active and so able to poison relationships between the two groups in the population. They were ordinarily young people who yearned to act as strong men opposed to every form of compromise and to the pacific influence of the Church. The following remarks made by a Ukrainian priest describe the situation very aptly: "We Ukrainians and Poles may be compared, in our contemporary political and religious antagonisms, to two lions that attack and mangle each other. Thereby we provide a spectacle for Europe and in particular for the states which are our neighbors and which watch our tussle and turmoil with satisfaction."

To the pertinence of these remarks I can myself attest.

That is the background against which the second Russian occupation, extended to the whole of Poland, must be visualized.

In so far as religion is concerned, this occupation, though attended by many cruelties and outrages, differed notably from the first, reflecting a change inside Russia itself. At the outset there was no overt attack on religion. Thus the Russians not only paid the expenses of the funeral in 1944 of the deceased Metropolitan of the Greek Catholic Church, Archbishop Szeptitski, but were officially represented at the obsequies. In the following December efforts were made to persuade this Church that its rightful place was inside the pale of Russian Orthodoxy. The Patriarch of Moscow sent a delegation to Lwów for the purpose. It was announced in the government press that the Greek Catholic clergy had been abettors of the evil policies of the Vatican, and that they were therefore to be considered as enemies of the Soviet Union. As has been indicated, there was some truth in the charge, because a few ardent Ukrainian patriots among the clergy had for a time expected great things of what they assumed would be Nazi policy towards the Ukraine. Secret police raided the residences of the Uniate bishops and prelates, confiscating all records. The successor to Archbishop Szeptitski, Dr. Joseph Slipyj, was arrested, tried, and deported to a concentration camp at Workuta. He is known to have been there as late as 1949. A similar fate was meted out to other bishops. A letter addressed to the "Pastors and Faithful of the Greek-Catholic Church" by the Patriarch of Moscow pointed out that, whereas the Russian Orthodox Church had supported peace, freedom, and the Russian cause, the Vatican had given aid and comfort to Hitler, "the greatest scoundrel the history of the world has ever seen." On April 29, 1945, some five hundred Greek Catholic clergymen met for a conference in the Cathedral of Lwów. This was surrounded by the secret police. The priests were arrested, and some of them were shot. Orders were thereupon issued that no Greek Catholic priest should conduct services without a special permit from the Soviet authorities.

The liquidation of the Greek Catholic Church and its enforced apostasy to Moscow was in process, even as it would soon be in Rumania. One cannot say definitely that this was a maneuver inspired by Communistic hatred of religion, for it resembles closely in conception and execution similar measures taken under the Tsars. Indeed, we might well confess that historians will find it extremely difficult to determine which of the steps to suppress the Church in the satellite states were suggested by Communist doctrine, and which were solely reflections of the traditional Russian colonization policies revived by Stalin in imitation of the Tsars Peter and Ivan. At any rate, announcement was made of the formation of a "Committee of Initiative for the Transfer of Greek Catholics to the Orthodox Church," headed by the Reverend Havril Kostelnyk, a theologian of some repute who had deeply resented the contempt visited upon his Church for nationalistic reasons by some of the Polish clergy. The committee issued two letters, one addressed to their fellow priests and the other to the Council of the People's Commissars of the Ukrainian Soviets. On June 18, 1945, the committee, which in the interim had been joined by twoscore more of the clergy, received a reply from the Ukrainian capital, recognizing it as the only "juridico-ecclesiastical body having unrestricted right to control Greek Catholic parishes in the western Ukraine," in order to promote the union of these parishes with the Orthodox Church. As a consequence it was instructed to report to the Council of People's Commissars the names of "deans, clergy, and superiors of religious houses who refuse to submit to the authority of the Committee of Initiative." The neck of every recalcitrant was now in the noose.

Representatives of the committee then made two trips—one to Kiev and the other to Moscow—to discuss the problems associated with reunion. Dr. Kostelnyk, who had meanwhile been ordained a priest in the Russian Orthodox Church, reported that 997 Uniate priests had recognized the authority of the Committee on Initiative. The total number of clergymen was more than 2,200, and it is not difficult to surmise the fate of the others. Meanwhile the two remaining bishops of the Greek Catholic Church were arrested and deported.* For all practical purposes, Greek Catholicism had been liquidated even though the tenacity with which deep religious convictions are held makes all reports of such overt actions misleading. There can be no doubt that this branch of the Catholic Church manifested great and memorable heroism, as in the time of the Nazi occupation. Archbishop Szeptitski in particular had issued a Pastoral Letter condemning the treatment meted out to the Jews, and had denounced the conscription of men and women for labor in Germany.

When Russian Communism came face to face with Roman Catholicism according to the Latin rite in those parts of Poland which had not been annexed, but which were nevertheless under Party control, it confronted one of its most doughty antagonists. This territory was now more strongly Catholic than it had previously been, owing to the liquidation of the

---

* *Osservatore Romano* of Dec. 12, 1946, described the arrest of the two bishops in the following terms: "The larger part of the Ruthenian diocese of Przemyśl was transferred to Russia, while the city itself and a small amount of adjacent territory remained with Poland. On May 14, 1946, Bishop Jiosofat Kocylowskyj was summoned by a Russian colonel of the Secret Police, a Polish major of the same arm, and Tiszezenko, the Ukrainian chief of the Russian Office of Transportation, and told to leave 'voluntarily' for Russia. The Bishop refused to do so, saying that he could comply only if the order came from the Pope. He was informed that in this case he would be deported by force. And so at 9 A.M., on the morning of June 20, the local commander of the Security Police, accompanied by a soldier, appeared at the Bishop's residence and declared he was under orders to transport him and the members of the Cathedral Chapter to Russia. The Bishop answered that he would not resign his See, and that in any event he would have to pack his luggage. At 6 P.M. soldiers dragged him out of his house, beating him severely. He was placed in an automobile, and this left immediately for the Russian border. On June 27, Bishop Lakota as well as Canons Resztyl, Kusyra and Hycelak were taken to the railroad station and asked to sign a declaration to the effect that they were leaving 'voluntarily' for Russia. All refused to do so. The train then took them across the frontier. The residences of the Bishops and Canons were plundered, and their property and personal effects were sold on the streets and in the market place."

Jews by the Nazis. The percentage, populationwise, may well have been higher than 93 in 1945. Despite all the grievous losses suffered, it was possible to reestablish within a short time a smoothly functioning ecclesiastical organization. Charitable institutions, educational establishments, and even the press were made ready for action. A notable revival of religious practice was reported from all parts of the country. Thus more than 2,000,000 persons went on pilgrimage to the popular shrine of Częstochowa during 1946. Against such an adversary, the Communists proceeded with great wariness. No earnest attempt was made immediately to alter the character of education, or to raise the issue of confiscation of properties belonging to the Church.

Nevertheless a mighty wave of propaganda, directed against the Hierarchy but primarily against the Vatican, descended upon the nation. It strove to prove that the Pope had aided the cause of Hitler and Fascism, and was therefore to be considered as an enemy of the Polish people. Two arguments in particular were employed. The first was that after the dismissal of the Polish Hierarchy in regions incorporated into Germany by the Nazis, the Church had recognized the jurisdiction of the German bishops. The second allegation, difficult to controvert, was that the Vatican favored the restoration to Germany of those territories which the Potsdam Conference of 1945 had ceded to Poland. The Holy See had manifested so often its detestation of Nazism, and had testified upon so many occasions to its affection for the Poles—for example, by according asylum to Cardinal Hlond and giving him almost unlimited opportunity to speak over the Vatican radio—that the accusation of sympathy with Hitler was likely to seem jocose. In addition Pope Pius XII had so promptly speeded up relief activities when it became possible to do so that no one in his right mind would believe that he had ever deviated from the policy of his predecessor expressed in the Concordat and in the Bull *Vixdum Poloniae Unitas.* It was, however, obviously impossible for the Vatican to foresee the treaty of peace and condone the expulsion of millions of Silesians whose loyalty to the Holy See was just as genuine as that of Poland itself. It could do so as little as it could have approved the German attack on Poland.

But on the basis of such arguments the pro-Communist government abrogated the Concordat on September 12, 1945, without previous notice to the Holy See. Surprisingly enough, the Polish courts were still in a position to rule that the government's action was invalid; and for a time relations between the Polish State and the Vatican remained nebulous. During the following spring the Primate of Poland, Cardinal August Hlond, returned from the exile into which he had been forced by the fact that he was in Rome when the war broke out. He had a long record of service to Polish national interests. Although conditions were still turbulent, his arrival attracted widespread attention, and popular demonstrations of respect and affection contrasted vividly with the criticism and denunciation meted out in the Communist press. He himself refrained from discussing relations between Church and State; but they formed the theme of Pastoral Letters issued by the Polish Hierarchy during April and June, which pointed out to the faithful that the materialistic view of life, as propounded by spokesmen for Communism, was incompatible with the traditions and the historic mission of Poland. The Letter of June 19 also criticized forcefully the administration of justice throughout the land, and observed that personal freedom and security were not safeguarded. It adduced cases of shooting of men, women, and even children without the formality of a trial and denounced conditions prevailing in prisons and concentration camps. This letter was confiscated, only twenty words of it having been approved by the official censor.

To be sure, terrorism was not halted by these protests. The Communists skillfully solidified their position in the period prior to the first postwar general election. Their methods, in so far as Catholics were concerned, deviated very little from the standard pattern. The government promptly discovered the Polish National Church, a quite insignificant movement of a schismatic character established by a handful of Polish priests who had returned from the United States after stormy passages at arms with certain American bishops of non-Polish extraction. This Church was now cast for the role of center around which "patriotic priests" could rally. In like manner, the two traditional Catholic political parties were revamped when a few members of both, having announced their readiness to co-operate with the government, were summarily installed as a joint "Board of Directors." The Hierarchy flayed these actions vigorously, urging the faithful to vote only for candidates who were not avowed enemies of the Church; and the Catholic press published pointed commentaries on the situation. Nevertheless the provisional government clenched its teeth and rammed through an election edict prepared in advance. The majority of the candidates standing against the government's list were clapped into jail; and the voters were terrorized by large contingents of Communist police, who had the assignment of seeing to it that "free elections" should turn out the right way. Foreign newsmen scrutinized the balloting carefully, so that some semblance of the truth about Soviet-sponsored democracy began to trickle through to the still far too optimistic countries of the West.

By the close of 1948 the Communists had managed to get the power into their hands. They redoubled their efforts to eradicate "religious prejudice" from the schools and to form youth organizations willing to imbibe the teachings of Marx, Lenin, and Stalin; and slowly and craftily they infiltrated the associations of teachers. Demands that textbooks and all other aids to teaching be revised in accordance with the "modern scientific outlook" began to be as common and similar as peas. A "Union of Militant Youth," similar to the German Freie deutsche Jugend, was strongly supported; and this began to build cells in the Polish Boy and Girl Scout organizations, which had been popular prior to Hitler's victory and were revived immediately after the liberation. The familiar motto, "A Scout Serves God and Country," was revised to read, "A Scout Serves Democratic Poland." Shopworn methods of infiltration were resorted to even in professedly religious schools and youth groups. Perhaps the most effective Communist recipe for the indoctrination of young people was the summer camp, which in Poland was combined with a free trip to the Soviet Union. The camps, often organized on a grandiose scale, offered "political education" to boys and girls by carefully trained Party instructors.

It may be observed for general edification that, although the methods of indoctrination in all youth organizations sponsored by totalitarian regimes are pretty much alike, the Russian Communist system differs in one important characteristic from the Fascist Balilla and the German Hitlerjugend: its brand of internationalism. It does not teach the young Pole, for example—as a Polish Hitler Youth organization might have done—that all good things without exception are found in his country, which, by reason of heredity or tradition, has a divine right to conquer other peoples. It tells him that the "true democracy" is to be found in the Soviet Union alone, and that his country will also become great when it in turn acquires "true democracy" through practice and imitation. Undoubtedly this doctrine appeals strongly to many youngsters; and in addition "true democracy" can be defined as the sole guarantor of "peace." In a sense, this system of youth formation resembles the system in the Catholic Church, which stresses the international solidarity implicit in the teachings of Christ, and holds that the nations will become noble and great when they have realized fully the ideals of Christian civilization. To be sure, the abyss between the two is deep and wide, unbridgeably deep and wide. While freedom of thought and decision, bounded only by a sense of obligation to the recognizable ordinances of God, are cardinal principles of the Christian order, there stands behind every youngster brought up under the Communist rule the man with the knout whose business it is to fit every human cog into the Soviet machine. Yet in some ways this man has an easy time of it. The law of God as taught by the Church is a law of love. And love is (let us remember) far more difficult, endlessly more challenging, than anything the Communist has to offer. Alas, it is so onerous that perilously few Christians fashion their lives in accordance with it.

At any rate, a preliminary climax in the Polish cultural and religious struggle was reached in March, 1949, with the issuance of a government declaration on matters affecting the relations between Church and State. The author was Wladyslaw Wolski, Minister of Public Administration. He mingled charges against some of the bishops of collaboration with the Nazis with charges that the clergy was harboring in its midst many "agents of Anglo-American imperialism." The government, he emphasized anew, did not intend to place any limitations on religious freedom; but on the other hand it would not "tolerate the abuse of freedom involved in inciting people against the state." Minister Wolski's declaration did, however, contain the assurance that religious institutions would "be free to perform their duties after they had become subject to proper government control and inspection." On March 25, the Bishops replied, demanding that the government recognize the right of parents to determine the kind of school their children should attend, and so end the subjection of children of Catholic parents to an anti-Christian training. They also asked that young Catholics be permitted to join associations conducted under the auspices of the Church. In the following September, Archbishop Stefan Wyszński, who had become Primate of Poland in January, appealed in the same vein to all who were giving religious instruction to young people. He urged that youth be led to believe "that justice is possible in this world, without recourse to violence, to prisons and to concentration camps, without the enslavement and exploitation of labor, and without the shedding of blood."

During the summer of 1949 a rumor spread that tears of blood had appeared on the face of the image of the Blessed Virgin in Lublin Cathedral. Huge throngs hurried to the city, despite the Bishop's official statement that there was no evidence that a miracle had occurred. Some mob hysteria followed, and a girl died of suffocation in the milling crowd. These events, which testified to the presence in the people of a deep undercurrent of religious emotion, caused violent outbursts of anti-Catholic comment in the Communist press. Just as the furore was at its height, the news came that the Vatican had excommunicated all who abetted and aided Communism. This action was followed in Poland by some days of awe-struck silence, for it meant that supporters of the regime would cut themselves off from the historic Church, part of the very lifeblood of Polish history. After a time the government saw fit to retaliate with a bitter attack on the Holy See; then it convened by order all the Catholic clergy in every district of the country to hear the reading of a decree of August 5. Those attending were asked to sign a statement that they supported the government against the Holy See, and that "the imposition of excommunication on persons helping to build the People's Poland is a horrendous act." Two priests were reported to have complied.

This decree was the first important legislation affecting the relations between Church and State. For the "constitutional act" passed by the Polish National Assembly on February 19, 1947—usually referred to as the "Small Constitution"—did not alter or abrogate the provisions of the Polish Constitution of 1921, which had conferred upon the Church most of its privileges and rights. It is true that a law of January 1, 1946, established civil marriage as the only kind recognizable by the State; but this also stated specifically that the parties concerned were not deprived "of the possibility of also adding the performance of ceremonies resulting from their membership in a religious association." It was not until June 27, 1950, that divorce was legalized in Poland; all annulment and separation proceedings previously had been matters for the ecclesiastic courts.

The decree of August 5, 1949, follows closely Article 124 of the Constitution of the U.S.S.R., not only in seeming to guarantee freedom of religion but also in providing a series of penalties for violation of such freedom. For example, Articles 4 and 5 of the decree read as follows:

Anyone who abuses freedom of religion by refusing to permit a person to participate in a religious activity or ceremony because of his political, social, or scientific affiliations or beliefs is liable to a penalty of up to five years in prison.

Anyone who offends religious susceptibilities by publicly insulting an object of religious veneration or a place set aside for the performance of religious ceremonies is liable to a penalty of up to five years in prison.

The fourth article obviously made it a punishable offense for a Catholic priest to refuse to administer the Sacraments to any person desiring to receive them, even though he had fallen under the Vatican's edict of excommunication.* The fifth, on the other hand, prohibits any godless person from making an offensive remark at a shrine, or from in any manner desecrating a church.

Article 8 is no doubt the most significant portion of the decree. It reads:

Anyone who abuses freedom of conscience and religion for purposes inimical to the existence of the Polish Republic is liable to a penalty of imprisonment for not less than three years. Anyone who makes preparations to commit an offense so defined is subject to a penalty of imprisonment.

Manifestly this Article could be and was interpreted in ways the government deemed useful or expedient. That it has been so used is clear from the record. More than 500 Polish priests have been held in prisons or concentration camps. The charges, in so far as they are known, have veered from accusations of friendliness to remnants of the old Polish Army, which for a long while carried on a form of guerrilla opposition, to charges that they had served as spies for the "Anglo-American imperialists." Up to this time, however, no bishop of the Catholic Church of the Latin rite had been tried or imprisoned.

Meanwhile the historic See of Cracow, where the patron saint of Poland lies buried, was presided over by an Archbishop of very considerable ability and fortitude, Cardinal Adam Sapieha. On the tenth anniversary of the invasion of Poland by the Nazi armies, he received a letter from Pope

* By special indult the Vatican ruled that, because Matrimony is a Sacrament conferred on the two contracting parties, priests might officiate even if bride or bridegroom were a Communist.

Pius which recapitulated the efforts of the Holy See to avert war and expressed regret that the stricken country had been invaded from both the east and the west. The Holy Father proceeded to say:

> The hour of trial has not yet passed. Catholic associations have to all intents and purposes been dissolved, the teaching of religion in the schools is interfered with. Many obstacles are placed in the way of the free development of institutions which have been entrusted to the care of the nuns or the clergy. The calumnies published by the press against the Catholic religion, against Ourselves, and against the bishops and priests; the stifling censorship imposed upon every Catholic publication; the denial of spiritual ministration to prisoners and those who are ill; the lack of free and secure communication between the Holy See, the bishops and the reverend clergy—all these things make more difficult the practice of religion amongst you.

The government reaction to this message was revealed primarily in the use of the old and trusted Communist device —seeking to set one Christian communion against another. Whereas in numerous instances the Communists had resembled the Nazis in their antipathy to religious sects—which Hitler referred to as *Sektenwesen*—they began in Poland to show favor towards each and every religious body which was in some way hostile to the Catholic Church. For example, Jehovah's Witnesses, at the time the favorite butt of ridicule and oppression in Eastern Germany, seemed in 1949 to be the very apples of the Polish Communist's eye. The government also, by using representatives of the Russian Orthodox Church as spokesmen, elicited approval of the new decree from the Protestant Ecumenical Council in Poland, and an expression of confidence in and support of the new state.

The year 1950 witnessed the first momentous blows against the independence and indeed the very life of the Church. First, a statute dated March 20 provided for nationalization of land held by religious orders, for retention by parish priests of parish lands of limited extent, and for a Church Fund to be administered by the government. This was more liberal than comparable statutes in other satellite states, but the intent was the same. Thus it stipulated not only that the government should hold all nationalized Church property in trusteeship, all income derived therefrom to be transferred to the Church Fund, but also that the government should determine the use of the fund. In other words, if a dissident Catholic Church could be created nothing would prevent the government from deeding over to it all the assets of those faithful to the Holy See. In addition the permission to parish priests to retain parish lands patently implies a line of distinction between them and their religious superiors. Here was a wedge that could be driven between bishops and clergy; and since 1950 persistent use has been made of it.

More important was the propaganda against Caritas, the central association of Catholic welfare agencies, which reached a new peak of efficiency. Its management was accused of graft, embezzlement, reactionary tendencies, close contact with Anglo-American imperialism, hostility to the "People's Poland," and many other crimes. Hundreds of workers for Caritas were promptly arrested. The whole organization was placed under government trusteeship, and a thorough investigation was ordered. It should be borne in mind that Caritas was an organization of central importance in the life of Poland. It functioned in twenty-five dioceses and in more than four thousand parishes. It maintained kindergartens, nurseries, recreation rooms, homes for the aged, dispensaries, and a variety of other welfare services. After the war it was financed to a considerable extent out of benefactions received from the Bishops of the United States and from Polish-American groups, and its activities were admired greatly throughout Poland.

The Hierarchy responded vigorously to the attack upon Caritas, first in a letter from Cardinal Sapieha to President Bierut. On January 30, 1950, the Polish Bishops, having met in conference to discuss the matter, issued a statement which the parish priests read in the churches of Poland wherever security police did not interfere. On February 16 the Primate (Archbishop Wyszyński) and Cardinal Sapieha addressed a longer and more explicit statement to the President of the Republic. Their letter indicates that the principal accusations against Caritas in the pro-Communist press were that it had received aid from the United States and was therefore allied with the machinations of that imperialist power: specifically, that "American elements, with Cardinal Spellman at their head . . . have seen in this institution a handy weapon aimed at the People's Poland. Caritas was to be a kind of Bishops' Marshall Plan." And it describes familiar Communist procedures graphically:

Diverse columns in the press and in radio communiqués are devoted to listing categories of alleged abuses designed primarily to put to shame in the eyes of the community the Catholic Church. Thus it is charged that allegedly the clergy and the religious orders obtained grants-in-aid from Caritas, though it should have been easy for the investigating authorities to determine that any such grants did not come out of supplies designated by Caritas for the poor. The Catholic League and other donors had stipulated that certain gifts were intended for the clergy and the religious orders, and these were distributed in accordance with the will of the donors. . . .

Caritas is often accused of having aided prisoners. Such assistance would indeed conform with the spirit of Christianity, but it should be noted also that the gifts were disbursed with the approval of the prison authorities. Quite apart from this propaganda campaign, so prejudicial to the Church and to Catholics, the Hierarchy condemns the steps taken by State authorities to mobilize the Catholic clergy, Religious Sisters and the faithful against Catholic charity—steps which are frequently violations of the freedom of conscience. Priests, nuns, and members of the laity are brought to conferences directed against the Church and to other gatherings and meetings in ways which may well involve terror and deceit. . . .

Abnormal moral pressure is brought not only by the heads of district and provincial administrations and by the mayors of towns, but also by members of the Party and officials of the security police. In some instances, organized hunts of priests have taken place. They have been pulled out of bed in the early morning by armed militiamen, who sometimes either did not permit the priest to celebrate Mass or forced him to interrupt Divine service and leave still clad in his liturgical garments.

Priests have often had to go into hiding. In order to influence people to fight against the charities of the Church, the authorities have arranged costly receptions replete with alcoholic beverages. We know of instances where warrants have been issued against priests who were invited to such functions and did not attend. The names of clerics long since dead have been published as among those who came to such receptions. Furthermore, the clergy is being drawn in also through the appointment of priests as members of the trusteeship body of Caritas, even though this is often done without their knowledge and consent.

All this will seem familiar to anyone who has studied the Party's procedures in other lands.

As the statement of the two leaders of the Hierarchy indicates, the government had staged an all-out effort to set up an organization of "patriotic priests" which would repudiate their bishops and thus lead to the signing of a "concordat" ending the Church-State struggle on such terms as the Government desired to offer. Some few priests did as a matter of fact swallow the bait. The statement refers to them as "men demoralized by war and prison camps." It says further that they "are in conflict with canon law or are blackmailed by the police authorities because they are subject to punishment."

Still there is no doubt that, subjected to threats and other means of terrorization, a considerable body of the clergy were frightened and even temporarily demoralized. Meanwhile an organization of laymen, who called themselves "Progressive Catholics," had been formed under the leadership of B. Piasecki, who in prewar Poland had been the head of a pro-Fascist organization known as Falanga. It calls to mind the Kreuz und Adler group, formed by Franz von Papen during the first year of Hitler's rule over Germany. The "Progressive Catholics" still enjoy a great deal of government support and are represented in the Polish parliament.

Russia now sent a "proconsul" to Poland in the person of Marshal Rokossowski. Vigorous measures were adopted to complete the sovietizing of the country. The Polish civil administration was reorganized to conform with the Russian pattern. Collective farming was stressed. But at the same time it became apparent that popular sentiment, especially among the peasants, was responding to this pressure in terms of more determined opposition. Suddenly it began to be whispered about that an agreement between Church and State was imminent. Cardinal Sapieha had left for Rome for an *ad limina* visit to the Pope. The Communist press surprised him, the Vatican, and everyone else by publishing an announcement that an agreement had been reached. And it was true that such a document had been assented to. The Polish Hierarchy issued a carefully worded comment indicating that the agreement was not to be looked upon as a Concordat, which only the Holy See was empowered to underwrite, but as a declaration of policy establishing a *modus vivendi* for the time being.

Before reviewing what look like major concessions by the government to religion, we may glance at Marshal Rokossowski's task and the extent to which he had fulfilled it. This was to reestablish the armed forces of Poland and to insure their

political reliability. In the opinion of competent observers he
has since succeeded to an ominous extent. Poland today has
armed forces which, if one includes the 60,000 men enlisted
in the security police, may well add up to 400,000. It is said
to have a far better air force than was available when Hitler
attacked; and there are indications that the navy has been reorganized under Russian command in several ports along the
Baltic Sea. While a succession of purges and trials seems to
indicate that the political dependability of the military establishment is open to question, it would be foolhardy to doubt
that the Soviets have obtained a formidable military auxiliary,
on the whole. This build-up has been accompanied by a ruthless, all-out effort to stamp out every conceivable threat to the
security of the government. Russian officials supervise the
operation of propaganda activities and the functions of the
far-flung espionage system.

In the circumstances an effort to avoid religious conflict was
obviously prudent. What is to be said concerning the agreement? The *New York Times* of May 4, 1950, reported that the
published text did not include secret annexes dealing with
bishoprics established in territories annexed by Russia. At
any rate, it incorporated concessions made by the Communist
government, at a heavy price to the Church. The concessions
were promises to refrain from interference with existing
standards of religious instruction in the schools and to confer
with representatives of the Bishops about a course of study,
assurance that an adequate supply of appropriate textbooks
would be made available, and agreement to bestow on teachers
of religion the status enjoyed by other members of the academic
fraternity. The University of Lublin, under Catholic auspices,
was authorized to continue its activities. Catholic associations
were to have "the same rights as heretofore, after satisfying
all requirements set forth in the decree concerning associa-

tions." The Catholic press received a certain amount of lat-
itude, military chaplains were permitted to serve, and even
the right of priests to minister unto prisoners was conceded.
The right of the Church to engage in welfare activities was
also recognized.

On the other hand, the Bishops accepted a number of important limitations on their authority. The most important are
these:

The principle that the Pope is the competent and supreme authority of
the Church refers to matters of faith, morals and canon law. In all
other matters, however, the Episcopate will be guided by the interests
of the Polish State.

Recognizing the premise that the mission of the Church can be fulfilled under differing social and economic systems, established by secular authority, the Episcopate will explain to the clergy that it should
not oppose the development ot cooperatives in rural areas, since the
cooperative movement is based primarily on the ethical element in
human nature which feels an urge to move towards social solidarity,
the objective of which is the common welfare.

In accordance with its principles, which approve the condemnation
of all criminal actions, the Church will combat the unlawful enterprises of underground bands and will denounce and punish under
canon law those clergymen who are guilty of participation in underground actions directed against the Polish State.

In accordance with the teachings of the Church, the Episcopate will
support every effort to strengthen the peace, and oppose, to the full
extent of its ability, every attempt to provoke war.

These were very significant concessions. They meant that in
order that the Church might continue to function as a religious
institution, the Bishops would abstain from criticism of what
was done by the Communist Party in economic, political, and
social organization. Indeed, the Hierarchy pledged itself to
support the government's plans. How well has this agreement

worked out in practice? Light is thrown on the problem in an interview given by Archbishop Wyszński to the Catholic paper of the Cracow archdiocese, *Tygodnik Powszechny*, and in a critique of this interview in *Trybuna Ludu*, organ of the Communist Party. The interview is dated April 27, 1952, and reads as follows:

Question: How does the agreement stand up in the light of the experiences of the two past years?

Answer: You are well aware that all forms of agreement between Church and State constitute an expression of the basic attitude of the Church, deriving from its social philosophy and theology. They are the expression of the Church's constant striving for agreement on the basis of co-existence or cooperation, so that the good of the Church and of the State may be fully achieved. Of course the basis of the agreements, thus understood, is so broad that difficulties could arise on both sides. Thus also the realization of the agreement signed two years ago is encountering various difficulties and is not proceeding without friction. But these matters are a topic of conversation between the Episcopate and the Government, and for that reason I shall not speak about them.

Question: Which points in the agreement do you consider particularly important?

Answer: From the Church's point of view, it is of immeasurable importance that the agreement recognizes the fact that the Apostolic See and the Holy Father are for the Church in Poland the final authority in matters of faith, morality, and jurisdiction. It ensues therefrom that the organizational character and the internal discipline of the Church cannot be interfered with. Such a declaration on the part of the government constitutes a basis for mutually loyal relations between the Church and the State.

In so far as the interests of the State are concerned, I am of the opinion that the readiness expressed by the Episcopate to support the struggle waged by the Polish Government and people in defense of the Western territories, and the obligation undertaken by the Episcopate to appeal to the clergy to support the economic expansion of Po-

land and to warn the faithful against pernicious acts of subversion
are of great importance. I spoke at length on these matters in November, 1951, and shall not revert to the subject again. Internal peace is
also of great concern to the Church.

Question: How should the outlook for the future be judged?

Answer: The situation is not easy . . . but the experiences of the
past two years have shown us that an agreement could be reached on
many matters. We are making every effort to insure that the agreement
will keep its binding character and that it shall be carried out in every
possible way.

The critique in *Trybuna Ludu*, May 7, 1952, may be sum-
marized as follows:

Public opinion cannot ignore the passive attitude of the Episcopate
towards the campaign against the Oder-Neisse frontier, which campaign is being conducted by West-German politicians and is patronized
and inspired by the Vatican. It must be remembered that the Agreement
pledged the Episcopate to oppose every form of revisionist campaigns
hostile to Poland. Polish public opinion cannot be satisfied with the
Primate's statements made last year on this subject, general in character as they were and unsupported by an expression of the attitude of
the Hierarchy as a whole.

Most of the clergy have adopted a loyal attitude towards the People's Government, but at the same time words of hatred for it can be
overheard from many pulpits. The faithful are incited to act against
the People's Government, and attempts are being made to create unrest
in the country. The Episcopate has done nothing to curb this hostile
propaganda, and quite often has acted as if it supported it. And although under the Agreement the Episcopate undertook to condemn and
punish clerics responsible for activities against the State, it still tol-
erates the presence of priests who have cooperated with diversionary
bandit gangs and taken part in murders and robberies.

In view of all these things, the Primate's statement that "we are
doing everything to carry out the Agreement as fully as possible" is
in striking contrast to the facts.

Behind the façade of these words, a tense struggle has been in progress. Perhaps the storm has centered on Article 3 of the Agreement:

The Polish Episcopate states that economic, historic, cultural, and religious reasons as well as historic justice shall demand that the Recovered Territories should belong to Poland forever. Basing itself on the premise that the Recovered Territories form an inseparable part of the Republic, the Episcopate shall address a request to the Holy See that those units of the administration of the Church now holding the rights of residential bishoprics shall be converted into permanent dioceses.

This article has placed the Polish Hierarchy in a very difficult situation. They are accused of failing to carry out one part of the bargain when, as a matter of fact, both Cardinal Sapieha and Archbishop Wyszyński have approached the Vatican more than once with a request that the permanent rule of Poland over the "Recovered Territories" be recognized. They have been supported by the Polish government-in-exile, which still enjoys diplomatic representation at the Holy See. The response was negative. However, it was reported recently that the Primate himself had appointed a Cathedral Chapter for Breslau, in Silesia, and had installed it. He has been quoted as saying that this action had the approval of the Vatican; but Rome has officially denied such an authorization, and has pointed out that until a treaty of peace with Germany has been signed no change such as that requested by the Polish Hierarchy can be sanctioned. According to Polish sources, the action of the Primate resulted from the fact that the government had forcibly removed from office the previous incumbents of the Chapter.

Meanwhile both sides followed with breathless interest the discussion antecedent to the adoption of a new Polish Constitution. The government induced a considerable number of clergymen to join the "Fighters for Freedom," perhaps as many as a thousand. If this figure is correct, one priest out of every twenty has become a more or less active propagandist for the Communist-dominated state. Such priests harangue their flocks whenever support is needed for some economic measure the government deems vital, such as compulsory deliveries of grain and other produce. Some of them are also eloquent organizers of public opinion for the retention of the occupied territories. As a whole, the group does not as yet constitute a substantial threat to the authority of the Episcopate; and it may also be conceded that some probably resort to Athanasius-like reservations in the face of the coercive power of the State. On the basis of what little can be gleaned from accounts furnished by escaped persons, the number enrolled is about the same as the number of those who utilize every possible opportunity to oppose the regime. The great majority of priests apparently follow steadfastly in the footsteps of their bishops. Nevertheless, in view of what was hoped for, the courage of the clergy seemingly leaves much to be desired.

Fidelity to religious practices appears not to have decreased, and there are the usual reports—usual in the sense that one nearly always encounters them in countries under totalitarian tyranny—that even the lax have taken to attending Church services regularly. However, the crucial struggle is being fought out for the minds and allegiances of the children, and the Communist Party seems to be winning slowly but surely, even as the Nazis did in the Third Reich. It has been predicted that, granted another generation of school control and camp indoctrination, of ceaseless propaganda and exciting appeal to the emotions, a large part of Poland's youth will take the Communist view of life for granted. The apostolate to them in terms of religious ideals and concepts of personal liberty is hemmed in on every side. There are reports to the effect that nursery schools in various parts of the country have been expropriated and transformed into "State Homes for Children." Such homes are, of course, centers of Communist indoctrination.

Against this background one must judge the debates recently in progress about the published provisional draft of a new Constitution. During March the Catholic press expressed concern lest it be considered as an abrogation or a watering down of the agreement of April 14, 1950, and it was immediately upbraided by its Communist counterparts. Yet during the year and a half that followed there was little to indicate that the Soviets planned to make a radical change of policy. It seemed that if the Church maintained silence concerning "Anglo-American Imperialists," and gave at least lip service to such central pillars of Communist propaganda as the "cause of peace," it could probably reckon with the termites within its structure rather than with the trampling and voracious bears outside.

But events in rapid succession towards the close of 1952 gave support to the belief that a major assault upon the Church was planned. Earlier, to be sure, it was reported that Bishop Czeslaw Kaczmarek of the See of Kielce, halfway between Warsaw and Cracow, had been arrested. At all events, towards the close of 1952 Bishop Adamski and his coadjutors, Bishops Bienick and Dennorz, were arrested in Katowice, populous diocese in the coal-mining region of the southwestern part of the country. Bishop Adamski had been an ardent Polish patriot. But he had urged the parents of the diocese to demand that religious instruction be reintroduced into the schools; and the Government viewed this as an unfriendly act. These three members of the Polish Hierarchy were subsequently removed to a village in the Carpathians, where they live under guard.

The Communists thereupon declared that a clergyman belonging to the "Union of Patriotic Priests" would be entrusted with the rule of the See of Katowice. His personal conduct appears to have been notorious, and his fidelity to the Church unstable. Because Katowice is from the ecclesiastical point of view a dependency of Cracow, Archbishop Eugenius Baziak, formerly Metropolitan of Lwów and until recently Vicar Capitular of the See of Cracow, refused to recognize the government appointment. He was thereupon arrested and brought to trial, together with a number of the clergy and laity of Cracow, for a variety of crimes. He and his alleged accomplices had concealed works of art, failed to convert foreign exchange in their possession, and established contact with a nest of "Anglo-American Imperialist spies" residing in the neighborhood of Munich. As is customary, the trial established the guilt of all concerned. At about the same time the Vatican announced that Archbishop Wyszyński was among the prelates designated to be elevated to the Cardinalate. Immediately a virulent campaign of denunciation and opposition began; and the press of the world reported that the Primate had decided not to leave for Rome, lest it prove impossible to return to his See.

No one could of course tell what was the portent of these events. Polish reality was grim. The Communist industrialization program had uprooted countless thousands of persons; and the countryside as one had known it was strangely changed and depopulated. Reports indicate that no fewer than 100,000 persons were incarcerated in slave-labor camps, most of them no doubt dissidents from Communism for intellectual, economic, or religious reasons. The desperately heroic escapades to which not a few resorted in order to flee the country testified to the state of affairs within this "People's Republic."

On September 14, 1953, Bishop Kaczmarek was brought to

trial in Warsaw. This was, so far as one knows, the second action of a punitive kind against a member of the Hierarchy according to the Latin rite. Arraigned with the Bishop in this spectacular trial were three priests and a nun. All were charged with crimes oddly reminiscent of those leveled against Slánský and his associates in Prague. They were said to have engaged in "espionage, anti-state propaganda, and diversionary activities." The name of Cardinal Spellman was adduced, even as the same prelate had earlier been defined as the infamous personage through whom Cardinal Mindszenty had dealt. As could have been anticipated, Bishop Kaczmarek dutifully appeared before the court in order to plead for leniency. He stated that he had been seriously misled, and that he would appreciate an opportunity to atone what perhaps were not so much evil deeds as aberrations. He was sentenced to twelve years in prison for espionage in behalf of the United States. His "accomplices" likewise drew heavy sentences.

Thus ended the latest recorded act in the drama of Soviet justice. While this trial was in progress, the text of the letter of protest delivered to President Bierut by the Polish Episcopate on May 8, 1953, was received in the United States. The letter indicates that the situation has greatly deteriorated. It comments primarily on a decree issued February 9 of the same year on the creation and filling of positions in the Church. Resembling similar legislation enacted in other satellite countries, the decree empowers the government to determine what posts are to be maintained or created, and who is to be assigned to them. The Bishops point out that therewith the independence of the Church inside the ecclesiastical sphere proper is abrogated. They go on to say that peculiarly enough the rights conferred by the decree upon the Government have been used chiefly in the Recovered Territories for refusing to recognize appointments by the Episcopate and substituting others.

The letter makes clear also that in every other respect hostility to the Church had acquired a momentum never known in Poland "save in tsarist times." Unions of dissident clergy were fostered by the government with every means at its command; religious instruction was curtailed in all the schools; the Faculty of the University of Lublin had been decimated, and most of its schools closed; the majority of Catholic publications had been "suspended," and instead those issued by dissident priests were liberally subsidized; and even Nursing Sisters were removed from hospitals. The Bishops said clearly that they had known that entering into an agreement with the Government involved "risks"; that these had been taken in the hope of improving relationships; and that the conclusion at which they had regrettably arrived was that hatred of the Church was the principal characteristic of the regime. Evidently the time was rapidly approaching in which there would be little difference between the treatment meted out to the Catholics of Poland and that which their confrères elsewhere under Russian rule had been compelled to endure. Meanwhile, however, signs of unrest in the nation as a whole patently increased. Defections by several who were able to go into exile exposed to the world the true situation in the Polish lands.

6 HUNGARY

PRIOR TO THE WAR unleashed by Hitler, Hungary comprised somewhat fewer than nine million persons. Except Austria, it was the most famous of the countries of Central Europe, primarily because of the romantic beauty of its capital city, the charms of its music and its cuisine, and the exotic appeal of its history. In religion Hungary was predominatingly Roman Catholic (Catholics constituted more than 65 per cent of the population); but there were important Jewish and Protestant minorities. The largest consisted of Calvinists, more than one-fifth of the population. In so far as religious affiliations were concerned, Hungary was no doubt also the most tolerant country in this part of Europe.

Today, without having suffered so much during the war as Yugoslavia or Poland, this unfortunate country has become a show place of Communist exploitation. The fate of Hungary is a poignant demonstration of the often forgotten truth that neither the mistakes of individual statesmen nor the Communist affiliations of persons in high places account for the success of postwar Russian policy. Every government official blunders. It was inevitable, the situation being what it was, that Moscow should attempt with every possible means to extend its sphere of influence westward. The true source of the debacle was the collective stupidity which all of us who should have been conscious heritors of Western civilization manifested in an hour of desperate crisis, and for which we do not even yet feel responsible. Our failure was rooted in prejudices and conventions, in outmoded though often reasonable assumptions, in shibboleths expounded wherever an audience could be assembled to listen, and, over and above all these, in the cultural history of the Western World.

Moderately liberal Americans often thought of Hungary as "an outpost of reaction." No doubt they were right from many points of view. The Hungarian people, one of the most gifted of Europe and also one of the most civilized, was in large part so galvanized by its role in history that it could not decide as to what it desired to be in the modern time. The soil of the country was very fertile, nurturing a sturdy and tenacious peasantry; but despite sporadic essays in land reform a landowning aristocracy, often devoid of interest in anything save the revenues upon which its standard of living depended, continued to maintain a swarm of virtual serfs who lived on meat fat and onions. The failure to solve any major problem incident to industrialization caused many Hungarian workers after 1918 to move politically far to the Left, while the wily Regent for a monarchy that no one was willing or able to establish waited for something to happen which would restore to the nation territories deemed to have been taken away unjustly by the Treaty of the Trianon. As a result Hungary, despite the ability of its citizenry and all the advances secured by determined advocates of social reform, remained to a striking extent a feudal country and therefore an absurd anachronism. Yet it was by no means alone at fault. Hungary suffered from the fact that the dissolution of the Austro-

Hungarian Empire had failed to bring about the establishment of a sound Danubian Federalism; instead, a veritable riot of competing national interests had come into being.

Other sources of social disorder can be found in the events which followed the close of the First World War. The fall of the monarchy denuded the country of strong leadership. Democratic forces under the direction of intellectuals of integrity rallied to form a government; but many of them may not unfairly be said to have lacked experience in distinguishing between obtainable objectives and ideals beyond reach. Their government quickly succumbed to a bold experiment in Bolshevist tactics which was tried at the same time in Berlin and Bavaria. Under Béla Kun, an erstwhile insurance agent who had been a prisoner in Russia and was now the power behind the Hungarian scene, a program of ruthless repression and enforced socialization was inaugurated. Troops and police raided the opposition, and "revolutionary tribunals" imposed death sentences which, although they reached an acknowledged total of 585, were only a sample of what was to ensue twenty-five years later. However, Kun's endeavors fell short of success—in large measure because occupation troops, primarily French, were present and in control. That fact enabled a counterrevolutionary movement to get under way; and by 1920 its army, commanded by Admiral Nicholas Horthy, had gained the upper hand. The Allies refused to permit the return of a Habsburg to the throne, and so a new government was formed as a Regency. It had to deal almost immediately with excesses by armed bands seeking revenge who, before they were curbed, tried and executed more than 300 persons. They were also virulently anti-Semitic, alleging that a disproportionately large number of Jews had been associated with Kun's regime.

As a result of the Regency's efforts to effect a measure of

"land reform" by purchasing large estates and parceling them out to small farmers, the Catholic Church became the principal landowner in the country. It held one-eighteenth of all the arable soil, and a great variety of other tangible assets. As a rule the Church treated its tenants well—so well, indeed, that many of them viewed the possibility of "land reform" with misgiving. One could, indeed, argue that such a "reform" might well prove to be an enterprise of questionable value. Perhaps a peasant could live better by working on a large estate managed in accordance with the principles of just labor legislation than on a small plot left to his own devices. The fact remained that there was a strong demand for ownership of the soil by those who tilled it. At any rate, a thoughtful, forward-looking churchman could not view the situation with equanimity. Although the Church estates produced revenue which was needed for the upkeep of numerous religious, cultural, and charitable institutions, a strong Catholic social reform movement insisted upon a wider distribution of property. A solution was not found. Either there ought to have been "land reform" in the sense indicated, or laws should have been enacted to insure a decent livelihood to the farm worker. Nevertheless one must note that Kalot, the organization of Catholic peasant youth founded by an indefatigable Jesuit, was one of the strongest associations of the kind in Europe. It had more than 200,000 members when Hitler marched into Hungary, and its educational program was directed with intelligence and moral fervor.

Perhaps the major reason for the Church's loss of appeal to poorer citizens in many parts of Europe was not Karl Marx or Charles Darwin, not Voltaire or Hegel, though they and others undoubtedly had a good deal to do with it. Something far more tragic was the matter. The poor man drifted away because of the Church's natural but too exclusive concern with its own rights and progress. It forgot that, although saving souls may ultimately prove to be the one thing necessary, people will not strive for spiritual redemption unless the ecclesiastical societies to which they belong accept them as they are, with a frank recognition of their needs, their aspirations, and their fears for the welfare of their children. Priests—the vast majority of them exemplary men—were tempted to think too exclusively about the great endeavor in which they were engaged. Prior to the First World War, Hungarian Catholics had an extraordinarily competent, farsighted, and saintly leader, Bishop Ottokar Prohaszka, whose services to all good causes, including social reform, were notable. He was succeeded in his influence over the nation by Cardinal Justinian Serédi, one of the most distinguished churchmen of the time; but, despite the numerous and often exemplary activities fostered by such leaders, the general situation was far from what could have been desired.

On the other hand, it must be pointed out that public opinion in the United States and elsewhere was far too prone to identify the Church in Hungary with "reaction." Few people took the trouble to familiarize themselves with the Christian Democratic Movement which had arisen in response to the appeal of Pope Leo XIII for social justice. Largely by reason of age-old antipathy to the Papacy, which lived on in countless minds that had forgotten both the Beast of Revelation and the doctrinal disputes of yore, there was little room in the Anglo-Saxon conception of what the postwar world was to be for any Christian social movement or organization. The term "conservative" engendered visions of mitered autocrats going about in clouds of incense to grind down the poor. This undertow of prejudice combined with general Catholic persistence in demanding that the interests of the Church be served, when other people could not possibly conceive of them as conformable with their own objectives, to set the stage for the tragedy of the postwar years.

Certain it should have been that what had happened once could happen again. Even supposing that Stalin had reformed and become a true democrat, one should have arranged a safeguard or two against the possibility of a relapse. A quick glance at history should have been enough to remind one that Béla Kun had failed after 1918 because Western forces insured the maintenance of democratic institutions. And as a matter of fact Hungary was ruled from 1945 to 1947 by the Allied Control Commission, on which the United States, Great Britain, and the Soviet Union were represented. Whether it was inevitable that the Western Powers would concede one position after the other cannot at present be determined. However, even after President Truman decided that Greece was not to be abandoned to the Russians, it was fashionable to believe that he had pledged the West to the support of "reaction." Not many critics stopped to think that the peoples affected were less interested at that time in "progress" or its opposite—there would be time to discuss such matters later on—than in the simple, stark fact that they were about to have the Russians at their throats.

Out of this somber complex of weakness and bad judgment and gullible interpretation of Stalinism the Communist Party in Hungary emerged as a claimant for absolute power. It came forth almost precisely as it had come in 1919. There had been very few Communists in Hungary. But once again a group of Party agents who had lived in the Soviet capital during the war and had been thoroughly indoctrinated arrived by plane at Russian Army headquarters.* They proceeded to recruit

* The following Communists who had been active supporters of Béla Kun and had subsequently lived in Moscow returned during 1945 to resume their beneficent activities: Mátyás Rákosi, Kun's director of economic production, who was Chief of the Hungarian Section of the Moscow Commissariat for Foreign Affairs

whomsoever they could. Violent anti-Semites and pro-Nazis, many with criminal records, were, as Hal Lehrman reported at the time, signed on the dotted line. Espionage and denunciation agencies were established. Nevertheless the anti-Communist population stood its ground well, though it was left unsteady by the sudden disappearance of the Regency, frightened by the brute impact of crimes against person and property by Russian soldiers, and cowed by shootings and arrests. It waited to see whether the Western Powers would give any indication that steps to protect Hungarian freedom would be taken.

Certainly the nation deserved a far better fate than would soon be meted out to it. To be sure, Admiral Horthy, who for years had waited like a cat for the mouse of opportunity to recovery Hungary's "lost territories," had welcomed the opportunity to do business with Hitler on this issue. Thereby he demonstrated anew the folly of Central European nationalism, which gobbled down small successes in the worst style of old-time autocratic dynastic imperialism, only to prepare itself for its own hour on the block. But on the other hand the Hungarian Prime Minister Count Teleki, alone among the European statesmen doomed to stand in Hitler's way, found the perfect symbol of opposition. He fought as long as he could against the alliance with Hitler and entry into the war. Then he took his life in protest. Cardinal Serédi,

---

from 1940 to 1945; Zoltán Vas, Chairman of the Planning Bureau and one of Rákosi's most intimate associates, who served during the war as a colonel in the Red Army with responsibility for indoctrinating prisoners; Erno Gerö, Chairman of the People's Economic Council, who had gone to Moscow at the close of the Spanish Civil War; Karoly Kiss, Minister for External Affairs, captured by the Russians, who gave him further training in Party matters; Mihály Farkas, Minister for Defense, who had worked with the Communist underground in Czechoslovakia; and József Révai, Minister for Public Education, secretary to Kun in 1919, who had gone to Moscow prior to the outbreak of war between Stalin and Hitler.

when he went to pay his respects at the bier of one who in the eyes of the Catholic Church had sinned grievously by committing suicide, provided one of the most dramatic moments in the history of opposition to Nazism. The Hungarian Army did what it was ordered to do. It fought with valor on the Eastern front and suffered heavy losses. We should not fail to respect its bravery and its sacrifices. One of the erroneous assumptions in recent historical writing is that good soldiers should pause on the eve of battle to decide by caucus whether what they are about to do is above reproach from every moral point of view. That is surely the proper business of the government that orders them to take the field.

During the period of Nazi domination, the Catholic Church fought with energy and charity to mitigate the persecution of the Jews. Numerous tributes have been paid to it for that reason. Cardinal Serédi stated the position of the Papacy on this question with eloquent courage. He was followed in office by Joseph, Cardinal Mindszenty, destined to become one whom the world would look upon as a martyr. The Church saved thousands of Jews from deportation to concentration camps, frequently hiding them in the rooms of convents and monasteries or spiriting them across the border, so that a substantial Hungarian Jewish minority survived. The pro-Nazi Party, known as Arrow and Cross, was shunned by every faithful Christian. In like manner the Church had assisted Polish soldiers who had been forced to flee after the defeat of the armies in which they served.*

When in 1944 the defeat of Hitler was foreshadowed by

---

* I shall not forget the Polish officer to whom, one fall afternoon in 1945, I gave a lift. As we drove from the outskirts of Naples to Rome, past the ruins of Monte Cassino, he told about the cemetery on the battle-scarred heights above the town, in which rest 1,200 soldiers of the Polish brigade who died in the attack. He was doomed not to return to his homeland. Gratefully he recalled the hospitality which had been accorded to him in a Hungarian convent.

the reign of terror which found in the Jew its major victim, the Papal Nuncio in Budapest issued countless "letters of protection" to Jews, enabling them to live in buildings which were the property of the Vatican and therefore entitled to diplomatic immunity. Nor did the Church itself escape paying a heavy price. Although Hungarians suffered less drastically than the Poles or Czechs at the hands of the Nazis many of their priests took the bitter road to Dachau. Others, including two bishops, were incarcerated in Hungarian prisons. During the winter of 1944 the Nazis executed the senior chaplain of the Hungarian Army. When defeat came the priests of Hungary did not flee. Only 12 out of more than 1,200 abandoned their rectories. Witness the death of William Apor, Bishop of Györ. Drunken Soviet soldiers entered his residence and tried to force their way into the cellar, where a number of women were hiding. The Bishop calmly met them face to face, in an effort to pacify them. He died in a fusillade of bullets, but the women were spared.

Yet this heroism was destined to earn no earthly reward. After 1945 there ensued instead one of the heaviest-handed enslavements of a people, and one of the direst persecutions of the Christian faith, of which history has record. Though we shall be concerned with the second, let us not forget the first. For the Communist Party the sole important question was how quickly and completely the opposition could be liquidated, regardless of the means or the cost to the population. The Hungarian people struggled to elect a non-Communist government and, despite great difficulties, succeeded. The November, 1945, election resulted in the triumph of the "conservative" opposition. Even after Communist intrigue and machinations forced out of office the government thus chosen, the Communist Party was defeated in the election of August, 1947, obtaining less than 23 per cent of the vote.

Nevertheless, with the help of the Russian Army and the Communist-infiltrated police force, all parties professing opposition to Communism were disbanded, the Independent People's Front was created, and it was announced that the People's Republic had been established. A single slate of candidates was presented to the voters in the election of May 15, 1948, and naturally the Communist candidates were chosen by an overwhelming majority.

We shall now review the developments which affected relations between Church and State and culminated in violent persecution.

The Catholic Church was a target first of all by reason of its material possessions. The Land Reform Law decreed during 1945 was drastic but could be defended in principle. It affected the holdings of wealthy owners and their buildings and livestock. Estates of more than a thousand acres were to be broken up completely. Owners of smaller properties were permitted to retain one hundred acres. However, the reform proved to be a poorly camouflaged prelude to the creation of collective farms—agricultural properties owned and exploited by the State. Communists, regardless of aptitude for farming or the validity of their claims, received virtually all the land which was redistributed. The State fared even better. By July 1, 1946, it was owner and manager of fully one-eighth of all the landed property in Hungary. None of the former owners received compensation. The new peasant proprietors were, it is true, compelled to make payments at regular intervals to amortize the cost of the land assigned to them. However, the moneys thus collected went into the State Treasury. By the beginning of 1948, the owners of one-hundred-acre estates, who had previously been affluent, were being pushed to the wall; for all farms larger than fifteen acres were taxed so heavily in grain and produce that it was utterly impossible to meet the levies. When a farmer succeeded in doing so, he found that he was forced to sell his surplus at prices fixed by the government; and these were so low that he was unable to make both ends meet and was forced into bankruptcy. Foreclosures became the rule.

By the close of 1948, the Catholic Church in Hungary had lost its wealth and material independence. To its other losses of this character must be added the elimination of revenues from the system of advowson, an economic survival from the Middle Ages. This arrangement made it legally incumbent upon stipulated wealthy patrons, and upon cities and towns, abbeys and foundations, to contribute to the support of the Church. Budapest, for example, was partly responsible for the upkeep of parishes within its boundaries. The 1945 Land Reform Law abolished all rich patrons as a matter of course; but cities and towns kept up the practice of advowson, often with ironical results. Thus in Budapest the patronage committee of the City Council, whose members traditionally had been clerical, very soon took on a Communist hue. This was, however, the committee entrusted under the law with reviewing the list of priests nominated by the Archbishop for appointment to pastorates. The responsibility, therefore, was now transferred to the Communist Party. It took persistent delight in vetoing all nominations of persons it looked upon with disfavor. Slowly, such committees also withdrew financial support. All that then remained to the Church were direct subsidies from the State, so that a relationship of complete financial dependence was established.

Meanwhile the fate of religious education was likewise being debated. Prior to 1948 Communist efforts to ban instruction in the tenets of the recognized faiths met with so much resistance that the traditional practices—namely, compulsory religion classes in the public schools and the maintenance of

private schools under Catholic, Protestant, or Jewish auspices
—were continued. But after the seizure of power the Minister
of Education, Julius Ortutay, presented a four-point program
dealing with religious influence in the training of youth. The
principal provision was that the private educational system
was to be nationalized, though a relatively small number of
institutions were suffered to remain under the aegis of Church
and Synagogue. Elementary schooling was the main target,
but the secondary schools also were grievously affected. The
government took over nearly three thousand Catholic gram-
mar schools, and more than a thousand that had been under
Calvinist supervision. Church authorities opposed these actions
resolutely, but the Ortutay program was adopted by vote of
Parliament on June 16, 1948. Therewith Communism won
the first round in the struggle for the mind of youth. The advantage was exploited with measures designed to curb and
suppress religiously motivated organizations, to curtail the
freedom of the press, and to subject to rigorous censorship all
that was said in the name of the Church. The charitable institutions, too, were nationalized. Hospitals, orphanages,
homes for the aged, nurseries—all became the property of
the government, which went on to demand that spokesmen for
religion sing the praises of the "People's Democratic State."

As usual, a State Office for Ecclesiastical Affairs was established, with full responsibility for regulating the endeavors
of the Churches. These sought to mitigate their impoverishment
by voluntary contributions from the faithful, and their appeal
met with a heartening response during the early years after the
war; but inflation, the confiscation and nationalization of
private property, and the imposition of crushing taxes on the
peasantry so drained the resources of the faithful that only
a few religious orders and the higher clergy could carry on
with what was voluntarily given. It should also be noted that

libraries, art treasures, and furnishings belonging to the Churches were nationalized by a decree of November 16, 1948, so that none of these could be sold. The Constitution of the People's Democracy, which had been ratified on August 20, proclaimed the separation of Church and State. This meant not only that all the ancient privileges of the Catholic Church were abrogated (for example, the Archbishop of Esztergom had been a member of the Regent's Council), but that in all truth two hostile powers had been established in Hungary: atheistic Communism, able to rely on the full might of the civil authority; and organized religion, able to exist only if it were subsidized by the State and if it remained content not to resist any propagandistic attack to which it was subjected. The sole unanswered question was whether under such conditions the Churches could survive and maintain their integrity. The prostitution of the intellectual had been woeful enough, as everyone knows who has studied the history of professors and clergymen cowed by Hitler. Would spokesmen for Christ now become the docile puppets of a ruthless and irreligious regime?

In a setting thus compounded of frustration and terror there emerged Joseph, Cardinal Mindszenty, and the drama of his opposition and torment, surely the most moving and widely known episode in the Catholic resistance to Communism. It has, however, perhaps not always been understood. When his name first drew notice outside his own country it was besmirched with the propaganda which laid low so much of the world, in that hour grim in its repudiation of Nazism and unwilling to face the dire possibility that Stalinism might conceivably prove to be still more mighty and no less evil. The Cardinal was widely reputed to be a reactionary busybody, a zealous friend and supporter of the Magyars (all of them of course disreputable), a devotee of Hitler, an arch-clerical schemer, and above all an anti-Semite. When Béla Fabian published his warmly human biography of the Cardinal in 1949, commemorating the friendship between the Jews of Hungary and the Prince of the Church, one could almost feel the surprise which was enkindled in many minds. Therewith the Communist Party slowly began to lose one of its most vigorously fought propaganda battles. It had every means at its disposal, including an official account of the trial of the Cardinal and his confession, which was translated into many languages. In the end, however, the testimony which the Party itself had provided about the methods of justice employed by its minions was subjected to careful examination in all free countries, and the results of that scrutiny were so conclusive that ever since no one who is not committed body and soul to the Party has believed any accusation levied by a Communist regime against its opponents.

The literature on the Cardinal is extensive, and much of it is very good. It presents a churchman who, despite a measure of physical frailty, had an extraordinarily dynamic and sanguine temperament. He could be relied upon to speak his mind, but the edge was taken off his candor by a sense of humor and a deep and readily communicated interest in the welfare of other human beings. The Cardinal was perhaps not of the intellectual stature of his great predecessor, Cardinal Serédi; but he had literary talent, considerable learning, and energy of mind. His name as we now know it was conferred upon him when he became Bishop of Hungary's most distinguished See and therewith, under the laws of the Regency, a nobleman. Born Joseph Pehm on March 29, 1892, he was of peasant stock, anchored for generations in the soil of western Hungary. He knew the simple people of the villages, their virtues and their weaknesses; and this insight stood him in good stead throughout his trying and absorbing career as a priest. Under the influence of a mother whose memory he would cherish and honor in a book, he proved himself a studious lad. Eventually he prepared for the priesthood, was ordained, and quickly earned a wide reputation as one who combined an ardent concern for the spiritual welfare of his people with a quite personal interest in their earthly well-being. The times through which he had lived as a boy and as a priest were stormy, but he weathered them. He was made an Archbishop of Esztergom and Prince Primate of Hungary on October 2, 1945.

A catalogue of the events which tried the soul of this spirited and zealous Prince of the Church would be a lengthy one, indeed. First there appeared, as might have been anticipated, a Communist-inspired "National Church" entrusted with persuading Catholics to sever their ties with Rome and the Vatican. The priests who served this "Church" were a fairly queer lot, who made their first collective public appearance after the Cardinal delivered, on January 20, 1946, an address in honor of St. Margaret, one of the patrons of Hungary. He said in his usual forthright way:

After a year of bitter suffering, Hungary finally saw the Tartars depart. They did not leave lightheartedly, for they had never enjoyed so much freedom or enjoyed so pleasant a life. Their experiences in Caracorum had been far more trying. There, in accordance with a rule laid down by Genghis Khan, they could neither bathe nor change their clothes. But they went back, because the Great Khan had died. . . . History teaches us that all things on this earth are transitory, even as were the achievements of Genghis Khan, Napoleon and Hitler. Through such men God sends the scourge of many sufferings to the world. When the bony hand of death touches such men, the peoples and the nations breathe once more.

These remarks alluded to St. Margaret's time, but their application to the Russian masters of Hungary was obvious. The

Communists staged a mammoth parade through the streets of
Budapest, demanding the Cardinal's head. The priests of the
"National Church" marched in the procession.

There followed the discovery of a series of alleged conspiracies against the government and the Red Army, each attributed to the instigation of the Cardinal. Both he and his
fellow churchmen were kept busy issuing denials. The major
import of the charges was that Catholic schools under the
tutelage of the religious orders were responsible for the widespread sabotage of the regime. Among the discoverers of plots
were divers alumni of such schools who for a variety of reasons, primarily no doubt financial, found it expedient to collaborate with the Communists, even as some of them had
previously fished in Nazi waters. On May 20, 1946, Cardinal
Mindszenty issued a Pastoral Letter in defense of Catholic
and, more generally, of religious education. It was a very frank
message, which contained such patently challenging statements
as this: "There are some who like to describe the Church as
a 'hotbed of reaction.' But those who consider everything
Catholic reactionary ought really to look for reaction in places
where all liberty is suppressed."

In order to account adequately for the complete candor of
such remarks, one must bear in mind that the peace treaty
with Hungary was not signed until 1947. It was therefore still
possible to hope that the Western Powers would maintain their
missions in the country and take steps to insure a modicum
of freedom. Unfortunately they would not do so. Meanwhile
the Cardinal, who was always a Hungarian patriot, had appealed to the ranking Catholic prelates of the United States
and Great Britain for assistance in preventing the expulsion
of Hungarian minorities from Czechoslovakia. These unfortunate people were driven out under conditions comparable
to those which had attended the casting out of the Sudeten

Germans. Later he denounced quite as vigorously the expulsion of German-speaking minority groups from Hungary. However, as soon as the treaty went into effect, the Cardinal and the Church were left to face the enemy unaided. It had been argued that he should have anticipated the development and adopted a more conciliatory tone; but the evidence garnered in other satellite countries shows that he would merely have made his own lot easier without changing in the least the direction in which the Communist Party was implacably moving.

The first effect of the treaty on religious activities was the subjugation of the Calvinist and Lutheran churches. Lutheran ranks had been seriously depleted by the expulsion of German "ethnic" groups. During the autumn of 1948 Bishop Lajos Ordass, undoubtedly the ablest and most courageous Lutheran leader, was brought to trial and sentenced to two years in prison. The Calvinists, on the other hand, were led intellectually by Dr. Albert Bereczky, who seemingly assented to every demand made by the State. Soon this Hungarian Protestant church heard Bishop Imre Ravecz say that "the most important and significant ordinances of the Hungarian form of society are in complete accord with Holy Writ." These developments were interpreted in some quarters as meaning that whereas the Protestant churches enjoyed complete freedom under Communist rule, the recalcitrant Catholic Church was having a difficult time because of the bigotry and lust for power which characterized its Hierarchy.

As a matter of fact, the Calvinist Church in particular was feeling the knout, not merely in outward persecution but also in inner conflict. Prior to the signing of the treaty and the Communist seizure of the government the dominant group in it was the one that had opposed the Nazis. These men, notably Bereczky, were persuaded that the traditional interdependence of Church and State had been evil, and that only separation could advance the cause of the Gospel. The coming of the Communists was interpreted as being in part a punishment visited upon the Church for sin. Drastic reform was therefore needed, and above all missionary effort to bring the masses to a realization of the true meaning of Christian teaching. Yet at the same time the gifted and realistic Bishop László Ravasz pointed out firmly that freedom was possible to the Church only if society recognized the value of freedom and insisted that religious education was a duty no parent could shirk if he hoped to remain a Christian. An ultimatum by the government to the Church, presented during the early months of 1948, resulted in the resignation of Bishop Ravasz as President of the General Synod and as a member of the Hierarchy. The Synod protested against this high-handed action, but in the end Bereczky gained the position of greatest prominence in the Church.

Passing over, for the moment, the situation thus created, we resume the chronicle of the Cardinal. Every new day brought disappointments. The government laid its heavy hand on the schools, the press, and Catholic Action. It induced a group of Catholics, in the name of progress, to promulgate criticism of the Primate. Outwardly it was still possible to pretend that Church and State were seeking agreement. Monsignor Zsigmond Mihalovics, director of Catholic Action in Hungary and later an exile, relates in *Mindszenty, Ungarn, Europa* that he went with a companion to attend a reception in honor of the President of the Republic late in 1947, only to find that Mátyás Rákosi, Secretary-General of the Hungarian Communist Party, was anxious to chat and have his picture taken in the company of Church dignitaries. The Party was still interested in camouflage and, as usual, was proficient in the art.

Events moved swiftly towards a climax during the summer

of 1947, when the government sponsored a year of commemoration of the Revolution of 1848, which had produced an outburst of heroic liberalism in Hungary. The Cardinal undertook a fateful counteraction. He dedicated the year to Mary, Mother of Christ, and solemnly inaugurated the observance on the Feast of the Assumption. Surrounded by all the country's bishops, he preached a sermon which blended deep anxiety over political and social trends with daring. Asking, "What is our purpose in observing this Year of Our Blessed Lady?" he answered, "We seek only what the deported Hungarians sought in Carlsbad." Three thousand had come together for a Mass on which the Gospel account of Jesus weeping at the sight of Jerusalem was read. He continued:

We all, every one of us, are deported Hungarians! Even if they have not yet driven us from our homes in the area between the Danube and the Garam, they have nevertheless deported us spiritually. For they have uprooted us from the traditions of a thousand years. Let us go back—back! Not back to Nature, but to That which is above Nature, to those things that are higher which under the banner of dialectical materialism are to be destroyed. Let us return to the world of the Transcendent, the highest peak in which, after God, is God's Mother.

During the weeks that followed, the Cardinal manifested an activity which seemed almost superhuman. Early in September he knelt with 100,000 pilgrims to pray at the ancient shrine of Szombathely. A week later he walked at the head of 100,000 men to the shrine of Maria Remete, some ten miles from Budapest. On September 22 he addressed a vast throng in the Cathedral Square of Eger. In October 100,000 working people assembled in the ruins on the heights above the Capital City. In the subsequent Eucharistic Procession 600,000 people participated. Thus did religious leadership evoke fervor in all corners of the land. It was magnificent, it was moving;

but the end was bound to be failure, unless, indeed, a miracle occurred. We may well believe that the Cardinal hoped in those days for such a marvel—not one which would summon down a legion of angels from Heaven, but one based on the impact of a united Catholic people, if not on the consciences, then at least on the political calculations of their rulers. But the Russians now entered the scene and grimly ordered the liquidation of the Cardinal.

To be sure, nothing was done precipitously. On January 10, 1948, Rákosi spoke for the Communist Party. He declared that nothing could be more desirable than an agreement between Church and State, but that the conduct and attitude of the Church made it impossible. That had, he said, become the cloak under which reaction plied its subversive trade. Its leaders were openly hostile to the new order. They had repudiated the noble traditions of 1848 by organizing a rival observance. They were opposed to land reform, to the Three Year Plan, and to peace. On February 15, Cardinal Mindszenty addressed an assembly at St. Stephen's Academy in Budapest, citing a number of Papal Encyclicals on peace to make the Church's position clear.* However, some of the quotations made could be easily interpreted as comments on the mentality and methods of the Communist Party. They were so understood. The Ministry of the Interior forbade the publication of the text of this address. Measures were taken in rapid succession to curb the Catholic press, to undermine Catholic charities, and to prepare the way for the transfer of all schools to the State.

Then occurred what is usually known as the tragedy of Pocspetri. On June 1 the pastor of this little town of 2,000 souls in eastern Hungary, acting on a request from the As-

---

* Texts of this and other addresses are conveniently assembled in *Cardinal Mindszenty Speaks: Authorized White Book* (New York, 1949).

sociation of Teachers, called the parents of his congregation together to vote on whether the schools should be removed from the jurisdiction of the Church. Two pads of paper were placed on the table, one for affirmative and the other for negative votes. All four hundred parents voted No. Two days later, the village council met to consider the same question. Rumors coursed through the town to the effect that the vote cast by the parents was to be nullified, and quickly an excited crowd gathered round the town hall, demanding that the will of the people be respected. The police were sent for, and they ordered the crowd to disperse. One officer drew his revolver and threatened to shoot. Thereupon a citizen named Kiralyfalvi entered the fray; there was a scuffle, and the policeman lay dead.

The pastor, Father Aszalos, seems not to have been present when the shooting occurred. Nevertheless he became the central figure in a highly theatrical trial designed to prove that he and the "reactionary Hierarchy" were responsible for the incident. First the poor priest was taken, together with Kiralyfalvi and other villagers to the notorious prison maintained by the secret police at Andrássy ut 60, Budapest. The trial was then conducted without benefit of defense counsel. To the great surprise of nearly everyone—including, it is said, the officials of the Ministry of the Interior—Father Aszalos pleaded guilty. Indeed he went on to say that the real culprits were his religious superiors, who were always stirring up opposition to the government. Left to himself, he added, he would never have argued against the secularization of education. Nevertheless he was guilty because he had failed to heed his own conscience. The sentence of death imposed by the court was changed later to life imprisonment.

The observance of the Holy Year continued, despite steadily mounting obstacles, into the summer of 1948. It had become necessary to secure the approval of the government for each pilgrimage, and most gatherings were surrounded by cordons of police. On June 13 many tens of thousands gathered in Budapest to participate in devotions honoring Our Lady of Fatima. Someone called for a cheer in honor of the absent Cardinal. The crowd responded. Police cars thereupon appeared, and the throng was attacked and dispersed. Many persons were arrested; some were deported to labor camps. This pattern was followed thenceforth, so that the year of devotion petered out in fear, dispersal, and helplessness. It was obvious that the Communists had been neither impressed nor cowed.

Cardinal Mindszenty had every reason to suppose that action would soon be taken against him. On November 18 he issued his last Pastoral Letter, defending the celebrations in honor of the Blessed Virgin and making a profession of faith. It stated:

Two of my predecessors were killed in action, two were robbed of all their possessions, one was taken prisoner and deported, one was assassinated. The greatest of them all went into exile. Karoly Ambrus visited and nursed the plague-stricken and himself died of their disease.

Of all my predecessors, however, none was as devoid of all means as I am. So systematic and so adroit a net of propaganda untruths—lies disproved a hundred times and yet repeated a hundred times—was never spun round any of my seventy-eight precursors in office. I stand for God, the Church, and Hungary. This responsibility has been placed on me as a result of the fate which has been meted out to our nation, standing now alone, an orphan in the world. When what happens to me is compared with the sufferings of my people, it is seen to be of trifling consequence.

A brave man, sometimes impetuous but always zealously mindful of duty and of love, was going by reason of the might of evil into his own Gethsemane.

On the day after Christmas, 1948, a van of police cars moved from Andrássy ut 60 to Esztergom to arrest the Cardinal. The sixteen officers armed with light automatic rifles carried out the mission assigned to them. The Cardinal took leave of his aged mother, having scribbled on the back of an envelope the now famous words: "I have taken no part in any conspiracy of any kind. I shall not resign from my episcopal See. I shall not make a confession. But if despite what I now say you should read that I have confessed or resigned, and even see it authenticated by my signature, bear in mind that it will have been only the result of human frailty. In advance, I declare all such actions null and void." On the following day it was announced to the world that the Cardinal was in prison.

Stephen K. Swift has made a careful study of available reports concerning the treatment meted out to the Cardinal while he was in the hands of his jailers, and this can be followed in detail in his memorable book, *The Cardinal's Story*. Because certain of the officers who witnessed the events managed to escape from Hungary and relate what they had observed of interrogation methods learned in Moscow, there is no reason to doubt the authenticity of the reports. These also corroborate what has been learned of Russian methods through victims who have escaped from other parts of the Russian-controlled world. It is therefore no matter for wonder that the Cardinal signed a confession. Indeed, as we shall see, he could proudly have attested to many things of which he stood accused. But the captors managed to break his spirit and make him say that he regretted what he had done. This ominous success gained by the interrogators, even if we had no other reason for opposing the Communist system with all the strength and ingenuity we can muster, would suffice to rouse the conscience of the world as it once did against Nazism: the successful employment of science to crush the soul of a human being and make him gainsay everything that has been dearest to the core of his heart during all his life.

The Cardinal was tried in the company of men deemed to have been his accomplices in a great conspiracy against the government. All pleaded guilty. Witnesses to the trial beheld a spectacle oddly reminiscent of the Reichstag Fire trials in Berlin during 1933, with the sinister difference that then even Göring could not intimidate the Court. Béla Fabian has pointed out the curious fact that those who conducted the trial of the Cardinal were former Nazis. The President, Dr. Vilmos Olti, had served the Hungarian Hitlerites even as he now served the Communists; and the leader of the prison interrogators, Dr. Martin Bodonyi, had worked for Nazi military tribunals under another name. The defense counsel assigned to the case had, however, been a member of the Communist Party since the days of Béla Kun.

Questions and answers succeeded each other much as they must have in the fearful prison. On the morning of February 8, 1949, the verdict was read:

"Joseph Mindszenty, the first accused, is sentenced herewith . . . to the cumulative penalty of penal servitude for life as the main penalty, to ten years' loss of office and ten years' suspension of political rights; further, the confiscation of all his property as supplementary punishment."

The charges against the Cardinal were circulated prior to the trial itself in an official *Yellow Book*, and the government subsequently issued a *Black Book* giving its version of the proceedings. The more carefully one reads these volumes, the greater one's astonishment is likely to be. We may discount in advance all the allegations which are known to have no foundation in fact. What is to be said of those which are probably true? A relatively minor charge is that certain sums of money obtained from abroad for Church purposes were not transferred at the official rate. For these derelictions the Cardinal accepted full responsibility and offered to make restitution, though he personally could have had nothing to do with them. At best they would have merited a small fine levied against the Archiepiscopal treasury. The second charge, and no doubt the most important, was that prior to the signing of the treaty of peace the Cardinal had endeavored to win the support of the Western Powers. This he was clearly entitled to do, in the legal sense; and morally he was under the obligation to make every effort to maintain civil and religious rights as he understood them. It was true that he had clung desperately to his belief that the United States would not permit the Russians to acquire unilateral rule over Hungary—a hope he shared with millions of other Hungarian citizens, and indeed with foreigners of every creed and persuasion who happened to be in Hungary at that time. In declaring that such beliefs constituted conspiracy against the State, the Prosecutor argued and the Court upheld the view that desiring anything short of complete Russian control was incompatible with the Constitutional provision that full liberty of opinion, speech, and assembly was assured.

One special charge was that the Cardinal had indirectly approached American authorities handling restitution claims in order to urge that the Crown of St. Stephen be sent to the Vatican to be held in trust there. Here he was daring but still prudent. Undoubtedly he had very good reason to fear that the Crown, most illustrious symbol of Hungary's past, would be shipped to Russia as soon as it was returned to Budapest. His maneuver was certainly not complimentary to the Communists; but they were bound by the Occupation Statute and later by the treaty of peace, which went into effect on September 15, 1947. The Cardinal's correspondence concerning the Crown antedates the treaty. Yet even this obliges the Hungarian government to respect Article 2, which reads:

1. Hungary shall take all measures necessary to secure to all persons under Hungarian jurisdiction, without distinction as to race, sex, language, or religion, the enjoyment of human rights and of the fundamental freedoms, including freedom of expression, of press and publication, of religious worship, of political opinion, and of public meeting.

2. Hungary further undertakes that the laws in force in Hungary shall not, either in their content or in their application, discriminate or entail any discrimination between persons of Hungarian nationality on the ground of their race, sex, language, or religion, whether in reference to their persons, property, business, professional or financial interests, status, political or civil rights, or any other matter.

Never has a peace treaty contained fairer pledges. Unfortunately there exists no sanction against their violation save a rebuke before the forum of the United Nations. Such a rebuke was of course administered.

The charge which laid the Cardinal most seriously open to criticism was that as a Monarchist he had conspired to bring about a Restoration, had conferred with the Pretender to the Throne, and had relied upon American intervention to achieve his aims. The testimony on these matters presented at the trial and outlined in the *Black Book* is confused; nor did the Cardinal receive an opportunity to comment on the accusations in any adequate or sustained way. He admitted that he was a Legitimist, that he had hoped the Regency would be succeeded by a Monarchy, and that at the request of Otto of Habsburg he had conferred with him while visiting the United States during 1947. These things did not constitute conspiracy against the State, and would indeed be permissible within the framework of a relatively democratic society. Whether reestablishing the Monarchy was in any sense practicable, whether it was the form of government best suited to Hungary, and whether the population of the country would have voted in favor of a Restoration are, to be sure, matters one could debate at length. But that discussion has no bearing on the issue that the Cardinal had conspired to plunge the nation into civil war and thus impose a solution by force.

A number of able jurists of varied confessional and political points of view have carefully reviewed the trial procedures. There is none of repute in the free world who has not held that the trial was a farcical travesty of justice.*

And so the Cardinal, indefatigable leader of his Church and of his people, entered through a narrow gate of infamy and pain the desert of penitential tribute to the power of iniquity. The ancient secret, that of the *mysterium iniquitatis,* the mystery of evil, was his to meditate upon even as hermits and martyrs, sages and great sufferers, the wise and the humble since the dawn of time had pondered it in times past. No doubt all he had to uproot from his heart were some vestiges of pride in his natural abilities and in his holy office—the pride he had sloughed off, surely, in the bitter days when he may well have asked the question which was on the lips of his Master, why God had forsaken him, and why he had been so grievously scourged for the sins of his time. They had humiliated him far beyond any boundaries which are set for humility to traverse. They had proved that theirs were the battalions and the torturers, the makers of decrees and the profiteers of power. The Archbishop of Esztergom, Prince of the Church and member of the Regent's Council, had become

* The trial of the Cardinal was directed by László Rajk, Minister of the Interior, who during September, 1949, was accused not only of having attempted to overthrow the Hungarian government and assassinate its principal officials but of espionage in behalf of the governments of the United States, Great Britain, and Yugoslavia. In short, Rajk was on trial for emulating Marshal Tito. Seven others were indicted as his accomplices. All were placed in confinement for some time previous to the convening of the Court. Testimony was introduced purporting to prove association with divers representatives of foreign powers. Nearly all of these have vehemently denied the allegations. Three death sentences were handed down and carried out. One victim was Rajk himself.

a convict devoid of honor or name, uncertain even whether he was looked upon throughout the world as a man who had betrayed his trust. No one could tell him that in his worst hour simple people were praying that the Lord God might have mercy on him—praying throughout Hungary, which he may have loved too well even as some other men love their wives unduly. The world into which he went from his trial was a world without prayer or peace. God had departed from it. One cannot avoid saying that. It was become a world in which endless shifts of prisoners move out of the gray dawn into the even grayer dusk, and it was necessary that it have in its midst a man stripped naked. It needed Job in the red hat of a Cardinal.*

After the condemnation of its most resourceful and coura-geous Christian leader, Hungary could no longer muster any-one to lead the resistance. During August, 1950, the Catholic Bishops signed an agreement with the government similar in every significant respect to that which the Bishops of Czecho-slovakia had signed. Despite it Cardinal Mindszenty's suc-cessor was arrested and haled before a court. A "Peace Move-ment" was formed among the clergy; and though at first only a few elected to join it, these gave it enthusiastic support. On October 23, 1951, for example, the Budapest Radio an-nounced that a meeting of the "reconstituted Board" of the movement had been held, at which Bishop Beresztocsky, the

* The fate of the Cardinal in imprisonment has been described by eyewitnesses who may be assumed to be reliable. Congenital frailty, and not mistreatment in prison, is responsible for his poor health. He has been permitted to celebrate the Holy Sacrifice of the Mass, although in complete isolation. Two visits from his mother have been permitted, and he has seen the Archbishop of Eger and the Bishop entrusted with the care of Catholics according to the Greek rite. Hungarian sources indicate that he has not been deported but is at Hüvösvölgy Prison in Budapest. There is no information as to views which the Cardinal may have expressed to his visitors, but all sources agree that he has been treated without undue harshness, and that the principal rigors of prison life are self-imposed.

chairman, reviewed the progress of the peace movement throughout the world, and lauded Stalin as the foremost enemy of war. Meanwhile the clergy of Hungary had also been called upon to sign an oath of allegiance to the Constitution. The great majority of priests complied during January, 1950, making the usual reservation that they pledged themselves to nothing that was antithetical to the Catholic faith.

Archbishop Jozsef Gröcz, successor to the Cardinal, attempted as best he could to guide the ship of the Church through the waters of persecution. Nevertheless during the summer of 1951 he and several other members of the Hierarchy—Bishops Andreas Hamvas, Joseph Petery, and Luigi Shvoy—were arrested. The subsequent trial, in which a number of less prominent clergymen also were the accused, offered a new version of the ordeal of the Cardinal. No doubt the major reason for this spectacle was the declaration of the Bishops that any service they rendered to the cause of "peace" was of a moral and religious character only, with no political significance. Archbishop Gröcz was sentenced to imprisonment on June 28, and a new series of assaults upon the Church ensued. A few days later, the remnant of the Hierarchy signed a profession of loyalty to the government. This in turn decreed that no one could validly hold office as a bishop, abbot, or provincial unless the State had approved his appointment. Indeed, even those who had assumed their offices after January, 1946, were declared subject to the same regulation. Religious orders were dissolved, and priests who had incurred excommunication by membership in the "Peace Movement" were appointed to important pastorates. Many priests and monks were deported to slave-labor camps. Under the pressure thus exerted, the bishops who still had freedom and the Abbot of Hungary's largest monastery took the oath of allegiance. Some of them even went

further and issued statements praising the government for its
zeal in promoting religious liberty.

Protestants also viewed the condemnation of the Cardinal
with profound alarm. Who was to carry on the struggle? Pastor Albert Bereczky, now well past fifty, had ministered during most of his service in the Church to a congregation of
working people. He had made a conscientious study of the
writings of Professor Karl Barth, renowned Swiss theologian.
This intellectual relationship gave rise to a strange and re-
vealing episode. During April of 1948, Barth accepted an
invitation to come to Hungary. But to the astonishment in particular of his Swiss and American admirers, who respected
him both for his vigorous reformulation of Protestant theology
and for the manner in which he had exposed the errors of
Nazism, Barth continued to refrain from criticism of the
principles on which the Communists based their bid for political power. It is difficult to do justice to his argument in a
few words. Perhaps, however, it can without gross unfairness
be interpreted as follows. Hitler, said Barth, was an incarna-
tion of evil because he misled many, not the least among whom
were those German churchmen who thought that the Nazi
cause was noble and invigorating. Stalin, on the other hand,
was the exponent of a view of life which every follower of
Christ knows full well is contrary to the Gospel. Accordingly
(he went on) there is virtually no reason to suppose that
Christians will be led into temptation by the Stalinist-Leninist
doctrine. Indeed, it might rather be that they would be led
astray by the materialistic West, notably the United States.
Barth's conclusion therefore was that a Christian ought to refrain from committing himself to either side in the debate
between East and West.

This teaching deeply shocked many persons on both fringes
of the Iron Curtain. When Barth appeared in Hungary, his

opinions were challenged by large numbers in the audiences which he addressed. More than once his reply to a query was difficult to fathom. For example, he professed to believe that a Christian faced with the problem of living in a State which did not respect the law should above all "not lose his sense of humor." For, he said, while no government will prove to be worthy of Christ, it is unlikely also that any will be of the Devil. It seemed to him that Evangelical Protestantism was called upon to take up a position "far more spiritual" in character than that adopted by Roman Catholicism. For had not the Papacy succumbed to the "anxiety" which had become the existentialist quality of the West? The true follower of Christ can entertain no fear save that for the salvation of his soul.

It is against this background of Barthian theory that the collaborationism of Bereczky and his associates must be seen. What from one point of view seems to be abject servility becomes in another perspective an abstruse, highly problematical, but possibly by no means dishonorably entertained desire to imitate St. Paul by accepting whatever government has been willed by Heaven. At any rate the Bereczky group began by lauding the Russian peace offensive, but soon went so far towards complete acceptance of the Communist position that fellow churchmen entertained grave doubts as to his fitness for the important post of Bishop of Budapest. Nevertheless Barth, in a letter from Switzerland on May 23, 1948, contended that these doubts should be put aside because the Church, fearing no one save the Lord, should not be afraid to accept as Bishop a clergyman who was a favorite of the government. He added: "It will be manifest in the fact that you rid yourselves of this minor anxiety that you have no anxiety whatsoever." But as time went on Barth must have begun to question whether Bereczky was not proving his own orig-

inal assumption—namely, that every Christian will realize
that Stalinism is incompatible with Christianity—to be false.
At any rate, in a private letter to Bereczky dated September
16, 1951, he wrote, "It seems to me that you are on the way
toward making your affirmation of Communism a part of the
Christian message." This would, of course, be the same error
of which the German Christian Movement had been guilty
under Hitler.

At any rate, the Protestant Churches in their turn were
compelled to negotiate an agreement with the government,
accepting the whole of the Communist program dealing with
finances, education, and the appointment of clergymen and
other Church dignitaries. When Bishop Ravasz resigned in
protest, the Calvinist Synod attempted to elect a worthy man
to be his successor. The government refused to endorse the
choice, and finally succeeded in gaining acceptance for Pastor
Roland Kiss, well known as friendly to the Communist position. Only a few indications of the extent to which infamy and
outrage prevailed thereafter can be adduced here. The gross-
est kind of interference in the work of the pastorate was resorted to, so that in the end notorious and criminal Communists were installed in ecclesiastical offices, while worthy
churchmen were dismissed, deported, and imprisoned. Only
eight Church schools survived the drive for the nationalization
of education. Relief and welfare organizations were forbidden; and the press was reduced to impotence by censorship
and suppression. Toward the close of 1951, two theological
seminaries were closed. Even more dire, if that be possible,
was the fate of the small Lutheran minority. Its leaders were
hounded, ousted from office and imprisoned.

By the close of 1951, civil and religious liberties were ex-
tinguished in Hungary to an extent which the Cardinal himself
could hardly have foreseen. Virtually everyone who had oc-

cupied a position of trust or responsibility in the country prior to 1945 was now impoverished and ostracized. The number of distinguished exiles was legion. Economic conditions had deteriorated so completely that even food, product of the rich plains, was lacking. Tens of thousands who could find no employment in the industries which were being created by fiat, by reason of age or of earlier religious and political affiliations, were marked for deportation. These wholesale shipments of human cattle aroused the indignation of the outside world. Lord Vansittart reported to the House of Lords that 100,000 persons had been earmarked for slave-labor camps. For a time this ghastly business was halted; but seemingly reliable information indicates that the shipments were resumed during 1952.

As elsewhere in the Russian orbit, the emphasis was on production and organization for war. Russian military and economic officials virtually took over the country. Criticism of the workers and particularly youth was everywhere part of the order of the day. Young Hungarians, the government declared again and again, had been inoculated with the diseases of pacifism and pro-Imperialism. Even the official Youth Organization, DISZ, was accused of "cosmopolitanism" and "adoration of the Anglo-American imperialist monster." On June 28, 1952, Matron Horváth, speaking for the Communist Party, reemphasized the need for continued intensive opposition to "clerical reaction." He expressed shocked surprise that some members of the Party still participated in religious functions and, indeed, permitted the Church to influence their children.

This would be as pertinent a note as any on which to end our account of the Hungarian tragedy were it not for the breath-taking events which have followed the death of Stalin. Years of draining away the substance of the people and of endeavoring to clamp the peasants into the vise of collective farming had created a movement of resistance which could no longer be curbed. Demands for return of the land that had been collectivized, together with farm animals, rose spontaneously from the farm folk everywhere in Hungary. Rákosi was removed from office, and Imre Nagy, a non-Communist, was restored to the office he had once held. On July 11 Nagy declared in a startling address that the collective farms would be dissolved if the majority of the peasants banded together on them so desired, and that their lands would thereupon be given back to them. It is true that men who took this proclamation literally often found themselves denounced as "kulaks" and enemies of the people. But a careful review of reports from those who have daily monitored official Hungarian broadcasts indicates clearly that the government, wedged in between the peasants' demand for liberation and the desperate need of the population for food, is far weaker than anyone would have deemed it to be a short time ago.

In the circumstances, it is safe to say that the average Hungarian recalls with grim irony the final speech delivered by Rákosi on May 10, during the "political campaign":

Let us be vigilant in all fields . . . and ruthlessly take action against all who sabotage the building of our happier future. Our People's Democracy must incessantly watch for conspiracies, sabotage, and espionage activities which, without exception, are initiated, organized, and financed by the United States. Even now the United States is making so-called liberation promises which mean nothing save that it seeks to restore the rule of reactionary lords over the liberated Hungarian people.

Not even the United States could have so stirred the people of Hungary to reaffirm, despite terror and need, its traditional belief in freedom as the bulwark of life, liberty, and the pursuit of happiness.

7 ALBANIAN INTERLUDE
AND BALTIC VISTA

I

LITTLE ALBANIA, where mountains rise in serried ranks behind a marshy, malaria-infested coast, was perhaps the first satellite to reveal the nature of Communist rule fully and unreservedly. Living uneasily under Turkish domination well past the nineteenth century in a country not unlike the Great Smokies, the Albanians have been the least known and the most handicapped nation in Europe. Like many a mountain folk in the United States—whether in Tennessee or in Vermont—they have been influenced culturally by the inaccessibility of their villages, the primitive state of their agriculture, and the dearth of modern means of transportation. Even proximity to the sea has been of limited value because delta silt has impeded navigation throughout history. Outside the cities, family and tribal solidarity remains stronger than national sentiment. But, while the Albanians have been dependent on foreign powers for security and prosperity, they are a patriotic folk and a martial one.

Communism came to this land not because of the abuses of capitalism or because of a yearning of workers to unite, but through a political movement which developed against the background of the World War. The independence of the country and the inviolability of its boundaries were guaranteed by the peace treaties after the defeat of the Austro-Hungarian Empire in 1918. At the same time the Great Powers held that Italy had a special diplomatic and strategic stake in the welfare of her neighbor across the Adriatic Sea. As a result Italian interests in Albania expanded greatly after 1920, and to every intent and purpose the foreign trade of the two countries was pooled. But Yugoslavia naturally sought to challenge the primacy of Italy in the Adriatic area, and its support is held to have largely made it possible for Ahmed Zogu, Prime Minister in a government constituted as a Regency, to take over the rule of the country during 1924. Shortly thereafter, a Republic was proclaimed, and Zogu was elected President for a term of seven years. A skillful diplomat and political leader, he improved relations with both Greece and Yugoslavia, and signed the Treaty of Tirana in 1926 with Italy. This, accompanied by a sizable grant of financial assistance from Italian banks, gave recognition to the common interest of both countries in maintaining the independence of Albania. A year later they entered a defensive alliance. When it was alleged that these developments conceded to Mussolini rights which he exploited unduly, Zogu curbed the opposition with dramatic swiftness. He proclaimed himself King, on September 1, 1928, and was responsible for a constitution which recognized no political liberties but insured freedom of religion. Zogu, a benevolent dictator, made an honest effort to improve the cultural and economic life of the country, building roads, fostering health and hygiene, erecting schools, fighting a vigorous battle against illiteracy, and modernizing the banking system. Albania even acquired a radio station, and air travel became a reality. The King brought in foreign experts, particularly Austrians. Some of them I have known; and while they had the usual reservations about the political institutions of Albania, they respected his energy and sincerity of social purpose.

At this point Mussolini was unfortunately smitten with irrational imperialist ambition: if Hitler could have his empire of the master race, he himself was called upon to reconstruct the dominions of ancient Rome. Italian troops landed in Albania on April 7, 1939, shortly after the fall of France. They quickly overpowered the small defense army, and Zogu had to seek refuge abroad. The crown was thereupon offered to King Victor Emmanuel III, of Italy, who docilely accepted it. It is worth noting that the reception accorded the Italians was not too unfriendly, because some sections of the population expected to profit from the political change. Using Albania as an advance base, the Duce attacked Greece on October 28, 1940; but the valiant Greeks put his armies to rout and occupied nearly half of Albania. The Germans, defeating Yugoslavia, took over the rest of Albania, but confined themselves to routine control. Two resistance movements were formed, the one pro-Zogu and primarily against Italy, and the other Communist with the Germans as its principal target. The second, the National Liberation Front, was the stronger, primarily because it boldly drafted men into its partisan forces and because it maintained ruthless discipline. British commandos in the Adriatic therefore quite naturally aided it. As a result, the Front was able to assume control of the country as soon as the Germans retreated.

The provisional government formed by General Enver Hoxha, commander in chief of the National Liberation Front, was recognized by the United States, Great Britain, and Russia in 1945. A republic was established during the following year. General Hoxha and his followers meanwhile made no secret of their devotion to the Communist cause, although their utterances took on the usual protective coloring. At a Congress in the little town of Permeti, on May 24, 1944, the Front had "guaranteed freedom of religion and of conscience, and equality of rights for all religions." Hoxha's partisans, like Tito's, were frequently seen at religious services. Albania, a turbulent and weapon-toting country addicted to blood feuds and similar practices, was one of the most tolerant of nations from the religious point of view. In 1930 nearly three-fifths of the total population of 1,003,000 were Mohammedans, while the members of the Greek Orthodox Church constituted another fifth. Catholics in union with Rome were noticeably in the minority, scarcely more than one-tenth of the professedly religious reported in the census, and were concentrated in the extreme north of the country. Their major religious, charitable, and educational institutions were in Scutari, an ancient town on a beautiful mountain-surrounded lake, afflicted with mosquitoes and malarial fever. Ancient ties with Italy, which Mussolini so wantonly divested of moral and diplomatic import, had led to the existence of a considerable number of religious of Italian origin in Albania, and also to the settlement of many Albanians in Italy. This fact would no doubt have given rise to some antipathy even under normal conditions. Yet on the whole few in Albania were apprehensive when the war ended. The age-old tradition of religious peace seemed to preclude violent change.

Albania had a rude awakening. General Hoxha was interested in nothing less than freedom of religion. Information concerning the fate of the Moslem majority is meager and difficult to come by. But laborious piecing together of news items from Albanian radio broadcasts and newspapers makes one surmise that the Communists have tried to neutralize the Moslem population by breaking it up into mutually hostile factions. It is known that purges of Mohammedan leaders who were insufficiently cooperative have occurred. Islam is today divided into several sects. Hoxha's aides sought first to play one of these against another, and selected the strongest, the *Bektashi,* for the role of principal collaborator; but there ensued a weird series of assassinations, or purges, impossible to interpret. All we really know is that government broadcasts beamed to the Near East stress that Albania demonstrates the ability of Communism to carry out its program successfully while granting complete freedom of faith to Mohammedans. The names of some Moslem leaders who have perished are known, as is that of Hafiz Musa Hashi Alija, who is currently cast in the precarious role of chief adviser to the government on Islamic matters.

News concerning the fate of the Orthodox Church is also much more fragmentary than one could desire. Historically, in Albania, this Church was free of strong confessional ties with Constantinople and Athens, and from time to time some of its leaders took under serious advisement the possibility of reunion with Rome. Accordingly Communist efforts after 1945 to "nationalize" Orthodoxy and to foster its allegiance to Moscow met with resistance. It was not until January, 1948, that a small delegation of the clergy visited Moscow, Kiev, and Leningrad. The official press reported that the head of this group had expressed, in behalf of his colleagues, the view that the "strength of the Russian Church" would insure protection against "all the other Churches, and particularly the Vatican," which might seek to "absorb and destroy the Albanian Church." During the same year, a Russian bishop visited Tirana, Albania's capital city; and the Orthodox Church Conference of that year convened in Moscow. This conference, it will be remembered, condemned both the Protestant Ecumenical Movement and the Vatican, "center of Fascism and of plots against the Slavic peoples."

The fact that the Primate, Archbishop Christopher Kissi, did not attend any of these assemblies was strongly indicative of a lack of appreciation for Communist conceptions of the role and functions of the Church. Indeed, it would have been strange if he had attended. The Orthodox Church, like all other religious bodies in Albania, had suffered from the Land Reform Law promulgated during August, 1945, which gave the Party the right to confiscate and nationalize property it has claimed elsewhere. By the close of 1948, Moslem and Orthodox ecclesiastics were completely dependent financially on the state. During the next year, the Archbishop was deposed and arrested. The government's published contention was that he "had worked against our interests and the interests of the people by collaborating with the Unitarian Church during the period of Fascist occupation." Two other prelates, Bishop Ireneo and Bishop Agathangjeli, were arrested. How many other members of the clergy have been taken into custody, deported to labor camps, or executed, no one knows. There is a report that Bishop Irenaeus Banushi was put to death during 1947.

However, the full fury of Hoxha's enmity fell upon the Roman Catholic Church. The Germans had withdrawn in November, 1944. A month later the government seized all printing establishments, and the Catholic press was abolished. At the same time a number of ecclesiastical offices were searched, and some members of the clergy were taken into custody. Religious youth organizations were banned, and only the Antifascist Youth Front, avowedly pro-Communist, was permitted to function. In February, 1945, the first "People's Court" to convene in Scutari sentenced one of the best known Albanian writers, the Reverend Lazarus Shanjoha, to death. He had favored close ties of friendship with Italy for many years, and so the sentence was ascribed to the National Liberation Front's fanatical detestation of all things Italian, and not to antireligious prejudice.

Ilya Ehrenburg, major Soviet propagandist, visited Albania during the November of 1945. Upon his return to Moscow he described Scutari, more than half the population of which was Roman Catholic, as a vicious hotbed of reaction. At the time of his visit the city was preparing for its first postwar elections. A handful of students at the diocesan seminary for the training of priests circulated mimeographed sheets urging that the recipients vote against the National Front. These sheets bore the signature of the "Albanian Union." Spurred on by Ehrenburg's denunciation, the government jailed and tortured some of the distributors. They revealed the names of the seminarians, who as a matter of fact constituted the complete membership of the Albanian Union. A spectacular trial of those held guilty of having plotted to overthrow the State with the help of "Anglo-American imperialists" became in reality a forum before which the Catholic Church was indicted for high treason. The Rector of the seminary and one of his fellow Jesuits were accused of responsibility for the conspiracy, found guilty, and executed. Others received heavy prison sentences. Nowhere else had a court acted more grimly.

The liquidation of virtually all Catholic activities followed swiftly, with more cruel and vengeful treatment of the clergy than has been witnessed even in Hungary and Yugoslavia. The Papal Nuncio was expelled, as were all priests and religious born in Italy. Education was reserved to the State, even nursery schools being taken from the Church. Catholic Action was suppressed. The seminaries were closed. Ecclesiastical property was deeded over to "the people," and the priests who were permitted to remain in office were restricted to one room in their rectories. The only Catholic bishop who is thought to have survived lives in an isolated mountain village. By the close of 1948, virtually every widely respected and well educated priest had been executed or imprisoned. Francis Gjini, Bishop, Abbot, and Albanian representative of the Papal Nuncio; George Volaj, Bishop of Sappa; Matthias Prennushi, Provincial of the Franciscans—all were put to death. Vincent Prennushi, Archbishop of Durazzo, died in prison.

Under this reign of terror, the Catholic population of approximately 100,000 was reduced to dire poverty, impotence, and silence. The laity suffered almost as grievously as the clergy. Catholics holding positions of public trust were ousted. Priests were forbidden to minister to the sick in hospitals or prisons. To consort in any way with a priest meant probable imprisonment or worse. By the middle of August, 1951, Catholics who still ventured to practice their religion openly were served by not more than sixty-two priests. On the third day of that month, the government published a decree concerning the status of the Roman Catholic Church. This document, having announced that the Church no longer "has any kind of organizational, economic, or political ties with the Pope," went on to ordain that the clergy must accompany religious teaching with the inculcation of sentiments of loyalty to the "people's power of the Albanian People's Republic," and that appointments to ecclesiastical positions must have the approval of the government. This decree was approved at a convention of Catholics meeting in Scutari in 1951. At the same time the government announced that Catholicism in Albania had repudiated all forms of allegiance to the Papacy, "enemy of the people."

The legal status of religious establishments was clarified by a law dated November 26, 1949. The principal stipulations were these:

All clergymen or lay officials must be approved by the State; and any who act illegally "must be dismissed from their posts immediately."

Any communication addressed to the public by a Church official—speech, message, or pastoral letter—must be submitted in advance for censorship.

The education of youth is conducted by the State, and "religious institutions have nothing to do with it."

Religious orders were not to assume management of any hospital or other charitable institution, or to possess real property.

Measures taken against the Catholic minority were so brutal that even Communist functionaries protested. At a Congress of the People's Party, held on March 31, 1952, General Hoxha sternly upbraided Tuk Jakova, one of the principal Communist Party leaders, for questioning the wisdom of the persecution. Hoxha's words, as reprinted, read in part:

Comrade Tuk Jakova, disassociating himself from the political program of the Party and of the State in so far as religion and in particular the Catholic clergy are concerned, has not evinced the right attitude toward this clergy or acted against it vigorously. Not seeing the very grave danger which is present in the reactionary clergy, Comrade Jakova has not hated them in an adequate way.

It would therefore appear that while Mohammedanism has been spared the full rigors of the antireligious crusade in Albania, the Christian Churches have suffered as perhaps nowhere else in satellite Europe. Bereft of leadership and of education, depleted through violent death, deportation to labor camps, and escape to other countries, they have been reduced to a status almost as primitive as that of the Churches

in the Soviet Union itself prior to the War against Hitler. They
are almost wholly isolated. Information concerning the cultural life of the Albanian people is limited to what can be
obtained from broadcasts over the government radio station.

Hoxha did not join forces with Marshal Tito when that
leader broke with the Kremlin, but was soon made aware that
Albania was wholly isolated and that his Yugoslav neighbor
gave asylum to dissidents who plotted a *coup d'état*. That
such an undertaking might well meet with success seems probable. But Italy retains its interest in the strategic and economic advantages of the Albanian area, and its assent would
be required; and currently, with the struggle for Trieste in
the foreground, no entente is conceivable. The Russians apparently maintain a small body of troops in the vicinity of
Tirana, but have in no other wise manifested great concern.
Apparently they consider Hoxha a negligible problem child.
It is apparent, however, that the Russian garrison makes impossible any attempt to overthrow the dictatorship from within
the country.

II

The fate of the three erstwhile Baltic Republics—Lithuania, Latvia, and Estonia—illustrates the sad truth that in
troubled and imperialistic parts of the world it does not pay
to be a small nation. Each of the three had a solid folk or tribal
core round which language, mores, and religious tradition
had developed. For brief periods each managed to acquire a
precarious independence. But they lay along the great Baltic
seacoast route from Western Europe. German colonization
efforts, spearheaded by the Teutonic Knights, went this way,
and later came solidly entrenched land barons. There were
periods of Swedish and Polish domination. Finally, as a result of the Treaty of Nystad, which in 1721 ended the Swedish

wars, and of the Third Partition of Poland, all three countries were ceded to Russia. At first the Czars governed rather benevolently, but by the middle of the nineteenth century the three had been absorbed into the "Northwest Territory"; and stern measures of Russification were resorted to. In Lithuania, for example, only Russian might be spoken. Monastic schools were closed. The Polish and Lithuanian languages were forbidden. Many thousands of persons were deported.

After World War I broke out, the three suffered by reason of the wavering fortunes of the belligerents. In 1918 they were the scene of sanguinary fighting between remnants of the German army, invading Bolshevik troops, and hastily formed armies of national liberation. The Poles also intervened. Finally, however, all three states were declared independent, and governments were formed. A period of uneasy tranquillity followed, but the predominatingly peasant population achieved a measure of prosperity. Then the Pact of August, 1939, between Stalin and Hitler and the subsequent erasure of Poland from the map of Europe inaugurated intense tribulation along the Baltic. Germans were evacuated from Latvia and Estonia. All three Republics were compelled to sign agreements with Russia permitting the establishment of military bases. Thousands fled, and countless other thousands were deported. Next came the aftermath of the Nazi declaration of war on Russia. In a very short time Hitler had the Baltic coasts under his heel, and the expulsion and liquidation of Jews began. Finally the German armies retreated, the Russians entered, and the status of the "Northwest Territory" was restored.

Elections followed, and as a matter of course pro-Communist governments were established. It should be noted that only in Estonia had a native minority of any size favored the Communist cause. Moreover, the religious affiliations of the populations were deeply rooted in tradition. Estonia, with a prewar population of 1,250,000, had about 900,000 Lutherans and approximately 215,000 Greek Orthodox. There was only a small group of Roman Catholics. Lithuania, on the other hand, with 3,000,000, was predominatingly Roman Catholic. Minorities of Lutherans, Jews, and Greek Orthodox constituted about one-fifth of the population. More than half of the population of Latvia belonged to the Lutheran Church, but there were substantial Catholic and Greek Orthodox minorities. The organizational activities of the Churches were varied and rich. In Lithuania, for example, with two archdioceses and four dioceses, more than 800,000 persons were enrolled in various lay organizations. The largest daily newspaper was in Catholic hands, and the total circulation achieved by the religious press was impressive. In Latvia likewise, publications under religious auspices numbered more than a fifth of those printed.

The first Communist occupation, dating from June 15, 1940, engulfed all three nations in tragedy. The Russians decreed that every organization established before their seizure of control "jeopardized public security," and religious institutions and organizations were suppressed. Their property was confiscated, and they were forbidden to maintain any contact with the outside world. Religious instruction was curtailed drastically, the clergy being called upon to sign a pledge that they would desist from teaching religion either in public or in private. Waves of Communist propaganda, much of it directed against religion, passed over the country, burying every attempt at counteraction. Within a year the Russians had destroyed every overt vestige of the autonomous culture which these small countries had fostered during the limited time of their independence.

It was done ruthlessly, brutally, barbarously. More than

60,000 Lithuanians were deported to Siberia. A number of priests were murdered, and some are said to have been crucified. In Latvia and Estonia the numbers deported appear to have been smaller; but the clergy of all denominations were hounded, slain, and shipped to labor camps. It is no doubt correct to say that no year in the history of predatory imperialism since the dawn of time has been characterized by so complete a lack of restraint. The individuality of the peoples was rooted out with implacable determination.

The Nazis drove the Russians out again, but in turn resorted to suppressions of their own. It was a time of dire distress for the Jewish minority, and of course also for anyone deemed to be opposed to their theories of race superiority. Deeply religious folk from the Baltic States were shipped to concentration camps. The Russians returned during the summer of 1944. This time large numbers of Lithuanians in particular fled to the West, the total being estimated at 80,000. Of the remaining inhabitants of the three countries, it is believed that more than 500,000 have been seized and sent off to Russian labor camps. There have been at least six round-ups of slaves. The first was in Estonia at the close of 1948, and it is believed that 50,000 persons were taken from their homes. The others have been carried out with the same irrational callousness. The deportations have stripped the countries affected of virtually all religious leadership which might have opposed Russian domination. Only 30 of Estonia's 250 Lutheran clergymen are still at work there, and comparable figures have been computed for Latvia. One Catholic priest out of five remains in Lithuania.

It is hardly necessary to state that the economies of the countries affected are exploited for the benefit of Russia. But one can grasp only with extreme difficulty the extent to which agents of Moscow dominate political and cultural activity.

Even Nazism was by comparison liberal. Officials assigned the task, direct the government, the press, and education. The Russian language is of course taught in the schools. A relatively recent report from Estonia reads:

Teachers of the Russian language must explain to their pupils the universal importance of this great tongue. It is the language used by Lenin, the greatest genius of the human race. It is the tongue in which Stalin addresses the toiling masses of the world. The Russian language will enable the student to understand Russian culture . . . and to acquire a knowledge of the world's most notable scientific achievements.

Training in the Russian language is accompanied by the dissemination of Communist classics, notably the works of Lenin, made available in cheap editions and foisted off on workers regardless of their wishes. Young people in particular are targets for Communist indoctrination, and nowhere have they been bombarded with greater vigor than in the Baltic area. There can be little doubt that in twenty years virtually all awareness of Christian thought and feeling will have disappeared, save among the rare survivors of an older generation.

All the usual devices—nationalization of Church property, suppression of religious education—have of course been resorted to here. The kolkhoz system has been widely introduced into Lithuania, largely in order to restore the efficiency of an agricultural system depleted of usable labor by the deportations. Although nearly all of these are reported to be under direct Russian control, the results appear to have been disappointing. A report assumed to be reliable has this to say:

The names of Estonian kolkhozes provide a most interesting commentary on Communist propaganda and on the strict hierarchical system which prevails in the Soviet Union. Stalin has 26 or 27 kolkhozes dedicated to him; Lenin has 25; Marx, 6; and Engels, only 2. The kolkhozes named after Stalin are larger than the others and are situated in the most fertile regions. Whereas ordinary kolkhozes have some 120 cows, Stalin's have from 450 to 700. Workers on Stalin kolkhozes receive higher wages than are paid on others. Stalin kolkhozes are never criticized in the press and are invariably run by well known, active Communists. Other living Soviet leaders also have kolkhozes dedicated to them: Molotov has 9 named after him; Voroshilov, 7. Zhandov, who in 1940 accomplished the Sovietization of Estonia, has 6. Other kolkhozes with Russian names are Stalingrad, Volga, Ukraine, Gorki, Pushkin, and Lysenko. Not a single one, however, has been named for a living Estonian except that adorned with the cognomen of the Soviet Union's wrestling champion, Johannes Kotkas.

About the only notable action against a prelate of standing which has been adequately reported is the trial of the Bishop of Danzig, Carl Maria Splett, who was brought to the dock for assisting the Nazi oppressors. The Bishop, a stanch and zealous man, protested his innocence; and there was no evidence whatsoever that he had in any way aided the infamous cause of the Nazis. He had, indeed, contended bravely against the depredations of Hitler's minions on the freedom and mission of the Church. Nevertheless *Osservatore Romano* reported, on February 3, 1946, that he had been sentenced to prison for eight years because he had "assisted the German occupants to the detriment of the Polish people." Bishop Splett is still in duress.

What we do know about the fate of these people rests upon an infinitely painstaking, imaginative piecing together of very small bits of information. Thus it is possible to say that there was considerable guerrilla resistance, particularly by peasants; that the armed bands were surrounded in the forest and mowed down; that villages were thereupon razed, as Lidice

in Czechoslovakia had been by the Nazis; and that of heroism
there is even yet no end. We are also able to say that Russians
were brought westward to take the places of the dead and the deported. But it requires a creative writer rather than a historian
to draw out of the drably reported facts their full significance;
and this has been done by the Polish poet Czeslaw Milosz in
a remarkable article in the Berlin *Monat*, from which I
quote:

> The letter I held in my hand stabbed me in the heart. It came from a
> family which had been deported to Siberia from one of the Baltic States
> during March, 1949, and was addressed to relatives in Poland. This
> family consisted of a mother and two daughters. The letter described
> in terse and arid words the labor they were called upon to perform on a
> kolkhoz somewhere on the other side of the Urals. The last letters in
> the several lines were written more heavily than the others; and when
> one read them from top to bottom they formed these words: "SLAVES
> FOREVER." This missive, addressed to somebody else, fell into my
> hands by accident. How many similar cries of despair expressed
> through a comparable code may have been received by others who,
> unlike my confidant, kept an anxious silence!

Milosz goes on to wonder whether this peasant woman, gone
into a dour exile from which virtually none return, be not a
symbol of a moral disaster of which the world of the West is
hardly aware. To be sure, the West knows there are slave-
labor camps, and realizes what goes on in them. But it cannot
rouse itself to a united, flaming moral protest which not only
would have meaning for the victims of Communism but would
clean out many of the breeding places, in our society, of infection that in turn produces more Communism. I have seen
no letter so dramatically pathetic, though I have read many
written under Russian bondage, filled with heartache and
despair. Nor can one have talked with refugees, be they simple folk or intellectuals, without gaining some insight into the

ultimate human meaning of the catastrophe which has befallen a country like Lithuania.

Lithuania, a Catholic land, lived by the precepts of the
Church with the fidelity that is characteristic of Ireland. During 1939, more than 1,600 priests served a communion of
nearly 3,000,000. Jesuits, Franciscans, and other religious
were firmly established. There were nine bishops. One-fifth
of all the books published in Lithuanian dealt with religious
subjects. There was a vigorous Catholic press. Education was
not divorced from religious teaching. All the things that are
characteristic of Catholic countries—shrines, pilgrimages,
seminaries, hospitals, organizations for the furtherance of
Catholic social action—were amply in evidence.

The shock of finding all this irretrievably wiped out (or so
it had to seem) must have been staggering indeed, even for the
more parochially minded. In the eyes of so many deportees
and escapees, I have seen utter bewilderment as if they had
witnessed the unimaginable transformation of everything familiar into a jumbled amalgam each minute part of which was
become terrifyingly strange. Human beings can survive great
catastrophes intact, sometimes even strengthened, provided
the basic communities in which their lives are merged—family, church, civil society—preserve their normal outlines.
Otherwise they cannot do so.

Very little news comes from Lithuania. What does come
indicates that the people have clung with moving fidelity to
their faith. Only one member of the Lithuanian Hierarchy
not in exile survives. He was recently compelled to attend a
Peace Congress in Moscow, but was not asked to address the
assembly. Fewer than one-third of the parishes still have pastors. It is reported that the Seminary at Kaunas still trains
young men for the priesthood, though the number has become
small. No new church may be erected, nor has any which was

destroyed during the war been rebuilt. Nevertheless people gather for prayer and worship even when there is no priest to minister unto them. How implacably the wheels of oppression grind may be deduced from the following comment:

Priests are obliged to pay income taxes in accordance with their rank. Thus a pastor must pay up to the amount of 100,000 rubles annually, and a curate up to half that amount. This means, in the case of a pastor, a sum as large as several of the salaries earned by the most highly paid civil servants. Of course it is impossible for the priests to meet these levies because the faithful, normally earning only a tenth of what it costs them to live, must slowly dispose of everything they own in order to exist. Ultimately the priests must pawn or sell not only everything they possess but also the property of the Church.

Thus broken fane and hunted priest and cowering faithful are symbols of Christianity in our day. What shall we say is the answer that comes from the heart of the West? Is Milosz right when he says that we not only forget about the 500,000 Lithuanians who have been deported to the slave-labor regions of Russia, but fail dismally as well to give our own industrial society dignity and richness? A peasant woman like the writer of the letter he cites must indeed have lived a narrowly circumscribed life. Yet somehow it had a rhythm which, regulated by the seasons, kept the sacredness of the seasons. Who does not occasionally think of the desiccated culture of the West, afflicted with a dry rot which must be in the bones of our education as well as in our social goals? An American, for example, who has observed the lives of so many of his countrymen abroad, veering from reading designed for minds unintelligent and smug alike to entertainment whose sole purpose is to provide a stylized commentary on raw passions, cannot but wonder whether the resources of pseudo-Christianity we fancy we have conserved will suffice for the long and bitter ordeal which lies ahead for us.

8 SOVIETIZING THE
BALKAN REGION

I

RUMANIA AND BULGARIA, both allied with Hitler during World War II, were of necessity doomed to Soviet rule once the fighting was ended. Yet it should be remembered that neither country had been an enthusiastic partner of the German dictator. Rumania in particular had suffered during the thirties from constant bloody clashes between the moderate supporters of the Monarchy and a fascist movement known as the Iron Guard. Many thousands of persons were executed or slain, and the civil liberties of the nation almost disappeared. In the end, the Germans gained control, and the Rumanian Army became part of their war machine. Bulgaria, too, had lived under virtual dictatorship; and when the Nazis found it possible to satisfy at least partially the expansionist desires of the regime, there came into being an uneasy alliance which the majority of the people undoubtedly opposed. This sullen and strong opposition made it unwise to involve the Bulgarian Army in Nazi military adventures, and the Russians could legitimately conclude that the warm friendship suddenly manifested in both countries when Red troops marched in was not wholly sincere.

The United States made a serious effort to insure effective democratic government in the Balkan region. For example, with Great Britain, it protested against the manner in which the Bulgarian elections of November, 1945, were conducted. The voting had led to a scarcely contested triumph for the pro-Communist Fatherland Front. The matter was debated at the Moscow Conference which convened in the next month, and the Russians indicated that possession was just about the whole of the law, although they did agree to include representatives of other parties in the government. From that time on, Soviet domination of the two countries slowly and implacably became more complete, and any likelihood that Western intervention could alter the course of events evaporated like a morning mist.

Except Greece, Bulgaria was the country in which the Greek Orthodox Church was strongest. Moslems were the only minority of notable size, Jews and Roman Catholics and Protestants being negligible in number.* Accordingly, as soon as the Russians had taken over and begun to establish a collectivist economy, the Orthodox Church was an object of immediate attention. There was a maneuver which has been a topic for speculative comment ever since. For many years the hostility between Bulgaria and Greece which had its roots in the struggle for Bulgarian independence had manifested itself also in the

---

* Prewar population statistics for Bulgaria reveal that 83.5 per cent were Greek Orthodox; 14.3, Mohammedan; 0.9, Jewish; and 0.8, Roman Catholic. Postwar (1948) estimates for Rumania indicate that 72 per cent of the population were Orthodox; 10, Roman Catholics according to the Greek rite; 7, Roman Catholics; 4.6, Calvinists; 2.3, Jews; and 1.6, Lutherans. Other Protestant groups, including Unitarians and Baptists, constituted about 1 per cent. Most Rumanian Catholics and Protestants belonged to German or Hungarian minority groups.

religious organization. Faithful to its Byzantine origins, the Greek Orthodox Church recognized (as we have previously noted) the Patriarch of Constantinople as its head, but accepted the Hierarchy of Greece as the center of ecclesiastical power. This Hierarchy had, however, ruled that the Bulgarian Orthodox Church was a schismatic body, and all pleas that its decision be altered fell on deaf ears. When the war ended, the Bulgarian Holy Synod met and elected the Metropolitan of Sofia president and head of the Church with the title Exarch Stephan I. He had long fished in the troubled waters of Bulgarian politics and was widely known as an anti-Communist, but now he began to manifest a zealous ardor in support of Communism which virtually knew no bounds. When he made representations to the Constantinople Patriarch that the curse of schism be lifted from the Bulgarian Church, an affirmative answer was received, owing no doubt to the weakness of the Greeks and the peril in which they at that time found themselves.

Much going and coming ensued. Stephan journeyed to Kiev, Moscow, and Leningrad. In turn the Patriarch of Moscow, despite his eighty years, made an official visit to Bulgaria. Not a few students of the situation reason that a plan had been concocted to make the Patriarch of Moscow head of all the Eastern Orthodox Churches, conferring a new and signal distinction upon the Russian capital, which would thus become not only the world center of Communism but also the "Third Rome," and manifestly rival the Vatican in importance as a seat of ecclesiastical authority. The plan—if it actually existed—soon ceased to bear any relation to reality; but it is interesting to conjecture as to what might have happened if the Greeks had been absorbed into the Russian orbit.

All this had a complex and sometimes confusing historical background. The services rendered by the Orthodox clergy

to the cause of Bulgarian independence, and to the resurrec-
tion of the Bulgarian language as a medium of literary expression, gave the Church universally recognized prestige.
After 1878, when national freedom was gained, the Orthodox
Church was a State institution, and the members of its Hierarchy were public officials. A portion of the national budget
was set aside to support the Church, which in addition owned
considerable property largely derived from bequests. The
case was comparable with that of a large state university in
the United States. Salaries of professors in such a university
are paid out of the state treasury; but it may own not inconsiderable wealth in its own right, is permitted to collect fees
from students and to charge for other services rendered. When
one considers the rural character of Bulgaria and the poverty
of most of its 6,000,000-odd people, the financial strength of
Orthodoxy reflected in such magnificent structures as the Archiepiscopal Palace in Sofia is genuinely impressive. Clergymen
of all ranks officiated on public occasions; and, though the
spirituality of the Bulgarian people may well have been far
from deep, they prized the Church as the primary agency of
the national culture.

Bulgarian education enjoyed a well merited repute, and the
theological schools established after 1878 ranked high among
the country's institutions of higher learning. The training given
consisted in the main of what we should call "general education," theology being taught as a field of specialization. The
result was that many leading citizens were graduates of these
schools. Religious instruction, normally by laymen, was likewise included in the curricula of elementary and secondary
schools. About 4,000 churches served the people, under the
direction of the Holy Synod. This body also fostered breadth
of view, and held membership in the World Council of
Churches prior to the war. On the whole, the religious situation

was idyllic, in spite of a rather constant exchange of uncomplimentary remarks with the Greeks.

The first approach to the Church by the Communists was made rather gingerly and was not unfriendly. They seemed, indeed, to regard this venerable institution as a political instrument worth keeping in repair. True enough, religious instruction was banned from the public schools, and the control of marriage legislation was reserved to the State. Previously the Church not only had married aspirants to wedlock, but had maintained an elaborate system of marriage counseling and of divorce courts—courts with rules far more lenient than those recognized by either Catholic or conservative Protestant Churches in Western Europe. But the State budget continued to provide for the support of the clergy, and the prosecution of priests and prelates for alleged subversive activities was minimal.

A drastic change took place when the Communist Party assumed complete control during December, 1947, following the return of Georgi Dimitrov from Russia. The Constitution signed on the fourth day of that month dealt with religion in the customary Soviet manner: guaranteeing freedom of conscience and religion, and specifically endorsing freedom of worship; on the other hand, decreeing separation of Church and State, and prohibiting political organizations based on religious belief and political activities by the Churches. During February, 1949, statutes were decreed which outlined in detail the relationship of the Churches to the government. Control over ecclesiastical matters was lodged in the Ministry for Foreign Affairs, which could hold the recognized authorities of each Church responsible. All such authorities had to be Bulgarian citizens, and to register with the Ministry, which might insist upon the removal from office of any clergyman it deemed undesirable. These laws, which subjected the Church to the domination of the State, clearly implied that Orthodoxy was to have an opportunity to qualify as the "people's religion." Note, for example, the language of Section 12:

Clergymen and other officials guilty of violating the laws, public order, or good morals, or of acting in a manner hostile to the democratic institutions of the State, may, over and above other applicable penalties, be provisionally suspended or removed from office on the request of the Minister for Foreign Affairs. Upon receipt of such a request from the Minister for Foreign Affairs, suspension or removal from office shall be effected immediately by the leadership of the respective religious denomination. If the clergyman is not removed by the responsible leadership, he shall be removed by administrative order.

We shall now see how the legislation described was put into effect.

In so far as the Orthodox Church is concerned, the story opens with the removal from office of Exarch Stephan I, who was said to be an overly ambitious prelate bent on skillfully juggling the disparate objects of Communist ideology and Christian tradition. Apparently Church and State agreed on his removal to the small town of Karlovo, the former because it deemed him too dictatorial and the latter because it no longer had any use for him. Ecclesiastical authority was lodged anew in the Holy Synod, which had already learned that the Communists took seriously ordinances abolishing religious marriage, prohibiting the teaching of religion in the schools, banning religious observances from military establishments, and subjecting the public to barrages of irreligious propaganda. Absolute dependence upon the State was associated with absolute surrender of traditional privileges.

It must be noted that the Exarch, during his tenure of office, had sounded almost every note in the scale which Dimitrov may have dreamed of as the ideal music for an ideal Church.

Here is a brief report written by one who was an unhappy eye-witness of the events described:

On the occasion of the anniversary of the October Revolution in Russia, the Exarch addressed a letter to all the Metropolitans in which he glorified the achievements of the Soviet Union. He also spoke glowingly of the role of the Slavic peoples in history. Finally he lauded Czechoslovakia and emphasized the need for very close relationships between Church and State. At about the same time, Marshal Tito visited Bulgaria, and the Exarch sent a telegram to Dimitrov in which he paid homage to the alliance between Bulgaria and Yugoslavia and expressed the hope that these two great peoples would continue to foster mutual assistance. But the message also stressed the role which the Church had played in the history of the two countries. During the summer of 1947 the Exarch paid a visit to Carlsbad as the guest of the Czechoslovak Government, and took the cure there. During his stay he delivered an address in which he praised the Government of the country; and when the time came for him to enter his name in the Golden Book of the City of Prague he expressed gratitude for the honor and paid his respects to the "Slavic ideal and to the contributions it had made to the triumph of peace and justice in the world." He hailed the formation of the Cominform as a step towards the safeguarding of Slavic solidarity.

The Synod which succeeded to the authority of the Exarch was scarcely less supine. Despite the fact that the Communist Party had ordered that courses in dialectical materialism be offered in the seminaries which trained young men for the priesthood, it commemorated the twenty-fifth anniversary of the death of Lenin. It likewise instructed the clergy to accept membership in the Fatherland Front. The situation is illustrated by an émigré from Sofia, who relates that the editor of the principal Orthodox theological journal had approved an article in which the author expounded the thesis that natural science alone could not answer all questions. He was summoned to the Ministry and made to apologize profusely for the aberration. At any rate, the Holy Synod was soon reechoing every banal attack on Anglo-American imperialism and applauding every appeal for the Moscow version of "peace." In the summer of 1949, its official journal expressed regret that the center of Roman Catholicism (the Vatican) and the heartland of Protestantism (the United States) had of their own free will blessed a new war and sung the praises of the atomic bomb.

These various attitudes received final binding expression in the series of resolutions on relations between Church and State which the Holy Synod adopted on September 20, 1948: the clergy were authorized to join pro-Communist organizations and to support the collective farm system; government decrees prohibiting the teaching of religion in the schools were endorsed; all priests were warned not to make any statement from their pulpits which might be considered to be political. The Synod assured the government that it stood ready to cooperate in any measure "for the reform of society in accordance with the principles of liberty, equality, and fraternity." For the seventieth birthday of Stalin it addressed a letter, dated December 12, 1949, to all pastors urging them to conduct Divine services for the welfare of the great Russian leader. It also formally endorsed the peace plea with all its might and main.

Yet all this does not mean that the rank and file of the Bulgarian Orthodox clergy betrayed their faith without a struggle. It took the pro-Communist Union of Orthodox Priests a long while to recruit members. Watched constantly by the security police, removed from office for dissident attitudes, often sent to slave-labor camps, the clergy witnessed with foreboding the working out of policies designed to seduce youth, secularize all welfare activity, and subject all preaching, whether oral or written, to censorship by an uncompromisingly Marxist ideological authority. Eventually only one theological school, at Plovdiv, was permitted to remain open. Two theological journals, one of them the organ of the Communist-dominated Synod, made propaganda at the government's behest. Everyone who gave any indication of fidelity to the Christian creed in its true significance and glory had to reckon with the possibility that he would speedily be sentenced to one of the dreaded prisons—Kolarovgrad, for example—which were always crammed with the unfortunate victims of tyranny.

The Orthodox Church having been transformed into an abject lackey of the State, Communist wrath descended on the religious minorities. Protestants were the first victims. Missionaries had come to Bulgaria from Turkey, and had established schools which, despite wars and upheavals, gave a good education to boys and girls. An exemplary woman introduced the kindergarten system and trained native teachers. By the close of World War I, hostility to Protestants had pretty largely died down; and although the small congregations did not grow rapidly they successfully maintained their identities. Their pride and joy was the American College, situated near Sofia. It was closed by the Nazis in 1942 and has not been reopened. The work of the Y.M.C.A. and the Y.W.C.A. was suppressed at the same time, and the Communist regime has not lifted the prohibition.

The legislation adopted during February, 1949 (often referred to as the Canonical Purity Laws) contained a number of provisions designed to render impossible any religious activity under the auspices of a Church or institution with headquarters outside Bulgaria. It stipulated, for example, that any Church or any clergyman desiring "canonical relations with or aid or gifts from" institutions, organizations, or official personages abroad must secure permission in advance from the Ministry for Foreign Affairs. It was presumably under this legislation that fifteen Protestant pastors were brought to trial for high treason during 1949. It was the first large-scale action against Protestants in any satellite country, though to be sure Protestant Churches had suffered grievously in Czechoslovakia, Hungary, and Poland. The pastors, none of whom had occupied a position of eminence, were confronted with a lengthy list of charges. In particular they had, the Public Prosecutor contended, given military, economic, and political information to representatives of hostile foreign powers. They were also accused of having "spread malicious rumors about Russia." Those indicted—the Reverend Basil Ziapkov, for example—made confessions of the length desired and pleaded for mercy. The Court pronounced sentences of varying severity.

Manifestly this trial was also a blow struck at the prestige of the United States, from which most of the support for the Protestant congregations had come. Its primary effect was, no doubt, that the curtain was rung down on any hopes Bulgarian citizens might have that diplomatic intervention by the West would blunt the edge of the Soviet sickle, or that Washington could defend the interests of Americans in regions under Russian domination. How complete the resulting loss of morale was can be deduced from the official statements issued by the other Churches on the subject of the ordeal to which Protestantism had been subjected. The Holy Synod of the Orthodox Church declared, for example:

In accordance with our Church's traditional solicitude for fostering the aspirations of the people and maintaining loyalty to the State, the Holy Synod has always exhorted its clergy to look upon themselves as preachers of the Divine Word and as guardians of the Holy Spirit, and to remain aloof from all political influences hostile to the country and its people. We must add that the pastors of the Holy Orthodox Church have consistently obeyed our admonition. Not one of them has been prosecuted by the authorities on account of religious activities.

The Holy Synod strongly condemns all subversive activities carried on by the faithful, all actions detrimental to our People's Republic, and anything which may threaten the independence and liberty of our people. And we condemn such things even more strongly when they are carried on by those who profess other creeds.

The statements made by the Catholic bishops, both of the Latin and of the Greek rite, contained professions of loyalty to the government but did not comment on the trial of their Protestant brethren.

The Catholic Church wielded an influence in Bulgaria which was wholly disproportionate to its size. Fewer than ten persons in a thousand professed to belong to this Church, which of course was also hampered by the division according to the two rites. But Catholics had played a stirring part in the struggle for liberation from Turkish rule, and so their heroes were eminent in the nation's song and story. Educational institutions created and developed by members of religious orders were likewise held in high esteem, and many of the graduates were prominent in the civil service and the professions. These institutions have been nationalized, and the Church itself is circumscribed by the laws affecting religion. During 1949, the Catholic Bishops acceded to the government's request and sent a message to the United Nations affirming the existence of religious freedom in Bulgaria. Subsequently the lot of both clergy and laity grew steadily worse; but the first spectacular and drastic action taken against the Church was the arrest of a bishop, more than a score of priests, and a number of laymen, on the usual charge of conspiring with a hostile foreign power. The Bishop and three priests were sentenced to death for high treason, and twenty-four priests and twelve laymen received prison sentences. Therewith an almost mortal blow was struck at the life and organized activity of the Church.*

* Most of the more than half a million Mohammedans in Bulgaria were of Turkish descent. During 1950 the government began deporting them to Turkey,

One may therefore summarize by saying that there has been virtually no religious struggle in Bulgaria, even though the victims are not few in number. This does not mean that all has been tranquil and serene. Georgi Dimitrov was not a man to give that sort of content to the word "peace." Nowhere have the Russians shown greater ruthlessness in carrying out the policies to which Leninism-Stalinism is committed. Marxist theorists consider the independent farmer as the greatest obstacle to social progress. They think it inevitable that industry should spawn the proletarian worker, and hold this worker to be at one and the same time a carrier of the Marxist virus and a member of the class majority in whose hands collective power over productive properties collectively owned and managed properly belongs. Accordingly there is only one way in which to speed arrival at the Communist goal, defined by Marx in the first volume of *Das Kapital*. The agricultural operation must be collectivized, so that eventually all tillers of the soil will cease to be owners of property and will work instead for the State. On this belief has been based the otherwise curious and paradoxical procedure of the Communists in Eastern Europe. In countries containing large estates, the Land Reform method is used to break them up and to parcel out small holdings; but as soon as this has been done the process is reversed, and the peasant owners are squeezed until they can only surrender their land for the organization of a "cooperative."

Therefore Bulgaria was almost made to order for Communist experimentation. Nearly four-fifths of the population earned a living by the soil; and, though after the First World

---

and now the number of Mohammedans expelled is in excess of 150,000. Moslem religious activities are, as a matter of course, subject to the existing laws concerning religion. Turkey has therewith been faced with a grave problem of refugee resettlement, and reliable reports indicate that she has dealt with it skillfully. Refugees are receiving farm lands in Anatolia, which has been sparsely populated. Naturally there need be no fear of Communist infiltration.

War a program of cooperative farming was inaugurated on a voluntary membership basis, the vast majority of farmers were small landowners of the type which once was so characteristic of the Ukraine. As early as August, 1945, the first of a series of decrees was promulgated, to liquidate the hated kulak and incorporate him into the kolkhoz, or State farm, system. At the same time a blueprint of industrialization was drawn, on the basis of the familiar Two- and Five-Year Plans. The blueprint required first of all cheap compulsory labor in quantity. The published legislation outlines the methods by which that labor force was to be obtained. The police received authority "to commit to communities for educational labor, or to a new place of residence, persons guilty of fascist or antidemocratic manifestations." It was also decreed, soon after the seizure of power, that many hundreds of thousands of persons should be "sent to the factories or shifted to industry." On none of these matters was any effort made to maintain secrecy.

Soon dams and electric power plants were being constructed in various parts of the country. The exploitation of Bulgaria's very modest coal deposits was greatly intensified. In order to supply the needed labor force, concentration camps were erected in a surprising variety of places. One of the better known is that at Belene, the inmates of which work at digging canals. Here are cooped up many prominent Bulgarian intellectuals, businessmen, and officers of divers political organizations once opposed to Communism. The Communists themselves have advertised widely this camp, where, it is estimated, 9,000 persons are interned under the most primitive penal conditions. If the accounts of prisoners who have escaped from it are to be credited (and there is no reason why they should not be), it is in all truth an infamous place. The methods of committing people to it have been spelled out in carefully devised legislation, which makes no provision for haling anyone before a court for trial and sentence. The Law on Labor Mobilization of Idlers and Vagrants, originally enacted on April 30, 1946, and subsequently amended announced:

Section 1. All Bulgarian nationals of both sexes, between 16 and 50 years of age [45 for women], fit for work but who have taken to idling and vagrancy or who spend most of their time in saloons, coffee shops, bars, pastry shops, and the like, shall be mobilized for compulsory labor.

Section 2. The purpose of the labor mobilization shall be to make the draftees accustomed to useful work, to develop in them a love of socially useful labor, to eradicate their bad habits, and at the same time to utilize their physical energies and their intellectual endowments for the increase of the population and the welfare of the country.

Section 3. The labor of the draftees shall be used on projects of general usefulness, such as road construction, railroad tracks, canals, dams, buildings, levees, river constructions, tillage of government or public farms, work in mines, quarries, factories, workshops and the like, according to the sex and age of the draftees.

The lot of the "draftees" in such camps as those in the Dobrudja, Bulgaria's most fertile area, has been described by persons who have escaped. A typical camp is that for women near the city of Tutrakan. It is a network of primitive barracks in each of which are to be found two rows of wooden bunks, each row in three tiers. The prisoners work on a large State-owned farm. The camp director gives the assignments. For example, the prisoner may be told to dig up such and such an acreage of sugar beets, or to spade a specified amount of soil in preparation for the planting of paprika. The daily wage is 900 grams of black bread. Failure to complete the task causes the ration to be diminished. As a rule each inmate works eleven hours a day. At ten P.M. there is a roll call, after which each prisoner solemnly promises to do everything she possibly can "for the building up of the People's Republic of Bulgaria."

There is an austere puritanical fanaticism about the regulations which is difficult for an American, inured to doing what he pleases, to comprehend.

Virtually all potential foes of the Communist regime in Bulgaria have been sent to such camps, which means that any person who deviates in the slightest degree from the established Communist norm invites the public prosecutor to get on with incarcerating him. It is difficult to believe that the system is as far-flung and well established as it is; but the Communist authorities themselves have made available a substantial amount of information on its extent. There are at least thirty slave-labor camps in Bulgaria, and it has been estimated that at least 500,000 persons have been confined in them during the seven years of Communist rule. Among the inmates have been whole families—men, women, and children. Before we condemn the Bulgarian Churches for cowardly behavior it may be well to ask what we ourselves might have done in the circumstances.

II

Rumania was not fully subordinated to the Communist Party until the close of 1947. On the eve of the invasion of the country, which had been the only one to lend full support to the Nazi cause, young King Michael overthrew the Iron Front government and its strong man, General Antonescu, by a *coup d'état*. The new Government, in which a general also served as Premier, accepted the terms of armistice. Nevertheless by March 6, 1945, the Communists were unmistakably in control, although a fellow traveler, Dr. Petru Groza, was selected to head a government in which they had the upper hand. At the Potsdam Conference the United States, Great Britain, and Russia agreed to sign a treaty of peace with Rumania as soon as a government should be formed which was "broadly representative of all democratic elements of the population." Later, at the Moscow Conference, the Western powers declared that they would believe such a government existed as soon as representatives of two political parties other than the Rumanian Workers' Party had been named to ministerial posts, and as soon as satisfactory guarantees had been given that freedom of speech and assembly as well as the right to vote without constraint had been assured. Dr. Groza complied by appointing the two desired ministers to the Cabinet without portfolio and by announcing that free elections would be held soon; but, as was to be anticipated in view of the fact that the Russian Army held the country in an iron grip, the Rumanian Workers' Party received 90-odd per cent of the vote. The ministers without portfolio promptly resigned, and there was nothing the Western powers could do about it save to register an emphatic protest. This they did in language suitably designed for the occasion.

The elections referred to were held on November 19, 1946. Almost precisely a year later the leader of the principal opposition party, Dr. Juliu Maniu, was sentenced to life imprisonment for high treason. Unquestionably this able and farsighted man, who had served the government and the people of Rumania well over many years and had been identified with every movement for reform and justice, was the foremost of the nation's citizens. King Michael abdicated on December 30 of the same year and fled from his native land. Thereupon the "People's Republic" was proclaimed, and every source of potential opposition to it was ferreted out and suppressed. A Constitution of the usual kind was adopted on April 13, 1948. Now no obstacle barred the way for putting the Soviet paradise plan into effect. The principal productive enterprises were declared the property of the State, and this likewise became the sole arbiter of the educational system. Collective farming was introduced. A novelty was that new elections were held during

December, 1950. As a matter of course, only one party appeared on the ballot. Some 80,000 persons appointed to local soviets were duly elected.

One of the distinguishing characteristics of this "uprising of the proletariat" was the extreme paucity of Communists. Another was the fact that the population had no democratic tradition to fall back upon. The country had lived under a fascist type of dictatorship without sensing that it had been very differently treated than it would no doubt have been under a liberal regime. When the war was over, most of Antonescu's Iron Men simply transformed themselves into a different metal. We may say without hesitation that opportunism and not conviction made Rumania's transition to Sovietism so absurdly simple. Nobody had believed it possible that a man like Dr. Maniu could be clapped into jail, brought before the courts on a trumped-up charge, and sentenced. But the People's Democracy managed even that, and it was small wonder that the average citizen began to think earnestly about his own throat.

As we ponder the evil fortunes which lay ahead for religious confessions in Rumania, it is helpful to bear in mind that this country, the easternmost colony of the Roman Empire, learned to know Christianity as early as the second century of the present era. Congregations formed there were represented at some of the earliest councils of the Church. Subsequently, after wars and invasions had run their course, the Rumanian ecclesiastical establishment was affiliated with the Eastern, or Byzantine, Patriarchate. As a result Greek Orthodoxy became the confession to which the great majority of the people subscribed after the independence of the nation had been achieved in 1878. The Church thus established occupied a position in the life of the country which was not unlike that of the Orthodox Church in Bulgaria. The clergy participated in the official affairs of the nation. In general, exception having been duly made for the Jews, the Orthodox Church dealt with other confessions in an irenic manner.

Rumania profited greatly if temporarily from its sponsorship of the Allied cause during World War I. Territories were assigned to it which had traditionally belonged to Bulgaria, Hungary, and Russia, presenting the government with a number of problems with which it had not previously been concerned. Transylvania, taken from Hungary, had a population divided almost equally between Roman Catholics and Protestants. The Russian Orthodox Church was predominant in Bessarabia, once deeded to the Czar by the West. The Rumanians dealt with the situation in a manner both intelligent and conciliatory. After the favored status of the Greek Orthodox Church had been defined, laws regulating the Confessions were passed during April, 1928. They carefully safeguarded the rights of the State and specifically forbade clergymen to embark on seas of foreign policy of their own charting, but acknowledged the right of the Churches to give religious instruction in public and private schools, and to conduct charitable enterprises. The government also signed a Concordat with the Holy See in 1927, with which the Vatican had no reason to be dissatisfied.

The Concordat conceded to the Catholic Church in all its branches, regular and secular, a large measure of legal protection. Stipulating that ecclesiastical properties must be used for the benefit of Rumanian citizens, and that the income therefrom was subject to audit by the government, it authorized the Church to create a "Sacred Diocesan Fund" to be administered by the Hierarchy. It also promised to add to the Fund if this proved to be inadequate to meet the expenses of necessity incurred by religious foundations. The Catholic clergy were asked to take an oath of allegiance to the King, to the Constitution, and to the laws of the nation. The government agreed not to intervene to secure the appointment of clergymen, but requested that it be informed in each instance. These laws were modified under the rule of the Iron Front, in order to make possible the persecution of the Jews. Christian communions appear, however, not to have been affected.

When a pro-Communist government was formed in Rumania, the situation changed immediately and radically. The laws adopted in 1928 were repealed by a decree of August 4, 1948. As usual in Soviet-inspired constitutions, freedom of conscience, of religion, and of worship was assured. Freedom was conceded to all creeds to organize and conduct their own ecclesiastical endeavors so long as they did nothing to jeopardize "public security and public order." The last proviso was, as always, the Trojan horse by means of which the conquerors would enter the citadel. For what were public security and order? The government reserved the right to determine; and in this case the "government" was and could only be the local soviet under which a poor cleric was to live and move and have his being. As a matter of fact, the system under which the Rumanian Communist Party functioned was simplicity itself. The list of electors registered in 1946 was kept up to date by striking off the names of all who had in some manner or other manifested hostility to the "people." The possessor of a name thus purged might retain the right to worship wherever he pleased, but was of course deprived of any opportunity to draw a salary from the State or to hold a position of public trust.

Indeed, the law went much further. Article 25 provided that

the Ministry of Religious Affairs shall suspend any decision, instruction, or directive, as well as any order having an ecclesiastical character, whether administrative, cultural, educational, or caritative, or pertaining to endowments, if it is not in keeping with the status of the denomination in the act by which it has been established, or is inimical to public security, public order or morals. Pastoral and circular letters shall be communicated in advance of publication to the Ministry of Religious Affairs.

While thus making apparent that the Church was deprived of all liberty of action in areas of moral judgment concerning actions taken by the public authority, the law further stipulated that the salaries of "clergymen and officers of the religious denominations" would be paid in accordance with the regulations governing the civil service. In this fashion it was determined that all clergymen, on the one hand, had the rights accorded to the civil service but, on the other, assumed corresponding obligations—among them an oath of allegiance to the national Constitution.

Subsequently, on August 12, 1950, a decree dealing with the security of the State imposed the death penalty for the following offenses: treason to the nation; rendering "service to the enemy, or causing prejudice to the power of the state"; and procuring or transmitting state secrets to a foreign or an enemy power. The decree was directed primarily against the dignitaries of the Roman Catholic Church, because they were in communion with Rome. On July 6, 1950, another decree had provided a basis for expelling from Rumania the Papal Nuncio, Archbiship O'Hara, and his two assistants, Monsignor Kirk and Monsignor Del Mesti. Most of the Rumanian members of the Nuncio's staff were sentenced to imprisonment. Therewith an initial climax was reached in two years of fierce attack on the Churches and on the Roman Catholic Church in particular.

At this point a more detailed review of the religious situation in Rumania may help to clarify what has happened. Prior to the outbreak of the Second World War, the 70 per cent of Rumanians adhering to the Orthodox Church were affiliated with the Patriarchate of Constantinople but enjoyed ecclesiastical autonomy. This Church, directed by a Holy Synod pre-

sided over by a Patriarch, had 7,833 parishes, fifty-seven religious foundations for men, and twenty-six similar foundations for women. The two Churches in union with Rome served
some 3,000,000 persons, slightly more than half of whom practiced according to the Greek rite. Catholics following the Latin
rite had fifty-seven religious foundations for men, and eighty-
one for women. Those of the Greek rite (usually termed, as we
have seen, Uniates) had seven foundations for men, and five
for women. Such statistics indicate that the Latin branch, in
which the clergy are bound by the law of celibacy, manifested
far more interest in monasticism, though the number of parishes available to them (638 in number) was much smaller
than the number of those which served Catholics professing the
Greek rite. It is therefore evident that any attempt to suppress
the religious orders would strike at a vital nerve of Catholic
life. Protestants were somewhat fewer than 6 per cent of the
population, and the Jews were about the same. One may also
note that Protestants were almost equally divided between
Lutherans and Calvinists, the first being ethnic Germans and
the second ethnic Hungarians residing in territories taken from
Hungary at the close of the First World War.

In outward appearances, the position of the Orthodox
Church was not greatly affected by the Communist seizure of
power. It is true that changes in the pertinent legislation gave
the government, and therewith of course the Communist Party,
control over all nominations and elections to Church offices.
This meant that all those who exercised authority would come
to be snugly tucked under the thumb of the Party. The most
notable illustration in Rumania is the Patriarch Justinian, who
has not hesitated to declare that the Christian Gospel has much
in common with the doctrines of Marx and Lenin. It is hardly
necessary to inquire how and why a prelate of his character
acquired rank and station. The Orthodox Church was by no

means abject or corrupt; but the tradition of ecclesiastical elections to which it subscribed provided the Communists with a golden opportunity of which they took full advantage.

To make clear the situation in which the clergy of the Orthodox Church have found themselves, a report by an eyewitness who has escaped from Rumania may be cited. On October 30, 1950, the clergy met in conference. A huge portrait of Dimitrov adorned the assembly room. No symbol of religion was anywhere to be seen. The Minister of Culture spoke concerning the relations between Church and State. He attacked the spirit of opposition which, he contended, still flourished in some sections of the clergy. A priest, he said, had reported that obedience to Georgi Dimitrov was out of the question because he might very well command that the cross be removed from the tower of the cathedral in order to make room for the half-moon. Thereupon the assembled clergymen were called upon to give a rousing cheer for Dimitrov. Later, the question rose whether the editor of the principal Church journal should be elected or appointed. Some one objected that if election were abandoned the editor might conceivably prove to be a man wholly without faith. When the matter was put to a vote only twenty clergymen expressed a preference for appointment. Nevertheless the chairman announced that a substantial majority favored this method. One priest arose and said, "It is obvious that dictatorial methods are being employed here." No one else ventured to interpose an objection.

Having taken the Orthodox Church in tow in this manner, the Communists began to bring pressure on Catholics professing the Greek rite to secede from the Holy See and to embrace Orthodoxy. Short shrift, indeed, was made of sundry legal scruples. The heavy hand of suppression was felt almost immediately. Bishops were arrested and sent to labor camps. A decree of December 2, 1948, stated tersely and bluntly: "Subsequent to the reverting of the Greek Catholic parishes to the Rumanian Orthodox Church, and in conformity with Article 13 of Decree 177/1948, its central organization . . . shall cease to exist." All properties belonging to this Church were transferred either to the State or to the Orthodox Synod. The subsequent martyrdom of the Greek clergy rivaled the witnessing of early Christian days. All the bishops were arrested for deportation, and two, Monsignor Vasile Aftenie and Monsignor Valeriu Frentiu, are known to have died in prison. Courageous members of the lower clergy are reported to have gone into hiding in order to minister secretly to the faithful. According to persons who fled the country, such priests were hunted down as ruthlessly as the clergy of southern France in the days of Danton and Robespierre.

Therewith the time had also come to attempt the liquidation of Catholics who worshiped according to the Latin rite. Their Church was the only one which had not expressed complete satisfaction with the state of religious freedom in Rumania on June 24, 1949. The first important and ominous debate between the government and the Catholic Bishops had begun in the summer of 1948, when they stated in answer to an inquiry that it would not be possible for them to repudiate the Primacy of the Holy See. The Minister of Culture replied that he entertained no objection to an understanding with Rome on dogma, although such discussions were necessarily subject to the scrutiny of the Ministries of Culture and Foreign Affairs, but that any other kind of dependence on the Papacy was illegal. When the Hierarchy failed to concur, the government launched against it a press campaign of the greatest vehemence, which made it very evident that the goal set was the absorption into a "National Church" of Catholics who worshiped according to the Latin rite. Such a goal has always been envisaged whenever

Communists gained control of a satellite country; but in Rumania it could be attained with relative ease.

The first blow was struck in July, 1948, when the Concordat with the Holy See was revoked. Other decrees subordinating the Church to the State were passed soon thereafter. The Catholic Bishops manifested heroic valor and steadfastness. When their schools were expropriated, their caritative enterprises forbidden, their press closed down, and their religious orders suppressed, they protested. It did not seem meet and just to them that children should be prevented from coming to church, faithful men and women carted off to labor camps on trumped-up charges, or that loud-speakers should blare from one end of the day to the other accusatory comments which were in essence monstrous blasphemies. Our time has grown accustomed to thinking that only patriotic feeling, only the sense of solidarity with the nation to which we belong, can engender the resolution to make every sacrifice that becomes necessary. Therefore the spectacle of a few elderly men who accept every scourge of tyranny with patience because the Lord Jesus has willed that they do so has for us a quality which transcends fortitude—a quality which is the ultimate secret aura of what men for thousands of years have called freedom of conscience. This freedom, perhaps more than any other, is the counterpart of obedience—*usque ad mortem,* even to the death, as the Catholic liturgy says over and over.

Here is just one quotation, from a letter addressed by the Bishops to the President of the People's Republic:

We believe, Your Excellency, that the moment has come when we should no longer keep silence by reason of patriotic considerations, but should rather give expression to our sorrow. The measures which have been taken by the Government are extremely injurious to the welfare of the citizens of the Rumanian People's Republic. Nor should we abstain from making an emphatic protest against what has taken place in so far as the Catholic Church in Rumania is concerned. We must rather manifest our profound indignation. Millions of citizens have been deliberately wounded in the innermost core of their human feeling by the very authority to which there has been entrusted, in the presence of the nation and of the whole world, the defense of the interests of the people. Internecine strife is being fostered, the country is in tears over rampant injustice, and a wound gapes which cannot be healed over except by doing away with laws and measures which have struck and are now striking at the Catholic Church in the Rumanian People's Republic.

All the Bishops who signed this and similar fruitless appeals have since been sentenced. The initial blow was struck at all dioceses save those of Alba Iulia and Iasi. In June, 1949, the Bishops of these sees also were arrested on charges of high treason. There remained only Bishop Augustin Pacha, more than eighty years old, who in turn was found guilty and sentenced to forced labor. Some of the prelates are said to have been deported to Russia; and of the whereabouts of nearly all of them nothing definite is known. Thus the Roman Catholic Church was stripped of leadership, the government recognizing only the Vicars-general of two dioceses in Transylvania. These likewise refused to conform with Communist directives. Thereupon a ruthless assault on the lower clergy was inaugurated. On the basis of reports received by the Vatican, it is estimated that at least six hundred priests and religious have been arrested, tried, and sentenced. Thus there was made manifest exemplary and moving fidelity.

That some would prove less steadfast was to be anticipated, and in due time the government found a man willing to be the leader of a "National Church"—Andreas Agotha, an unfortunate priest whom the Holy See promptly excommunicated. Under him a congress was convened at Targul-Mures, on April 27, 1950, which created the "National Catholic Church," urged the clergy to support the Stockholm Peace Resolution, and endorsed the formation of a "Catholic Committee of Action" to support the policies of the "People's Republic." The participants were few, and one of the Vicars-general still in office ordered the clergy of the diocese of Iasi to read a declaration denouncing the congress. He was promptly arrested and has died in prison. A second congress convened at Gherghani five months later, after an appeal by Agotha to all "peace-loving" priests and faithful. Months of open persecution and of strenuous pro-government campaigning followed. Under the protection of the government, the "Rumanian National Catholic Church" convened at Cluj on March 14, 1951, and took over the administration of all Roman Catholic establishments. Some 225 clerical and lay delegates attended and set up a "Council" of 27 members which declared its readiness to cooperate with the government in every manner desired. Delegates who approved of this capitulation received salaries and other benefits. Those who resisted were hounded down and imprisoned.

Meanwhile, under a decree of August 1, 1949, action was taken against religious orders and communities. Five convents and monasteries were designated as the places in which all monks and nuns doing educational or welfare work should live in accordance with rules laid down by the Minister of Culture. Once there were as many as 1,800 nuns in Rumania. Virtually all have returned to their families or are active as isolated parish workers. The majority of the monks are in prison. It is safe to say that by the close of 1950 the Roman Catholic Church was a flock dispersed, without shepherds, harried by the secret police and exposed to the constant threat of enslavement in forced-labor camps. Sometimes the actions taken against the surviving faithful have a flavor which is not only bitter but melodramatic and grimly ludicrous. Thus a priest was sentenced to a prison term for referring in a sermon to the destruction of Jerusalem by the Emperor Titus—which was deemed to be a cryptic reference to Marshal Tito. More generally every device of propaganda and repression is used to curtail the influence of religion. Popular religious festivals are forbidden, electric power failures interfere with the work of well frequented parishes, and frequenting the Sacraments makes a man subject to investigation.

The chronicle of the Church which worships according to the Greek rite is quite as harrowing. On October 1, 1948, the government announced that the 1,500,000 persons loyal to this Church had been summarily turned over to Orthodoxy. This action followed a campaign of vilification and suppression rare even in the annals of Communism. It is described in part in a letter signed jointly by the Greek Catholic Bishops at the time:

During this campaign [i.e., during the week following September 26, 1948] Iuliu Hossu, Bishop of Cluj, was confined to his residence, so that he could not communicate with the Uniate clergy or in any way protest against the actions to which our Church was subjected. In Cluj all priests and layfolk who ventured to disregard the measures taken against the Bishop, and who came to call on him, were arrested. In like manner all those who witnessed his arrest were taken into custody. Moreover Bishop Suciu of Blajm was arrested by the Security Police just as he was leaving the Church at Copacel, which he had just consecrated. He was taken to an unknown destination and kept in a cave during two days, so that he could be prevented from getting in touch with the clergy and the faithful. . . .

We think that prudence suggests that we do not at this time enumerate all the abuses and acts of violence of which the clergy, the priests and archpriests, have been made the victims in an endeavor to obtain their signatures. They were warned and threatened, as Bishop Suciu also was, to remain silent concerning everything that had happened.

These appeals were naturally of no avail. The government prepared to convene a "Congress" at Cluj which would ratify union with the Orthodox establishment. The meeting was held on October 1, 1948, and the thirty-eight canons, prelates, and priests who had been "elected" to represent the Church did as they were ordered to do. The government press reported that they had approved "unanimously and with great enthusiasm" union with the Orthodox Church and "the definitive severance of ties with Papal Rome." On December 2, 1948, still another decree transferred all the property of the Uniate Church to the Rumanian State without compensation. Much of it was subsequently turned over to the Orthodox Church. All the Bishops have been jailed or have disappeared. It is known that two, Vasile Aftenie and Valeriu Frentiu, have died in prison. The Pastoral Letter signed by the Episcopacy on June 29, 1948 (The Feast of Saints Peter and Paul), is surely one of the most touching and spiritually stirring of the documents which chronicle the persecution of the Church by the Communists. After summarizing the reasons why the Uniates had acknowledged the supremacy of the See of Peter, recalling the sufferings which had been borne by past generations for the sake of unity with Rome, and dealing with the present controversies, the Letter said:

We must suffer for the Gospels of our Redemption in order to possess the merit of having for our part met the test, just as our fathers did as, looking upon the Rood of the Lord, they heard in their hearts these words: *Dico enim vobis: Omnis quicumque confessus fuerit me coram hominibus, et Filius hominis confitebitur illum coram angelis Dei; Qui autem negaverit me coram hominibus, negabitur coram angelis Dei.**

The ties which bind us to the Pope, the Bishop of Rome, are not of human making but are of Divine origin; and it is our duty to bear

* The passage cited is from the twelfth chapter of the Gospel according to St. Luke and reads in translation: "And I say to you, whosoever shall confess me before men, him shall the Son of man also confess before the angels of God. But he that shall deny me before men, shall be denied before the angels of God."

by reason of them outrage and blows and threats and imprisonment and, it may be, destitution. These things truly mean glorifying the Lord Jesus. They will prove that we desire to insure for ourselves, even in this day of passing suffering, an eternal meed of renown which will be beyond weight or measure.

The men who signed this Letter all have witnessed to the faith they thus professed. And in their company stand devoid of eloquence but not of holiness and fidelity, the many, many thousands, chosen from amidst the humble and the poor, who have suffered persecution and enslavement in Vhalitza or in the region between the Danube and the Black Sea. In order that we may understand their ordeal, let me quote from eye-witness accounts of the camps built to house those who toil at digging a canal in the Dobrouja:

Approximately 30,000 prisoners are stationed there. The majority of them are intellectuals. They are digging a canal between the Danube and the Black Sea, or are building roads, bridges, and so forth. Practically all the work is done by hand in the same manner and with the same methods as those which were employed for the erection of the Egyptian pyramids. The food is very poor. As a rule, the daily menu consists of corn meal with a soup made of onions or beans. The sanitary conditions are indescribable, and for this reason the death toll is extremely high. Prisoners work more than twelve hours a day. Some of them were sentenced by the courts. Others were not. But this makes no difference, for even those who did receive sentences are not released when their terms are over.

The Uniate Churches are not among the great religious bodies of the world. But we might well pause in reverence while passing their temples of worship to commemorate those who in far-off countries have so nobly and sacrificially clung to their faith. Such a tribute would by no means preclude one from bearing in mind that others, too, have felt the crushing weight of Rumanian tyranny—Lutherans, Armenians, and Moslems among them.

All the news which has trickled out of Rumania during recent years merely indicates that the trends thus established continue. The Patriarch Justinian and the Holy Synod subservient to him tirelessly echo Soviet propaganda in every form. Thus they released, on April 3, 1952, a violent attack on the use of biological warfare in Korea, which reads in part as follows:

After the savage destruction of towns and villages, hospitals and schools, monuments of art and places of worship, the enemies of mankind, greedy for world domination, dropped huge quantities of insects, bearers of death by plague, cholera, typhus and other frightful diseases on the territory of the Korean Democratic People's Republic and a part of Northern China.

The indignation of the faithful is all the greater because recourse to this weapon, which not even the Fascists dared to employ, is the most odious infringement of the rules of international law, and the most criminal assault upon humanity. . . .

As worshipers of the Creator of life and not of death, the servants of the Lord of Peace and not of enmity, we demand the immediate prohibition of bacteriological warfare, which we condemn with all our vigor as a weapon which devastates the earth.

This same Patriarch has supported every Communist maneuver with the most abject servility since early in 1950. Then, at his behest, the Orthodox Church officially joined the National Rumanian Committee for the Defense of Peace, and organized more than 8,000 local committees "to explain to the faithful the problems of the partisan peace movement." He did everything possible to drum up support for the Stockholm Peace Plea, and his attacks on the Anglo-American warmongers and imperialists are legion.

Meanwhile the effort to promote the Communist view of

life through the schools and the youth organizations continues unabated. It has often been pointed out that this program of indoctrination has three aspects. The first is a compendium of all the arguments against religious belief which have been formulated by psychologists, sociologists, and anthropologists in many countries. On the one hand, the compendium joins forces with Marx by viewing religions as derivatives from the class struggles of the past. On the other hand, it reflects a pseudo-Nietzschean quest for a new morality. The second aspect is the identification of religion with "capitalism," the most detested of all enemies, and the contention that the Churches are mere pious instrumentalities through which the "warmongers" rouse the masses to hatred of "democracy." On this level the Communists seek to identify their view of life with "peace," and thus to confuse persons who have been taught to consider Christianity as the Gospel of Love. The third aspect is one which also characterized Nazism. The Christian Churches, the Roman Catholic in particular, are described as sappers of the virility of mankind, prevented by yearning for eternal bliss from getting the necessary work done on this earth. By comparison the Stalinist-Leninist doctrines are described as the sole ideological foundations on which society can rest.

There is nothing anyone resident there can do about this tidal wave of propaganda save to endure it in silence.

9 JEWRY UNDER SOVIET RULE

WHAT HAS BEEN THE fate of the Jew under Soviet rule? It is not easy to answer. Not a few gullible souls, influenced by the *Protocols of the Fathers of Zion* and similar products of a riotous imagination, have believed that Communism is the creation of conspiratorial Jews. On the other hand the legend that the Soviets had suppressed anti-Semitism and were, in fact, the supreme advocates of racial tolerance persisted during more than twenty years. This fiction was specially attractive during the period of Nazi rule, when Stalin the foe of race prejudice could be opposed to Hitler the instigator of the greatest pogrom in history. Spokesmen for the Communist Party, often at a loss for arguments to support praise of any other aspect of the Soviet system, could always elicit approval of this achievement. The consequences were curious and pernicious. Perhaps no group in the Western World has been as vigorous and persistent in its hostility to Communism as the band of survivors of the Russian Jewish *Bund,* who carried their memories of brutality and stupidity into exile. Yet they could not prevail against one of the most deeply rooted of Western illusions.

It is true that the anti-Semitism of Czarist times was banned from official Soviet literature, and that Lenin in particular condemned it. But the underlying causes remained and were indeed intensified by the social phenomena which attended the Revolution. In the older Russia the overwhelming majority of Jewish communities sprang up in the West, notably in the Ukraine and White Russia; but the First World War brought German invasion to these provinces, so that many Jews appear to have migrated eastward together with other segments of the population. This migration was primarily one of artisans, traders, and white-collar workers. Considerably more literate than their neighbors and for obvious reasons far less attached to the Imperial regime, Jews frequently displaced Czarist civil servants and so helped to tide over many an anxious moment in the early history of Bolshevism. Less frequently they rose to positions of power within the Party. Coreligionists who were not so fortunate suffered as a result, because the rigors, deprivations, and cruelties of the new government were often attributed to them. Serious waves of anti-Semitism were set in motion, even while the economic and religious dislocations caused by the new order of things meant ruin and death to large numbers who clung to the traditional beliefs and ways of life. Exception having duly been made for the small number who were snugly cabined on the Soviet ship, the lot of the Jews in Russia during the twenties was perhaps even worse than that of the rest of the population.

One reason why this was so happens to be the Zionist Movement, which at the outbreak of the First World War probably had more followers in Russia than in any other country. This movement gave the Jewish minority, poverty-stricken, despised, and beset with pogroms, a goal towards which to work in solidarity.* But to both Lenin and Stalin a "Jewish national

* Dr. Carl Dienstmann, former German diplomat, reported in the *Frankfurter Allgemeine Zeitung*, March 19, 1953, that notions still prevalent that Soviet

consciousness" was as unthinkable a mirage as eternal salvation is to a modern naturalistic philosopher. For what was, in
their view, the Jewish nation? The answer given by the foremost devisers of Bolshevist theory was that it could only be an
escape mechanism resorted to by "bourgeois" elements who
resisted being absorbed into the working proletariat. Zionism
was therefore curbed in every manner which suggested itself
to the Communist hierarchy. The study of Hebrew in particular
was frowned upon, and as early as 1919 schools teaching this
counterrevolutionary language were closed. It was asserted
that Hebrew was an obstacle to assimilation. Later in the
twenties, the establishment of a Jewish State in Palestine was
looked upon as a major goal of British imperialism, and therefore a product of despicable reaction.

A later writer, Alfred A. Skerpan, has reported the discovery of a "small book" by M. Shakhnovich, entitled *Komu
Sluzhit "Religiya Izrailya"?* (Whom Does the "Religion of Israel" Serve?), issued at Leningrad in two editions in 1929 and
1930.* This brochure, I may add, incorporates declarations

Russia had not instigated persecutions of Jews were erroneous: "During the years
between 1926 and 1928 I was Consul in Odessa. This was the time in which the
concept of the protection of the rights of minorities was fostered in the Soviet
Union too, and gave rise to the foundation of minority enclaves in the form of
autonomous republics and areas. The numerically strong Jewish population in-
dulged in the hope that the District of Odessa could become such an enclave
and made propaganda to that end. These wishes were ended as if by lightning
when the GPU undertook arrests on a vast scale. Several hundred Jews were
taken into custody during a single night, and by administrative decision were
deported to Siberia. It was believed that the Odessa movement had its origins
in Zionism, which sought to make Odessa an outpost of Jerusalem. The local
leaders of Zionism were without exception included among those arrested. The
idea of a Jewish enclave was therewith made politically dangerous and was not
alluded to again. Somewhat later the government established Birobidjan as a
substitute enclave for Odessa."

* See Skerpan's article "Aspects of Soviet Antisemitism," *Antioch Review*,
Vol. XII, pp. 287–328 (Fall, 1952). This is one of the most fully documented
essays on the subject which have appeared to date. Skerpan also says (p. 301):
"The enemy of the workers, Lenin had stressed, was not the Jewish *worker*, but
rich Jews, like the rich Russians and the rich of all countries; 'the Jewish worker

that were reported at the time to the *Commonweal* by Jewish observers who had studied developments in Russia. The religion of the Old Testament, according to Shakhnovich, was primarily a series of recipes for accumulating wealth on earth. He held common people, especially workers, in contempt and regarded the rabbis as spokesmen for the predatory bourgeoisie. Indeed, it would be difficult to find in the armory of Nazism any shafts capable of direction against the Jews which are more virulent than those poisoned by Shakhnovich. Perhaps Hitlerites like Rosenberg had read and utilized this little book. Synagogues were called hotbeds of reaction. We may note that while the Russian Government termed anti-Semitism a crime in the Penal Code adopted in 1926, it had outlawed Zionism six years earlier.

During the Second World War, the attack on Judaism subsided as did the expression of hostility toward the Orthodox Church. Yet this era of good will was preceded, it should be recalled, by the purges which cloaked with somber drama both the two years after 1936. A number of prominent Jews were brought to trial, and at the same time others were ousted from employment on the staff of the Secret Police and from the cooperatives of several cities, notably Moscow. Yet it cannot be demonstrated that Stalin was indulging in overt anti-Semitism. The wholesale removal from office of persons deemed unreliable may well have been undertaken with an eye on the civil service as a whole rather than on a particular group. On the other hand, the outburst which followed the signing of the Stalin-Hitler Pact in 1939 cannot be so interpreted. The domi-

is our brother,' he said, but the Jewish bourgeois is an enemy, not as a Jew but as a bourgeois. In view of the fact that before the revolution only about one-third of the Jews in Russia were classified as workers, peasants or craftsmen, the distinctions made by Lenin actually left almost two-thirds of the Jews open to attack on 'class' grounds. This loophole, like the loophole of 'anti-Zionism,' was to be utilized in the future as an instrument of Communist Party activity, within the Soviet Union and abroad."

nant Russians found in their ill-fated agreement with the German dictator an excuse for giving free rein to their fear, dislike, and suspicion of the Jew. Maxim Litvinov was doubtless the most eminent target, but he was by no means the only one. Of course it can be maintained that the decree which at this time dismissed three-fourths of Jews employed by the State and even curtailed the number of Jewish members of the Communist Party accordingly was a quite typical Stalin ruse, expressing no point of view and reflecting no philosophy but bidding for popular support, particularly in the Ukraine, where Jews had traditionally been unpopular.

At any rate, the policy was continued during the war, at least to the extent that no official steps were taken to curb widespread overt attacks upon Jews. In the West, anti-Semitic moods were of course fostered by Nazi propagandists. In the unoccupied parts of the country feeling rose against Jewish évacués. The story of the plight of this minority, pieced together by Solomon N. Schwarz after extensive and careful research, is a tangled and tragic one.* It is probably correct to say that the Jews had never suffered more in Russia, or borne it with so little realization on the part of others of what they were compelled to endure. Suffice it to conclude that the facts, once they became known to a still incredulous world, forever dispelled the fancy that Communism was the best protector of minorities.

With the coming of the peace, two new factors emerged to affect the position of Jewry. The first was the return westward of many thousands of Polish Jews who had been deported to, or had escaped to, the Soviet Union. A not inconsiderable number of native Russian Jews managed to join this exodus; and with them came innumerable authentic reports of what was really happening in the land of Stalin. These narratives

* Solomon N. Schwarz, *The Jews in the Soviet Union* (Syracuse, N.Y., 1951).

filtered down to the public through pro-Zionist organizations in various countries. When, as a result of the establishment of the United Nations and the emergence of Russia as a world power, political alignments in the Near East became a matter of major concern to the Kremlin, Zionism was for still another and major reason an issue with which it was not disposed to deal lightly. The official Russian attitude towards Israel was at first guardedly friendly, but soon grew very hostile.

On October 21, 1948, Ilya Ehrenburg published in *Pravda* an article which was read with mingled interest and consternation throughout the world. In essence Ehrenburg said that Jews living in Russia or in countries over which it held dominion must stop thinking of Israel as a "homeland" or a "Jewish state," and must instead make up their minds that only a world-wide triumph of Communism would bring to an end Jewish suffering and distress. For after such a victory, he contended, there would be no more Jews. Israel could not be viewed as a country which had achieved nationhood, for "the toilers" were not in control. Indeed, they languished under bourgeois rule, which in turn was dependent on "Anglo-American capital." And what after all was the state thus created? It reminded one, he said, "of a ship, an ark, a raft, bearing people who have been caught in the bloody deluge of racism and fascism."

As we have seen, Soviet antipathy to Zionism was by no means new; but this declaration of open hostility was nevertheless unexpected. Some of the hypotheses which have been advanced to account for it are: that the Russians looked upon attempts by Jews to emigrate to Palestine as expressions of dissatisfaction with the glorious achievements of the Communist heartland; that they professed enmity to Israel because the support it had received from the United States was bound to make it an integral part of the community of Western states; that for political and strategic reasons an appeal for Arab ap-

proval was far more advantageous than manifestations of
friendship, however tepidly worded, towards a Jewish state
which the Arabs necessarily looked upon with disfavor; and,
finally, that since Germany had become the key to the solution
of the European problem it would serve the purposes of Russia
better to relegate Jews to the ash can and woo former Nazis
with effective but camouflaged friendliness. Every one of
these theories can be supported on the basis of evidence that
has been accumulated since the appearance of Ehrenburg's
article.

At any rate, the ideas he expressed were quickly dissemi-
nated through every medium of expression at the disposition
of the Communist Party. Why, it was asked, should any Jew
desire to go to a "Jewish homeland" when he could stay where
he was and enjoy all the advantages of the "most progressive
society in the world"? In Poland, Czechoslovakia, and Hungary, Zionism was identified with "reaction," and all Jews
who responded to its appeal were flayed as weak-kneed and
socially illiterate betrayers of the working class. The campaign was conducted with special vigor in Rumania, where
many Jews desired to migrate. On December 15, 1948, an article in *Unirea*, organ of the Rumanian Democratic Jewish
Committee, stated:

. . . the process of re-enrollment of the Jewish working masses for
constructive democratic work was hampered by Zionist nationalistic
activities which have misled parts of the Jewish population by false
propaganda. In that action, the Zionists were assisted by other imperialist American agencies in different ways.

Zionism in all its forms is a nationalist, reactionary political movement sponsored by the Jewish bourgeoisie, which tries to isolate the
Jewish working population from the peoples among which it lives, to
keep it back from the ranks of the progressive forces which fight national and international capitalism.

The stage was now set for the liquidation of Jewry in so far as its religious and cultural solidarity were concerned. In view of the fact that information is sporadic and has come in driblets from a great variety of sources dependent upon localized experiences, it is extremely difficult to visualize the conditions under which Jewish groups have lived and carried on. Even such a question as "How many Jews are there in the Soviet orbit?" must be answered tentatively. It is estimated that approximately 1,800,000 persons of Jewish origin, many of them deportees from the satellite countries, now live in the Soviet Union. Of these some 300,000 live in Moscow. There is another heavy concentration in Central Asia, where Tashkent, the capital of Uzbekistan, has acquired a large Jewish population. Among the satellite countries, Rumania has the largest Jewish population despite a considerable emigration to Israel: the present total is believed to be about 250,000. In 1951, Hungary had 143,000 professing Jews, the great majority of them in Budapest. Of the once vast Jewish population of Poland, hardly more than a fragment remains, the estimated total being 45,000. There are probably fewer than 15,000 Jews in Czechoslovakia, and fewer than half as many in Bulgaria. Statistics from Yugoslavia profess to be more precise. The figure for December, 1950, was reported as 6,244. In short, the total Jewish population in Communist-dominated Central Europe, including dissident Yugoslavia, is less than half a million. In 1930 it numbered in round figures 5,000,000. Such was the toll of Nazism and war.

We shall now attempt to lift the veil, in so far as possible.

In February, 1951, Hayim Greenberg, editor of the *Jewish Frontier*, published a letter he had addressed to the Soviet Ambassador to the United States, and to which he had received no reply. One paragraph in his very interesting epistle reads:

Not a word has been heard about Birobidzhan for a long time. We do not know how large is its population, whether its Jewish community is growing or not. Are there Jewish schools in Birobidzhan? A Jewish newspaper? Do Jews come to settle there? If not, what is the cause? What has become of this project for a Soviet Israel? Has the Soviet Government changed its mind about the plan? Have the Jews disappointed? We have no answers to these riddles. Local Communist propagandists know more about Tibet than they do about Birobidzhan.

I read this part of Mr. Greenberg's letter with particular interest because of personal experiences, after the war, with members of the American committee which advertised the wonders of this Soviet version of Zion and raised money for its support. There seemed, if one listened to the promoters, to be literally no opportunity for social or cultural advancement which could not be found in this paradise, made available to Jewry by a benevolent Stalin. But if one asked how many people lived there, or what they did, no information was obtainable. But many young and eager persons seemed anxious to believe in the idea, regardless of whether it could or could not be put into effect.

Nothing even remotely resembling a progress report about Birobidjan could be obtained, even though it was known that large numbers of Jews resident in western provinces— perhaps as many as 300,000—had been removed to Siberia during the years after 1947. Neither the United States Embassy in Moscow nor interested newspaper correspondents could secure permission to enter the region. The Russian newspapers referred occasionally to Birobidjan, but only in connection with routine reports as to whether the quotas for agricultural produce had been met. To all intents and purposes, the famed paradise was as remote from reality as a skyscraper in Capri. It was not until March 29, 1951, that *Naaretz*, a newspaper published in Tel Aviv, Israel, was able to present some scanty information gleaned from professional Russian journals. The population was reported to be 140,000, of whom fewer than a third were Jews. It was further indicated that during 1949 and 1950 only a few hundred Jews arrived in the province, the majority of whom were relatives of persons already residing there. Meanwhile many thousands of Jews were settled elsewhere in Siberia. During the same years, Jewish Communist leaders were removed from their posts to make room for non-Jews brought in from various parts of Russia. There was no mention of specifically Jewish cultural activities, nor could it be ascertained whether Yiddish was still taught in the schools. All propaganda concerning the province abruptly ceased, and there were indications that it had been absorbed into the larger district of Khabarovsk.

All this fitted into the pattern of events throughout Russia. The campaign inaugurated by Ehrenburg was extended to cover every aspect of Jewish life. After 1950, only a handful of Jews (the name being applied not to those who retained any semblance of fealty to the religious traditions of Judaism, but to those of Jewish origin) held positions of trust in the Communist Party. There were numerous indications that anti-Semitism had become fashionable. All Jewish publications were suppressed, and the best known among their editors or contributors disappeared. Every cultural, welfare, or fraternal organization round which even a vestige of Jewish community life might be formed was systematically liquidated. Some synagogues still remained open in Moscow; but it was doubtful that any existed outside the capital city. The rabbi in charge of the synagogue on Spasoglinichevsky Pereoluk, Moscow, reported that he served a community of some 10,000 persons. If there actually are two other synagogues in Moscow which are used for worship, the conclusion must nevertheless be drawn that the vast majority of the city's Jews no longer have any communal religious life.*

Reports of mass deportations of Jews from western Russia do not include dependable information about the numbers detained in slave-labor camps. Rumors persist that the percentage is sizable.† Beyond any question is the intensity of the propagandistic attack on Jewish "nationalism" and "cosmopolitanism." Anyone suspected of these crimes against the State was liquidated without hesitation. Indeed, it is said that only five persons have been permitted to leave Russia for Israel. A relatively spectacular incident dramatized the atti-

---

* Birobidjan was the theme of an article in the New York *Herald Tribune* of Nov. 9, 1949, by Joseph Newman, its correspondent in Moscow. Newman reported his conversations with Carlos Melman, an Australian carpenter who had migrated to the Soviet Union during 1947 in quest of paradise, and who, because he had Australian citizenship, was able to leave Russia again. He stated that the Jews constituted approximately one-fourth of the urban population but were less numerous in the villages. Most of the people were engaged in collective farming and worked an average of twelve hours a day. The wage was just about enough food to keep them alive. The capital city had neither a sewage system nor a water supply. Most of the inhabitants lived in dilapidated wooden houses.

† Perhaps the most dramatic account of what happened to the Jews under Soviet rule is provided in an article by Julius Margolin, "When the Red Army Liberated Pinsk," in *Commentary*, Vol. XIV, pp. 517–528 (Dec., 1952). The author, a citizen of Palestine, happened to be visiting relatives in Poland when the war broke out between Germany and Russia. He was in Pinsk when that city was unexpectedly subordinated to Soviet rule. All the residents fancied that the coming of the Red Army would mean liberation from tyranny. Instead he was obliged to ask the question: "How could the Soviet government, in the space of one winter, have made an enemy of everyone in the territory it occupied, regardless of class, national, or political differences?" Mr. Margolin describes the steps which were taken with meticulous care. Perhaps no more graphic or harrowing account has been set down. He reports, for example: "The liquidation of the Jewish political bodies and organs of Jewish social life in Pinsk was completed by the spring of 1940. The heads of the Bund had been arrested and deported; in April the Zionists were singled out and each of them condemned to eight years in concentration camps. Systematically and unpityingly, every active element that might conceivably have offered resistance to the 'reeducation of the masses' was rooted out. All independent thought, all potential opposition was outlawed."

tude of the Kremlin towards the Zionist State. The first ambassador from Israel to the Soviet Union, Mrs. Golda Myerson, arrived in Moscow to assume her duties just at the time when the Jewish community was preparing to observe the New Year and the Feast of the Atonement. Thinking that the establishment of diplomatic relations with the new Zionist State warranted some jubilation, a sizable crowd poured into the synagogue and gave vent to its feelings. Then the government came down with a heavy hand. Those who were held to be the "instigators" of the "demonstration" were imprisoned. The sole surviving Yiddish newspaper was suppressed, and the Jewish Anti-Fascist Committee was abolished. The price paid was a heavy one, but there could now be no doubt that a sense of Jewish solidarity did exist in Moscow, and that the Zionist success had kindled its imagination.

So absolute had tyranny become in Russia by the close of 1951 that Jewish citizens resident in that unfortunate country no longer had any association with the outside world, unless perchance they had a way of listening to foreign radio broadcasts. Nor could they let anyone have news of themselves save possibly through one who managed to escape. Nearly all the Russians who have come over to the West are army officers stationed in the satellite countries, particularly Germany; and though conversations with them were illuminating in so far as life under Soviet rule is concerned, I found none who had any first-hand knowledge of Jews or of their special problems. Some, indeed, still believed that Communism was the handiwork of Jewry. So we are left to surmise that there has been created in the minds of persons who still cling to Jewish traditions a feeling of absolute isolation and complete hopelessness in so far as this world is concerned. It may very well be that a comparable mood blending resignation with despair has spread to all the satellite countries also, now that, as of

1953, the various offices of the Joint Distribution Committee have been closed. During centuries of persecution and tribulation, Jews had managed to help one another across national boundaries. They had developed methods of mutual aid and comfort which were perhaps unique in the annals of mankind. The fact that these methods have now been abrogated illustrates as well as anything possibly could the character and power of the Communist dictatorship. One must also assume that there are many who as a consequence of the propaganda to which they are perennially exposed believe that the Western World is a place where ruthless capitalists enslave and starve the poor. How stark and grim the picture of human destiny thereby painted on the wall of the imagination must be, we can only surmise.

One of the most significant reports bearing on recent Russian attitudes towards Jews has to do with the removal of Jewish officers and soldiers from the Red Army stationed in Germany. These reports are fragmentary and, coming from men who have escaped to the West, must be received with due caution. Nevertheless it is reasonably certain that the purge of Jews began in 1946, when the Russian forces in Eastern Germany were commanded by General Vassily Chuikov, and that it has continued ever since. We do not know whether comparable purges have been carried out elsewhere. It may well be that the measure was adopted in Germany only, on the ground that the presence of Jewish soldiers was distasteful to the former Nazi officers whom the Russians have persistently sought to recruit.

The pattern of policy towards the Jews in satellite countries has conformed to the Russian original, but with important deviations: Jewish charitable and cultural institutions have been nationalized; the schools of Talmudic teaching have been closed; and the surviving Jewish press consists of a handful of pro-Communist sheets, all strongly opposed to Zionism. Nevertheless official attitudes towards Jewry are formed in accordance with the requirements of Soviet policy at any given time and in any place. Thus Communists in East Germany, where there are only 2,600 Jews, have maintained a barrage of propaganda against the West German Federal Republic on the ground that their own treatment of Jews has been vastly better. They have accused Chancellor Adenauer of settling the problems of restitution not for humanitarian or ethical reasons but for the profit of both German and Jewish "capitalists." More recently German Communist journals have introduced some rather veiled criticisms of Israel and Zionism; but no cases of overt anti-Semitism have been reported. Indeed, measures of such a character would be utterly pointless, in view of the fact that East German Jews are so pitifully few and so completely without influence. Yet there have been indications that all Jews will be purged from the Communist Party. On January 14, 1953, Julius Mayer, head of the League of Jewish Communities in East Germany, and seven other persons who had been chairmen of local Jewish communities, sought asylum in West Berlin. Most of these were at least nominally affiliated with the Socialist Unity Party, so that it may be assumed that some warning was given them. Most observers feel that nevertheless East Germany will be forced to adopt a policy of anti-Semitism, if the process of incorporating it fully into the Russian orbit is speeded up.

It was in Czechoslovakia that the most spectacular events took place. Virtually every form of Jewish communal activity had been suppressed shortly after the Communist seizure of power. In the summer of 1950, only one of Prague's old synagogues was open on weekdays as well as Saturdays. No young men were being trained for the Rabbinate, and the

Chief Rabbi of the capital city reported that there was no demand for the religious instruction of youth. But all this paled into insignificance as the world learned of the arrest and trial of fourteen prominent Communists. The arrests, made on charges of treason and Titoism, were followed by wide-scale man hunts in which lesser folk were the victims. Death and life imprisonment were meted out to persons found guilty of listening to the Voice of America or of comparable crimes against the State. These things were done against the backdrop of economic depression of the most virulent kind. Nationalization, collective farming, loss of trade with the West, and heavy demands by Russia for its war machine, had gravely impoverished the people. Nor did the creation of a no man's land along the country's western border halt the flight of refugees. Representatives of foreign governments and interests were dealt with in heavy-handed fashion. Thus William N. Oatis, Prague correspondent of the Associated Press, was tried and sentenced for espionage. And Israel was startled when Mordecai Oren, leader of the extreme left of its Pamam Party, disappeared. A man who had clung to the Communist Party line with the tenacity of a leech, Oren had gone to East Berlin during the winter of 1951 to attend a meeting of the pro-Stalinist World Federation of Trade Unions. Hearing that one of his friends was being purged in Czechoslovakia, he journeyed to Prague. He called at the Israeli Legation to say that he was leaving for Vienna on New Year's Eve. Yet nothing was heard of him there or elsewhere for three months. An official inquiry elicited the information that he had been jailed for mysterious and terrifying crimes against the security of the State.

The Slánský trial of November, 1952, is surely one of the most shocking and surprising episodes in Communist jurisprudence.* Each detail of the proceedings was made public with every means at the government's disposal, with the result that the full transcript was available throughout the world. Two questions present themselves: Why was it deemed desirable to proceed against these men, and why was the advertising considered advantageous? In response to the first query, we can only adduce what was said in behalf of the Czechoslovak State. The defendants had associated in varying ways with persons and groups outside the country. Most of them were Jews. And as Jews they had aided and abetted the people of Israel at great cost to the Czechoslovak people. All three charges were constantly reiterated, but it was the second that gave the trial its macabre novelty. Indeed, not even the Nazis, for all their psychotic anti-Semitism, had staged any comparable drama prior to the slaying of Herr Von Rath in 1938. No doubt the principal reason for recourse to this method of pillorying previously trusted members of the Party was that an excuse was needed for the abysmal failure of the Communist economic policy.

But why was the grim business so profligately advertised? We can only guess. During the struggle for Jewish victory in Palestine, arms and supplies had been purchased in Czecho-

---

* The Library of Jewish Information (American Jewish Committee), in its bulletin "Jews Behind the Iron Curtain" dated April, 1952, printed a partial list of Jewish Communists who had been removed from their posts. The list contains 24 names, including: Rudolf Slánský, Secretary General of the Communist Party and later on Vice Premier; Otto Sling, member of the Central Committee of the Communist Party and its District Secretary in Brno; Bedrich Rejcin, Major General and Chief of Army Intelligence; Vavro Hajdu, Deputy Minister of Foreign Affairs and Chief of the West European section of that ministry; Gustav Bares-Breitenfeld, Deputy Secretary General of the Communist Party and chief of its propaganda section; and Bedrich Geminder, representative of the Czechoslovak Communist Party in the Cominform. Other prominent Jews disappeared in strange ways. Thus Eduard Goldstücker, once Czechoslovak Minister to Israel, was transferred to Stockholm in 1951 but never arrived there. There were also a number employed at diplomatic posts abroad who at this time elected to seek political asylum.

slovakia. But after 1950 Moscow was courting the Arabs; and it may well be that it was primarily for their benefit that the spotlight was turned on. One cannot be certain of the impact of these disclosures on the Arab world, but certainly the effect elsewhere was woefully disappointing from the Communist point of view. In the United States and Great Britain it removed the last vestiges of belief that the system created by Lenin and Stalin was the antithesis of Nazism. Even in Czechoslovakia itself, the men condemned to death had scarcely been hanged when it became necessary for the government to embark on a long series of explanations and exhortations. People were asking, Why did all the accused confess their guilt so readily, and for what reason was an attack on the Jews deemed necessary? President Gottwald, speaking over the Prague Radio on December 17, declared, "Zionism has become a dangerous and vicious enemy." It was subject to "American bosses" who were shamelessly exploiting the sufferings of the Jews under Hitler; and the collusion of the condemned men with these "bosses" had led to their treasonable guilt. Will Herberg has observed, "As far back as the spring of 1949, American Communists were denouncing the government of Israel as a 'tool of American imperialism,' and of course they were merely echoing Moscow's instructions." *
It is as ironical as anything could well be that Jews who had long since renounced any ties which bound them to their tradition and the faith it enshrines should have died because they were ordered to implement what at one fleeting moment was Moscow's policy towards Palestine—a policy designed to weaken the position of Great Britain, a country with which the defendants were at their trial found guilty of "collaborating."

* Cf. Herberg, "Anti-Semitism and the Left," *Commonweal*, Vol. LVII, p. 372 (Jan. 16, 1953).

In Hungary the Jews found themselves in a specially tragic situation. A considerable number of them held government positions, owing to the fact that former associates of Béla Kun had returned to the country in 1945. As a result large sections of the embittered peasant population were once more violently anti-Semitic. Yet in all truth the plight of the surviving Jewish community was desperate. Virtually the whole of it was affected by the nationalization of trade and industry, a Communist fetish which to all intents and purposes wiped out small business. By the close of 1950 hardly a Jew in Budapest could have existed if it had not been possible for him to sell some item of personal property. A campaign against the "nationalists" and "cosmopolites" who favored the establishment of Israel added to the misery and confusion. One of the charges levied against the several defendants in the trial of Laszlo Rajk was that they had favored "reactionary, chauvinistic Zionism." These strangely submissive "criminals" confessed that persons who favored Israel were traitorous advocates of American imperialism and treacherous indulgers in espionage.

It was possible for the government of Israel to negotiate an agreement permitting the emigration of 3,000 persons as late as 1950; but the quota was not filled, even though more than 30,000 applied. In 1951, the Hungarian government announced that a large-scale deportation of "vagrants" had been authorized, so that the "unemployed" of Budapest might find work and sustenance on kolkhozes and in cooperative industries. As has been said, this news attracted so much attention that the shipments of human merchandise to a laborious utopia were delayed. Even so, sizable numbers of poor victims were deported. On January 17, 1953, Lajos Stoeckler, president of the Hungarian Jewish Community, was arrested on the ground that "substantial amounts of American dollars and Swiss francs" had been found in his home, which, it was contended, had been made available to him by the Joint Distribution Committee; and since that time the "Joint" has served as a primary target for propagandistic abuse. On the other hand, Hungarian Communist organs have so far tried to distinguish between anti-Semitism and anti-Zionism far more circumspectly than was done at the Slánský trial. It was contended during 1952 and part of 1953, for example, that the United States had launched a vicious anti-Semitic campaign in connection with the Rosenberg case, whereas Hungary had been concerned only with the "lackeys" of a "foreign espionage agency." This thesis was oddly enough credited in various parts of Europe.

As a matter of fact the deterioration of the Hungarian economy and the increasing bleakness of the cultural scene led to bitter popular outbursts of feeling for which the surviving Jews were convenient scapegoats. These the government was unable to curb or suppress. Thus during February, 1950, the head of the Jewish community in Tokaj and his wife were beaten to death. The murderers were not brought to book, nor were Jews residing in this area permitted to go elsewhere. Thus the pathetic survivors of Hitler's efforts to wipe out the Jews of the countries he conquered are now subjected to the spleen of their frantic neighbors. It is reported that 75,000 of the 125,000 Jews probably still in Hungary have applied for emigration visas.

The situation in Poland, where the forty-odd thousand surviving Jews for the most part eke out an existence in certain industrial cities, is not clear. Community life has not been fully suppressed. But what survives, in the form of libraries, theaters, and sport organizations, serves virtually no purpose other than to provide sounding boards for Communist propaganda. Thus there still is a Jewish newspaper, but it is a Party organ. Institutions for the training of rabbis have been closed, and religious holidays are no longer observed. Emigration to Israel was permitted during a brief period during 1949, and it is estimated that more than half the total Jewish population applied for visas. They had previously been subjected to a violent barrage of anti-Zionist propaganda, flavored with choice morsels of news about the ties which bound Israel to the United States, monster of imperialism.

Jewish groups in the Balkans seem to have managed despite incredible difficulties to conserve a measure of their solidarity, and have no doubt also been heartened by their relative proximity to Palestine, which has made emigration somewhat easier. Religious worship is sanctioned under the supervision of the Committee of Democratic Jews, which is charged with seeing to it that the causes in which the government happens to be interested are served. Rabbis have thus been compelled to refrain from supporting "Zionism" and "imperialism" as well as to express their whole-hearted approval of "peace." Every obstacle has been placed in the way of religious instruction for young people. Rumania's traditional system of Yiddish education operated 69 elementary and 23 secondary schools until June, 1948, when all these establishments were closed. A year later two schools were permitted to reopen, and assurances were given that two others would be licensed later. The Ministry of Education announced that the instruction in these schools would be inspired by lofty patriotism and would "wipe out the bourgeois mentality of Zionism which is unfortunately widespread among Jewish youth."

The purge of Government officials which began in March, 1952, led to the dismissal of Aurel Vijoil, Minister of Finance, and of the notorious Anna Pauker; but, though other Jews were arrested and sentenced, anti-Semitism does not appear to have been a factor. Indeed, reports coming out of the country indicate that the Jewish community felt "indescribable relief at the disappearance of vicious and brutal individuals whose deeds engendered hostility to the Jews among the population." And indeed this was some cause for rejoicing despite the bleakness of the general outlook. The great majority of Jews who were economically productive belonged to the fraternity of small businessmen, so that the nationalization program and the inflation which accompanied it reduced them, their children, and their aged dependents to the direst poverty. Except for a small handful of veteran Communists, Jews are dubbed "capitalists" and made to suffer also for support given by them in the past to liberal causes. Accordingly they became "unproductive elements"—in the language of the Party—and consequently subject to deportation. It is believed that most of them who have been sent to labor camps are toiling in the regions bordering on the Black Sea. Tracing the fortune of any individual through that morass of misery has become impossible.

Until 1951, emigration from Rumania to Israel was relatively easy. It should be noted, of course, that each such emigrant was a profitable business venture for the government, which exacted payments both from the individual and from the international agencies which assisted him. But a campaign against Zionism was in full swing by the beginning of 1952, and prominent spokesmen for the movement were arrested on charges of "cosmopolitanism" and "nationalism." Since March of that year no visas have been granted for Palestine.

The small remaining Jewish community in Bulgaria has been completely subordinated. Reports in the Party press reveal that cultural life, traditionally organized around a core of libraries and reading rooms, has been transformed into a vehicle of Communist propaganda. The *American Jewish Year*

Book, 1951, carried a detailed account of the fortunes of one library in Sofia, which sponsored a series of lectures and concerts as well as meetings. The persons in charge complained, however, of poor attendance and a dearth of public interest. Closer scrutiny revealed that although the library had been made the recipient of many "Marxist-Leninist classics" and of books in the Russian language, the total number of volumes remained the same. Why? Because all publications reflecting a "nationalist Jewish tendency" had been removed. Lecture topics included: "The Great Stalin Pact for the Reconstruction of Nature," "The Celebration of the Anniversary of Lenin's Death," and "The Leading Role of the Soviet Union in the Anti-imperialist Camp and Its Fight for Peace and the People's Democracy." This literary and cultural fare appears to be standard for all such organizations.

During January, 1953, a climax was reached in the history of Communist-Jewish relations when fifteen doctors were arrested in Moscow on charges of plotting to assassinate prominent Russian leaders. In the group were nearly all the prominent Jewish physicians of the Russian capital. Shortly thereafter Josef Stalin died, giving rise once more to a multitude of international rumors. Then very suddenly, on April 4, the dramatic news was given to the world that the accusations levied against the doctors had been false, and that all had been released from prison. The action was accompanied by a series of steps described as "peace feelers," and the world was left to wonder whether vast and portentous changes were in the offing.

Certain it is that, after the dropping of charges against the doctors, the Kremlin took steps to establish a new and more conciliatory policy towards Jewry and in particular towards Israel. We do not know what this portends, or to what steps it will lead; but the tragedy of the Jew in Russia and the Cen-

tral Europe which Communism controls is heartrending. To
have been ground between the two millstones of totalitarian
oppression; to have hoped that escape from one might mean
salvation, and then discovered that the other was almost
equally implacable; to have been sealed off from virtually all
association with World Jewry, and left to find that the treason
of dissenters from Jewish tradition everywhere bred new
armies of the hostile and the venomously critical; and to have
stood by helpless while all vestiges of hallowed religious and
community living were systematically destroyed—these are
some of the evils, apart from the blighted hopes for emigration, dire poverty, and the constant threat of forced labor,
from which the Jew has suffered in a dark time.*

* Since this chapter was written, a new book—*The Jews in the Soviet Satellites*,
by Peter Meyer and others (Syracuse, 1953)—has appeared. It adds many
harrowing details to what was previously known about the plight of the Jews
under Soviet rule, and the reader of this volume is referred to it. In particular
it reinforces the view that the year 1950 marked the point at which the position
of Jewry began to deteriorate abysmally.

CONCLUSION

━━━

W HAT OF THE FUTURE? We must, I believe, make any attempt at prophecy depend on a resolute distinction between predictable weaknesses in the structure of the Russian
dictatorship and our estimates of how noticeably the appeal of
Marxist-Leninist doctrine may wane. Whether internal dissen-
sion will sap much of the strength of the Kremlin is anybody's
guess. I do not profess to know the answer. But concerning the
impact of the Communist doctrine there are some things to be
said. I shall limit myself to a brief discussion of two: First,
there is no indication that a Christian view of how to make
modern industrial society function to the advantage of the
majority of men has gained in popularity—indeed, the number
who ardently support such a view may be smaller than was the
case some years ago. Secondly, although the Marxist community is rent by schisms of an unusually virulent character,
the fact remains that, in many parts of the world, some version
of Marxism is all that the dominant intellectual caste is willing
or able to peddle to the masses.

While the reasons for all this are complex, one can without
difficulty note that, even as the intellectual lost faith, the com-

mon man lost hope. God departed from the room in which the professors, the research workers, the improvers, and the artists were talking—departed silently and ominously. And the worker, doomed to the treadmill of proletarianism, felt that only those spokesmen for the contemporary mind could do anything to bring about his liberation who talked aggressively in terms of the here and now. The result is that in many troubled areas religious leadership has simply been shoved aside. Churches are there, liturgies are the same, sermons are preached on modern variations of old themes; but not many of the people who come to worship really know why they do so. Perhaps the majority feel they are clinging for dear life to an heirloom. They do not believe that their daily bread will come because they pray for it. This skepticism is, of course, a disease. But it is a universal plague, and in all probability no remedy will be easily found. The "daily bread" to be earned under the auspices of industry is not the peasant's wheat, harvested in the sun. But that it depends upon the foresight, honesty, and social conscience of industry's leaders—and therewith upon fundamental natural virtues—is generally forgotten.

On the other hand, Marxism. There can be no doubt that, although it has lost followers in some parts of the world, it has recruited other devotees elsewhere. The primary source of strength is the paradoxical fact that, whereas the struggle of several backward populations for independence finds the democratic powers in the role of "capitalistic exploiters," the simultaneous drying-up of colonial opportunity creates population problems that in turn produce grist for the Communist mill. Wherever people have had experience with the Russian system, however, they have repudiated it as soon as any opportunity presented itself. This does not, of course, mean that Marxism has been discarded. Various kinds of "revisionism" became popular, as is currently the case in Western Germany.

Looking into the darkness of Russia, one might well bear in mind that its dictators have never dissented from the view expressed by Marx in his commentary on the Gotha Socialist Congress of 1875. As soon as the proletariat has "taken over" the means of production, he declared, it must consolidate its gains and protect them against its enemies. Therefore freedom must temporarily be postponed. Only when "the fountain sources of communal wealth gush freely" will it be possible to declare that the "revolution" has ended, and that every citizen is "free to act in accordance with his abilities and needs." There are still many people in the world who believe that the horrors witnessed since Lenin brought his Party to power are interim manifestations of dictatorship, to be followed by the dawn of the communal millennium.

Nevertheless it may not be too venturesome to suggest by way of conclusion that while Marxism is still being purveyed, its salesmen may be acquiring a universal reputation not as prophets but as medicine men. In so far as Europe and the United States are concerned, at least, the laws of economic society are demonstrably other dicta than those enunciated in *Das Kapital*. Very few working men any longer believe that Lenin and his followers have ushered in the proletarian millennium. To be sure, this waning of Marxist faith has not been followed by a reinvigoration of other social gospels; and the observer may indeed sometimes wonder whether the present hour may not be one of an intellectual and spiritual vacuum. As for Russia, if students of its present politico-economic structure are to be credited, it may well be that the brutal utopianism of Stalin has been superseded by a new gregariousness of the profit-takers of the Revolution. Gradually a new caste has been formed—that of a prevailingly bureaucratic and military aristocracy, as well prepared as any feudal society in history has been. Granted that there now exist some few millions

of successful Russians, who have finally liquidated the uprising of 1917, and granted also that they are ready as well as
willing to defend their heritage, it will be a heroic optimist
who will assert that any mass protest against the existing
tyranny would have a chance for success. Only a slow and radical spiritual reorientation might eventually put back into the
bloodstream of Russian life carriers of justice and mercy. It
is difficult to put faith in predictions that such a reorientation
can be effected from within Russia itself. The old order is too
distant and outmoded; no new one seems in the making. Perhaps the signs of the times are correct, and the redemption of
Russia will once more come from the West. We do not know
how it can come. Yet anyone who can visualize the possibility
must also know that reckoning with it implies a profound and
searching examination of current cultural and religious strategy. For him the mandate of the hour would not be the closing
of gates and the erection of more barriers. It would be rather
the brave going down every road which leads to the heart of the
East. Such a prospect is too momentous and problematical to
be discussed here at any length.

I shall, however, venture to reiterate what must by this time
surely have become fairly obvious. It is probable that, unless total and all-destructive war should be unleashed as a
consequence of what would be the most calamitous accident in
history, there will be no major change in the political and
social alignments now existing in the world. There may, of
course, well be border dislocations. Thus the Russians may re-
linquish their grip on East Germany. Or a Communist Party
subservient to them could conceivably triumph in India. At
any rate, the core of the non-Soviet area is Anglo-Saxon—is,
from an ideological point of view, the tradition of Magna
Carta and the Common Law. This tradition can be extended to
peoples at present subjugated only if it proves possible to

create, through the agencies entrusted with the establishment of international order, a code of minority rights which will be respected. Such a code (already adumbrated in the proposed Covenant of Human Rights and the stillborn Genocide Convention), the Russians would of course not immediately respect. But I am sanguine enough to believe that if it were adopted and vigorously advocated it would, as an idea, generate so much radiant force that it would in the long run cease to be merely evolutionary and would become truly revolutionary. We have said often enough that the ultimate victory for justice is not to be had merely through giving away material things, however necessary these may be. Why not, therefore, when a new concept of human relations is in our possession, develop and use the resources which are latent in it?

SELECTIVE BIBLIOGRAPHY

GENERAL

Newspapers and periodicals: *America; Catholic News; Christ und Welt; Christ unter Wegs; Christian Century; Civiltà Cattolica; Commonweal; Foreign Affairs; Frankfurter Allgemeine Zeitung; Le Monde; New York Herald Tribune; New York Times; Osservatore Romano; Stimmen der Zeit; Time.*

Publications, Mid-European Studies Center.

Memoranda. Basic to this study are the several memoranda prepared under the auspices of the Committee for a Free Europe, Inc., by scholars familiar with developments in each of the countries in question. Since some of the authors have requested that their names be withheld, it seems to be best to preserve the anonymity of all.

RUSSIA

Berdyaev, Nicholas, *The Origin of Russian Communism,* transl. G. French. London, 1937.

Bolshakoff, Serge, *The Christian Church and the Soviet State.* New York, 1942.

Carr, Edward H., *The Bolshevik Revolution, 1917–1923.* New York, 1951.

Chamberlin, William H., *The Russian Revolution, 1917–1921.* New York, 1935.

Cianfarra, Camille M., *The Vatican and the Kremlin.* New York, 1950.

Dallin, David J., *The Real Soviet Russia*, transl. J. Shaplen. New Haven, 1944.

Deutscher, Isaac, *Stalin: A Political Biography*. New York, 1949.

Eckardt, Hans von, *Ivan the Terrible*, transl. C. A. Phillips. New York, 1949.

————, *Russisches Christentum*. Munich, 1947.

Fedetov, G. P., *The Russian Church Since the Revolution*. New York, 1928.

Fülöp-Miller, René, *The Mind and Face of Bolshevism*, transl. Flint and Tait. New York, 1928.

Gurian, Waldemar, ed., *The Soviet Union: Background, Ideality, Reality*. Notre Dame, Ind., 1951.

Kravchenko, Victor, *I Chose Freedom*. New York, 1946.

Paléologue, Maurice, *La Russie des Tsars*. Paris, 1922.

Pares, Bernard, *Russia*. New York, 1945.

Sheen, Fulton J., *Communism and the Conscience of the West*. Indianapolis, 1948.

Souvarine, Boris, *Stalin: A Critical Survey of Bolshevism*. Chicago, 1939.

Stepun, Fiodor, *Vergangenes und Unvergängliches: Aus meinem Leben*. Munich, 1948–1950.

Timasheff, N. S., *Religion in Soviet Russia, 1917–1942*. New York, 1942.

Treviranus, G. R., *Revolutions in Russia: Their Lessons for the Western World*. New York, 1944.

THE SATELLITE COUNTRIES

Periodical and Occasional Publications

Aussenpolitik. Stuttgart, 1952.

Bonner Berichte aus Mittel- und Ostdeutschland. Bonn, 1951–1953.

Commentary. New York, 1947–1953.

Documents. Paris, April, 1950.

Life. New York, 1952.

Mitteilungen. Wirtschaftspolitische Gesellschaft, Frankfurt, 1950–1953.

Der Monat. Berlin, 1950–1953.

The Network, ed. Ruth Fischer. Various issues.

New Leader. New York, 1945–1953.

Publications: European Affairs Division, Library of Congress, Washington, D.C.; Library of Jewish Information, New York; University of Chicago Round Table, Chicago, 1945–1953.

Books

Amery, Julian, *Sons of the Eagle: A Study in Guerilla War.* London, 1948.

Anonymous, *Expulsus.* Königstein, 1953.

———, *Injustice the Regime.* Bonn, 1952.

———, *Kirche in Not.* Limburg, 1953.

———, *Kirche und Staat im Kanton Bern.* Bern, 1951.

———, *Report on Germany.* Office of the High Commissioner for Germany, 1950–1953.

Baldwin, Roger, ed., *A New Slavery.* New York, 1953.

Borkenau, Franz, *European Communism.* New York, 1953.

Chamberlin, William Henry, *The European Cockpit.* New York, 1947.

Gide, André, *Return from the U.S.S.R.,* transl. D. Bussy. New York, 1937.

Hesse, Fritz, *Das Spiel um Deutschland.* Munich, 1953.

Hogye, Michael, Protestant Churches in Hungary (manuscript).

Kohn, Hans, *The Idea of Nationalism.* New York, 1944.

Kolnai, Aurel, *The War Against the West.* New York, 1938.

Krivitsky, W. G., *I Was Stalin's Agent.* London, 1940.

Lehrman, Harold A., *Russia's Europe.* New York, 1947.

Maritain, Jacques, *The Rights of Man and Natural Law,* transl. D. C. Anson. New York, 1943.

Meyer, Peter, and others, *The Jews in the Soviet Satellites.* Syracuse, 1953.

Schmidlin, Josef, *Papstgeschichte der neuesten Zeit.* 4 vols., Munich, 1933–1939.

Schnabel, Franz, *Deutsche Geschichte im neunzehnten Jahrhundert.* Freiburg, 1948.

Weber, Alfred, *Farewell to European History,* transl. R. F. C. Hull. New Haven, 1948.

INDEX